NARRATOLOGY
Introduction to the Theory of Narrative

Third Edition

Since its first publication in English in 1985, Mieke Bal's *Narratology* has become the international classic introduction to the theory of narrative texts. *Narratology* is a systematic account of narrative techniques and methods, and their transmission and reception, in which Bal distils years of study of the ways in which we understand both literary and non-literary works.

In this third edition, Bal updates the book to include more analysis of film narratives while also sharpening and tightening her language to make it the most readable and student-friendly edition to date. Bal also introduces new sections that treat and clarify several modernist texts that pose narratological challenges. With changes prompted by ten years of feedback from scholars and teachers, *Narratology* remains the most important contribution to the study of the way narratives work, are formed, and are received.

MIEKE BAL is Academy Professor of the Royal Netherlands Academy of Arts and Sciences. Her website is at www.miekebal.org.

MIEKE BAL

Narratology
Introduction to the
Theory of Narrative
Third Edition

UNIVERSITY OF TORONTO PRESS
Toronto Buffalo London

© University of Toronto Press Incorporated 1985, 1997, 2009
Toronto Buffalo London
www.utpublishing.com
Printed in Canada

ISBN 978-0-8020-9687-6 (cloth)
ISBN 978-0-8020-9631-9 (paper)

First edition 1985
Reprinted 1988, 1992, 1994

Second edition 1997
Reprinted 1999, 2002, 2004, 2006, 2007

Third edition 2009

This third edition is a complete revision of *Narratology: Introduction to the Theory of Narrative*, which was a translation, revised for English-language readers, by Christine Van Boheemen, of the second, revised edition of *De Theorie van vertellen en verhalen* (Muiderberg: Coutinho 1980).

Printed on acid-free paper

Library and Archives Canada Cataloguing in Publication

Bal, Mieke, 1946–
    Narratology : introduction to the theory of narrative / Mieke Bal. – 3rd ed.

    Rev. ed. of: Narratology. 2nd ed.
    Includes bibliographical references and index.
    ISBN 978-0-8020-9687-6 (bound)   ISBN 978-0-8020-9631-9 (pbk.)

    1. Narration (Rhetoric).   I. Title.

PN212.B313 2009   808.3'93   c2008-907728-8

University of Toronto Press acknowledges the financial assistance to its publishing program of the Canada Council for the Arts and the Ontario Arts Council.

University of Toronto Press acknowledges the financial support for its publishing activities of the Government of Canada through the Book Publishing Industry Development Program (BPIDP).

Contents

Preface to the First Edition

This introduction to narratology aims at presenting a systematic account of a theory of narrative for use in the study of literary and other narrative texts. It does not provide a survey of the major different trends in the field of narrative theory. There are other books available that provide such a survey. The choice for a systematic, hence limited, approach has been made for the sake of understanding, of the possibility of exchange of opinions, and of emancipation from intimidation. The choices I have made in this book were born from the conviction that a systematic account of one theory, which proceeds from definition, showing at every step its own structure and the necessity of its own phases, is easier for beginners in the field to understand than a plural survey of many different theories, involving names, terms, and, especially, heterogeneous arguments. For the same reason, names of predecessors have been reduced to the absolute minimum and, wherever possible, accounted for in special paragraphs at the ends of the chapters. The theory presented as a whole is also better accessible in the sense that whoever uses it will understand it the same way. This agreement of users has the advantage of a greater intersubjectivity. Teaching it becomes easier, learning it more feasible, because the risk of misunderstanding is reduced. Finally, the use of a method of analysis that every participant in a discussion can master helps students overcome the feeling of intimidation that a brilliant but unexpectedly structured interpretation by a teacher often entails. It is that feeling – the feeling that the teacher, while conveying the desire to master literature, may at the same time, by the very brilliance of his or her performance, intimidate – that brought me to the development of the present account. Once

I was able to use a theory, I noticed a progression in the quality of my interpretations as well as in my capacity to teach.

These remarks lead to an instrumental view of theory, indeed of this particular type of theory, provided the 'instrumental' refers to the practice of learning and teaching, not to the relation between the text and the theory alone. Conceived as a set of tools, as a means to express and specify one's interpretative reactions to a text, the theory presented here holds no claim to certainty. It is not from a positivistic desire for absolute, empirical knowledge that this theory and its instrumental character should be considered to have been generated. It is, quite the opposite, conceived as it is because interpretation, although not absolutely arbitrary since it does, or should, interact with a text, is in practice unlimited and free. Hence, I find, the need for a discourse that makes each interpretation expressible, accessible, communicable. Secondly, the tools proposed can be put to varied uses. I have myself used this theory for both aesthetic and political criticism, and found soon enough that these cannot, or should not, be separated. Hence, the need of more theory, beyond narratology: a theory that accounts for the functions and positions of texts of different backgrounds, genres, and historical periods. If the need for that broader kind of theory makes itself felt more acutely, narratology will have served its purpose just fine.

One need not adhere to structuralism as a philosophy in order to be able to use the concepts and views presented in this book. Neither does one need to feel that adherence to, for example, a deconstructionist, Marxist, or feminist view of literature hinders the use of this book. I happen to use it myself for feminist criticism, and feel that it helps to make that approach the more convincing, because of the features a systematic account entails. The scope of narratology, in my view an indispensable tool, is a limited one.

The examples given are various. They come from different linguistic communities, including Dutch, my native language. Many Dutch examples have been replaced by others from more accessible literatures. A few, however, have been kept; they are provided with a short bibliographical note at the end of the book. Examples are drawn from different levels of aesthetic elaboration; not only from well-known literary novels but also from works of children's fiction and journalism; there are even fictitious examples. The latter form a kind of series.

The date of appearance of this book qualifies its place in the discussion of literary studies. It comes late, if one considers it a result of structuralism. Coming after the vogue of anti- or poststructuralist theoretical works, it aims at an integration of different types of theories, at showing the necessity of a rational critical discourse within whatever view of literature one may hold, and at pursuing steadily the study of narrative as a genre, which stretches far beyond literature in the narrow, aesthetic sense.

Soon after its appearance in Dutch, Christine van Boheemen found it useful in her teaching of English and American literature. She undertook the heavy task of adapting examples to an international audience, and of translating it into English without any guarantee of publication. If it appears today in its present form, it is due to her generous and competent efforts, for which I want to express my deep gratitude. I also thank Jonathan Culler, who believed in the enterprise from the start and encouraged me to pursue it, even when facing difficulties of sorts which I would rather spare the reader. The same holds for Henry Schogt and Paul Perron, loyal supporters in Toronto.

Nobody but myself is responsible for misunderstandings the theory presented here may provoke. Feedback of any kind will always be most welcome; it will help to increase the usefulness of the book for the audience it aims at: those who, beginners or not, share my interest in narrative as a mode of cultural self-expression.

1985

Preface to the Second Edition

Here is a sequel to the preface. Ten years later, the book was still enough in demand to warrant reprinting it. But I was less and less comfortable with it, and so I proposed to revise it. There were three problems with reprinting it as was. First of all, I was more and more uneasy about the tone of it, the references to 'being sure' and all those remnants of the positivistic discourse of my training that inhere in structuralist thought. I also changed my opinion, or perhaps my mood, regarding the somewhat arid presentation of concepts with examples only relating to the concept being presented. This became so conspicuous as I became a bit looser in my own critical practice. Even more decisively, my recent work has been less oriented towards literary narrative than to narrative in such diverse domains as anthropology, visual art, and the critique of scholarship. And then, of course, there was the problem of all the newer work on narratology I had not known when I first wrote it.

These three problems had me wavering between rejecting it altogether and revising it; between slight and thorough revising. I have moved on to other things since I wrote this book. Yet, the demand for the book did make it obvious that it is an instrument functioning in the public domain that I cannot simply take away. Negotiating my way through all this, I have, I hope, solved two out of the three problems mentioned. I have changed the tone wherever I could, trying to emphasize more the role of narratology as a heuristic tool, not an objective grid providing certainty. To this alleviation there is one exception. I have decided to keep the somewhat illusory abbreviations, such as EN = external narrator. These abbreviations were never meant to suggest greater certainty, only to suggest a mode of quick notation. Although I find them a bit off-putting myself, users have assured me that they are helpful. But readers are, obviously, welcome to ignore them. Regarding the second problem, I have added examples of a very different kind from those in the earlier editions. In addition to ad hoc examples of just one concept at the time, I have inserted short samples of how I have myself 'used' these concepts in works of criticism not given over to technical demonstration. These examples stand out as later additions and, whenever they are a bit longer, they are graphically marked off from the main text. Together, they form a range of works that show simultaneously how narratology can intervene in other disciplines as much as in literature, and what my own intellectual itinerary has been since I first published this book.

In trying to address the third problem, that of other work on narratology that has been published since 1985, I have been less happy. Narrative is more important than ever, not only in literary studies but also in history, where the awareness of narrative construction has grown tremendously; in cultural studies, where cultural memory, documented in mostly narrative form, is a popular subject of study; in film studies, which has itself bloomed over the past ten years, with its inevitably narrative subject matter. But it seems that with the growth of the study of narrative, interest in what makes narratives 'be' or 'come across' as narrative has only declined. Partly, narratology is to blame for this discrepancy, with its positivistic claims, formalist limitations, and inaccessible, idiosyncratic jargon. It is my hope that more modest claims, together with a more accessible presentation and more insight into the way narratology can be used in conjunction with other concerns and theories, may arouse renewed interest in its possibilities.

But, whereas narratology has continued to be elaborated and discussed, little of the work I found was geared towards the beginning narratologist in the way I wanted this book to be. Most work on narrative texts is not based on narratological analysis, and those that are invariably fall back on Genette's classical theory, which I had integrated into this book in so far as it was helpful, and criticized in so far as it was not. The exception is the work based on Bakhtin's theory of dialogism, which offers a different view on narrative. I have integrated this view as best I could without sacrificing consistency. I have continued to pay little attention to reception-oriented theory. This is not a statement on its importance but simply a matter of economy. Within the self-imposed limitations of this book, reception is not an issue of narratology per se, except where communicative figures such as narrator and focalizor can be assumed to have their symmetrical counterparts, their addressees.

Instead, it must be understood that the entire theory presented here is a readerly device, a heuristic tool, that provides focus to the expectations with which readers process narrative. In order to emphasize this I have reversed the order in which I presented the three layers – fabula, story, text – in the earlier edition. It is by way of the text that the reader has access to the story, of which the fabula is, so to speak, a memorial trace that remains with the reader after completion of the reading. Other new work has simply been added to the 'Remarks and Sources' at the end of each chapter.

1997

Preface to the Third Edition

The changes in this third edition compared to the second are numerous. These consist mainly of small clarifications, new examples, and sharper formulations based on teaching experience, reviews of the earlier editions, and helpful comments by colleagues and students. In order to further increase readability, any formulations that now seemed redundant to me have been excised. Concepts that seemed easily to come across as arid, such as the formal categories of the analysis of time, have been presented with more nuance. Relations among the more detailed examples have been established, with the result that throughout the book, extensive analyses emerge without the length required for detailed case studies.

Systematic changes were inspired by three considerations: length, relevance, and updating. For this edition, it became first of all desirable to limit the increasing length of this book, so that it could remain available for students. To that effect, and to vary and update examples, I have decided to replace some of the long case studies I had added to the second by shorter ones. I also eliminated longer analyses of paintings. Although I remain convinced that this theoretical framework can be productive for such analyses, I am more sceptical than I was in 1997 about the interest among art historians to make more than casual use of it. For clarity's sake I limit the examples to discourse, literary or not, and film. But the inclusion of film comes not only from a desire to acknowledge the relevance of narratology for this increasingly important field. I have also, since the second edition, been engaged in making films, and thus encountered the narratological issues from within that medium, so to speak. The experience has been extremely useful, both to realize and to relativize, or rather, specify the importance of narratological issues for the construction – as much as for viewing – of visual narratives.

There was yet another, quite practical reason for the changes in examples. I also wished to integrate a few more literary case studies. These are meant to increase the visibility of the practical usefulness of the concepts offered, and the way they do, indeed, foreground literary considerations. At the suggestion of many I have also offered reflections on the relationship between fiction and reality, in order to enhance the relevance of narratological analysis in contemporary culture.

The concern for relevance also led to a few more drastic changes. While many sections have been modified internally, in Part One I added a section on 'Description Contested' and in Part Two one on 'Nuances of Anachrony,' while some restructuring resulted in a new section, 'Why Characters Resist Us.' Both serve the purpose of integrating new debates, of foregrounding the relevance of the concepts presented, and of making more general discussions on texts visible. In the discussion of character I have offered a more detailed account on how characters emerge, both in the story and in the fabula. These additions have allowed me to introduce modernist texts, notoriously difficult to analyse narratologically. At the end of the three parts I have attempted to pull together the concepts and issues presented in each, sometimes through an extensive example. Especially Part Two ends on an analysis of a textual fragment in view of its 'cinematic' quality.

In trying to address the ongoing need for updating – in other words, the need to take into account other work on narratology that has been published since 1985 – I have limited myself. Theoretical consistency is always at risk of becoming dogmatic. Yet, both theoretically and didactically, consistency is indispensable. With every new publication that I considered, I carefully weighed these two opposing considerations. Narrative is more important than ever, not only in literary studies but also in history, where the awareness of narrative construction has grown tremendously; in cultural analysis, where cultural memory, documented in mostly narrative form, is a popular subject of study; in film studies, which has itself bloomed over the past twenty years, with its inevitably narrative subject matter. But it seems that with the growth of the study of narrative, interest in what makes narratives 'be' or 'come across' as narrative, and to what effect, has only declined. Partly, narratology is to blame for this discrepancy, with its positivistic claims, formalist limitations, and inaccessible, idiosyncratic jargon. It is my hope that more modest claims, together with a more accessible presentation and more insight into the way narratology can be used in conjunction with other concerns and theories, may arouse renewed interest in its possibilities.

But, whereas narratology has continued to be elaborated and discussed, little of the work I found was geared towards the beginning narratologist in the way I wanted this book to be. Most work on narrative texts is not based on narratological analysis, and those that are tend to fall back on Genette's classical theory, which I had integrated into this book in so far as it was helpful, and criticized in so far as it was not. I have continued to pay little attention to reception-oriented theory, but not to reception. Within the self-imposed limitations of this book, reception is not an issue of narratology per se, except where communicative figures such as narrator and focalizor can be assumed to have their symmetrical counterparts, their addressees. Finally, much new work in narratology comes from cognitive approaches. Although I am a bit sceptical regarding the general claims of this approach, I have integrated what I found helpful and added relevant references to other publications.

Instead of developing a reception theory of narrative, it must be understood that the entire theory presented here is a readerly device, a heuristic tool, that provides focus to the expectations with which readers process narrative. In order to emphasize this I had already reversed the order in which I presented the three layers – fabula, story, text – in the first edition. It is by way of the text that the reader has access to the story, of which the fabula is, so to speak, a memorial trace that remains with the reader after completion of the reading.

Other new work that did not require inclusion has been added to the 'Remarks and Sources' at the end of each chapter, with short notices concerning their particular contribution and sometimes the reasons why I have not integrated their views. I thank many readers who have offered comments on the second edition, especially Vincent Meelberg and Peter Verstraten.

2008

NARRATOLOGY

Introduction

I begin with a series of definitions. I do this to empower the student of narrative who can fall back on such definitions, test them against analyses and interpretations, and check their consistency. They are not meant to hold the truth of their object; rather to make it accessible. *Narratology* is the ensemble of theories of narratives, narrative texts, images, spectacles, events; cultural artifacts that 'tell a story.' Such a theory helps to understand, analyse, and evaluate narratives.

A theory is a systematic set of generalized statements about a particular segment of reality. That segment of reality, the corpus, about which narratology attempts to make its pronouncements consists of 'narrative texts' of all kinds, made for a variety of purposes and serving many different functions. Although everyone has a general idea of what narrative texts are, it is certainly not always easy to decide whether or not a given text should be considered narrative, partly or wholly. This is not a problem at all; delimitation is not the point of a theory geared towards facilitating analysis.

Instead, if characteristics can be defined, if only tentatively, these characteristics can serve as the point of departure for the next phase: a description of the way in which each narrative text is constructed. Once this is accomplished, we have a description of a *narrative system*. On the basis of this description, we can then examine the variations that are possible when the narrative system is concretized into narrative texts. This last step presupposes that an infinite number of narrative texts can be described using the finite number of concepts contained within the narrative system.

This book presents an exposition of a coherent, systematic narratology and of the concepts pertaining to it in this sense. Readers are offered an instrument with which they can describe, hence interpret, narrative texts. This does not imply that the theory is some kind of machine into which one inserts a text at one end and expects an adequate description to roll out at the other. The concepts that are presented here must be regarded as intellectual tools for interpretation. These tools are useful in that they enable their users to formulate an interpretive description in such a way that it is accessible to others. Furthermore, discovering the characteristics of a text can also be facilitated by insight into the abstract narrative system. But above all, the concepts help to increase understanding through encouraging readers to articulate what they understand, or think they understand, when reading or otherwise 'processing' a narrative artifact.

The textual description obtained with the help of this theory can by no means be regarded as the only adequate description possible. This is not the point either. Someone else may use the same concepts differently, emphasize other aspects of the text, and, consequently, produce a different description. For reading is an activity of a subjective nature. The point is, if the description of a text is understood as a proposal that can be presented to others, the fact that the description is formulated within the framework of a systematic theory carries with it one important advantage: it facilitates discussion of the proposed description. This is a 'democratic' use of a theory. This is why, even now, I do not relinquish the system of narratology.

With this in mind, we can return to the question of the corpus of narrative texts. Of what does this corpus consist? At first glance, the answer seems obvious: novels, novellas, short stories, fairy tales, newspaper articles, and so forth. But, with or without motivation, we are establishing boundaries, boundaries with which not everyone would agree. Some people, for example, argue that comic strips belong to the corpus of narrative texts, but others disagree. If these people hope to reach agreement, they will wish to explain how they have arrived at their decisions. In this case, the explanation is very simple. Those who consider comic strips to be narrative texts interpret the concept *text* broadly. In their view, a text does not have to be a linguistic text. In comic strips, another, non-linguistic, sign system is employed, namely the visual image. Other individuals, sharing a more restricted interpretation of what constitutes a text, reserve this term for language texts only.

As this simple example demonstrates, it helps to define the concepts we use. A definition works best if it is formulated so clearly that everyone who works with the concept shares the same understanding of the notion as it was originally defined. This ideal situation is sometimes difficult to realize, as, for example, when the concept in question has been used so often that it has begun to lead a life of its own and is understood somewhat differently by every user. Such is the case with very common and seemingly obvious notions such as *literature, text, narrative,* and *poem,* and also with the more specific concepts which will be introduced later in this book, such as 'focalization.' It is, of course, always possible to use a definition that is valid only for the particular study (lesson, discussion, thesis, article) with which one is engaged. The readers will then decide whether or not they will adopt the definition for use in other contexts; but at least the concepts under discussion have been clarified. A disagreement about the status of comic strips would quickly be settled if the definition of a text were first agreed on. In other words, definitions are like a language: they help to provide the 'dictionary' so that one person understands what another means. But no more than a dictionary can definitions enforce themselves.

Presenting a theory about narrative texts entails defining a number of central concepts. Much of this book consists of just such definitions. But let me begin with some basic terms. Within the scope of this *Introduction,* then, a *text* is a finite, structured whole composed of signs. These can be linguistic units, such as words and sentences, but they can also be different signs, such as cinematic shots and sequences, or painted dots, lines, and blots. The finite ensemble of signs does not mean that the text itself is finite, for its meanings, effects, functions, and background are not. It only means that there is a first and a last word to be identified; a first and a last image of a film; a frame of a painting, even if those boundaries, as we will see, are provisional and porous.

The following definitions are such cases as mentioned above, where others use slightly different concepts and definitions. Within the framework of this book, however, I have selected these: *A narrative text* is a text in which an agent or subject conveys to an addressee ('tells' the reader) a story in a particular medium, such as language, imagery, sound, buildings, or a combination thereof. *A story* is the content of that text, and produces a particular manifestation, inflection, and 'colouring'of a fabula; the fabula is presented in a certain manner. *A fabula is* a series of logically and chronologically related events that are caused or experienced by actors. These three definitions together constitute the theory this book elaborates.

These key concepts imply other ones, that I will discuss in due course. Take the last one, the fabula, for example. Its definition contains the elements 'event' and 'actor.' An *event* is the transition from one state to another state. *Actors* are agents that perform actions. They are not necessarily human. *To act* is defined here as to cause or to experience an event. And this series of definitions can go on.

The main point of this theory – the basis of its usefulness for analysis – is the division in three it proposes. The assertion that a narrative text is one in which a story is told implies that the text is not identical to the story. What is meant by these two terms can be clearly illustrated by the following example. Take the familiar story of Tom Thumb. Not everyone has read that story in the same text. There are different *versions*; in other words, there are different texts in which that same story is related. There are noticeable differences among the various texts. Some texts are considered to be literary while others are not; some can be read aloud to children, others are too difficult. Evidently, narrative texts differ from one another even if the related story is the same. It is therefore useful to examine the text separately from the story. The concept of text itself requires some further examination. Here, 'text' refers to narratives in any medium. I use this word with an emphasis on the finite nature and structuredness of narratives, not the linguistic nature of it; to keep this in mind I will use it interchangeably with 'artifact.'

The example of 'Tom Thumb' can again be used to explain the next distinction, that between story and fabula. This distinction is based on the difference between the the way in which the events are presented and the sequence of events as they 'occur' in the imaginative world of the fabula. That difference lies not only in the language used. Despite their having read different texts, readers of 'Tom Thumb' would agree, I expect, as to which of the characters deserves sympathy. They applaud the clever boy and they rejoice at the giant's misfortunes. In order that Tom might triumph over his enemy, readers are quite prepared to watch unabashedly as Tom exchanges crowns so that the blind giant unwittingly eats his own children. Readers are, in fact, delighted by this trick. Evidently, this rather cruel fabula is presented in such a way in all of the texts that the readers are willing to sacrifice one group of children for another. When 'Tom Thumb' is told in another sign system – in a cartoon film, for example – more or less the same reactions are evoked. This phenomenon demonstrates that something happens with the fabula which is not exclusively language-based.

These definitions suggest that a three-layer distinction – text, story, fabula – is a good basis for a further study of narrative texts. Such a distinction carries with it the assumption that it is possible to analyse the three layers separately. That does not mean that these layers exist independently of one another. They do not. The only material which we have for our investigation is the text before us. But, even this statement is not correct; the readers have only the book, paper and ink, or the strokes of paint on a canvas, the light in a dark (movie) theatre, the sound coming out of speakers, and they must use this material to establish themselves the structure of the text. That a text can be divided into three layers is, instead, a theoretical supposition based on a process of reasoning, of which I have given a summary above. Only the text layer, embodied in the sign system of language, visual images, or any other, is more or less directly accessible.

The distinction in layers is an instrumental and provisional tool. The reader wishing to analyse a text distinguishes different layers of a text in order to account for particular effects which the text has on its readers. Of course, the reader, at least the 'average' or 'natural' reader – not the analyst – does not make such a distinction. In this *Introduction*, written as an instrument for examining texts, the theory is based on the notion of distinct layers, a distinction that is necessary for a detailed analysis. It is, therefore, inevitable that what is in effect inseparable should temporarily be disjoined.

Within this framework, the following topics will be discussed. I will first present them in the order one tends to think of them, and then reverse that order. The fabula, understood as material or content that is worked into a story, has been defined as a series of events. This series is constructed according to certain rules. We call this the logic *of events.* Structuralists often work from the assumption that the series of events presented in a story answers to the same rules as those controlling human behaviour, since a narrative text would otherwise be impossible to understand. If human behaviour is taken as the criterion for describing events, then the question immediately arises of the function of the agents of action, the actors. French semiotician Greimas' suggestion that the actors be described in relation to the events provides one possible answer to this question. However, two other elements in a fabula can be described.

An event, no matter how insignificant, always takes up time. This time has a hypothetical status: in a fabula the events have not actually occurred, or at least, their reality status is not relevant for their internal logic. Nevertheless, the time is often important for the continuation of the fabula and deserves, consequently, to be made describable. If Tom

Thumb had not had seven-mile boots at his disposal, he would never have been able to flee from the giant in time. The difference between the time that Tom Thumb needs to escape from the giant's grasp and the time that the giant needs to wake up is, in this case, decisive for the happy ending of the fabula. Furthermore, events always occur *somewhere*, be it a place that actually exists (Amsterdam) or an imaginary place (C.S. Lewis' Narnia). Events, actors, time, and location together constitute the material of a fabula. In order to differentiate the components of this layer from other aspects, I shall refer to them as *elements*.

Still following the order of structuralist theory, these elements are organized in a certain way into a story. Their arrangement in relation to one another is such that they can produce the effect desired, be this convincing, moving, disgusting, or aesthetic. Several processes are involved in ordering the various elements into a story. These processes are not to be confused with the author's activity – it is both impossible and useless to generalize about the latter. The principles of ordering which are described here have a hypothetical status only, and their purpose is to make possible a description of the way content material comes across in the story. I distinguish the following:

1 The events are arranged in a sequence which can differ from the chronological sequence.
2 The amount of time allotted in the story to the various elements of the fabula is determined with respect to the amount of time which these elements take up in the fabula.
3 The actors are provided with distinct traits. In this manner, they are individualized and transformed into characters.
4 The locations where events occur are also given distinct characteristics and are thus transformed into specific places.
5 In addition to the necessary relationships among actors, events, locations, and time, all of which were already describable in the layer of the fabula, other relationships (symbolic, allusive, traditional, etc.) may exist among the various elements.
6 A choice is made from among the various 'points of view' from which the elements can be presented. The resulting *focalization*, the relation between 'who perceives' and what is perceived, 'colours' the story with subjectivity.

The result of these several processes is a specific story which is distinct from other stories. I shall refer to the traits which are specific to a given story as *aspects*.

A fabula that has been ordered into a story is still not a text. A narrative text is a story that is 'told,' conveyed to recipients, and this telling requires a medium; that is, it is converted into *signs*. As was evident from the definition of a narrative text, these signs are produced by an agent who relates, who 'utters' the signs. This agent cannot be identified with the writer, painter, composer, or filmmaker. Rather, the writer withdraws and calls upon a fictitious spokesman, an agent technically known as the *narrator*. But the narrator does not relate continually. Whenever direct speech occurs in the text, it is as if the narrator temporarily transfers this function to one of the actors. When describing the text layer, it is thus important to ascertain *who* is doing the narrating.

A text does not consist solely of narration in the specific sense. In every narrative text, one can point to passages that concern something other than events, such as an opinion about something, for example, or a disclosure on the part of the narrator which is not directly connected with the events, a description of a face or of a location. It is thus possible to examine what is said in a text, and to classify it as narrative, descriptive, or argumentative. Such an analysis often helps to assess the ideological or aesthetic thrust of a narrative. The one question that still remains is how all of this is narrated. There is often a noticeable difference between the narrator's style and that of the actors. As a result of this division into three parts, a division based on the three distinct layers previously discussed, some topics that traditionally constitute a unified whole will be treated separately in different stages of this study. An example of this is the anthropomorphic figure, called 'actor' in the study of the fabula, 'character' in the study of the story, and 'speaker' in the study of the text.

The network of definitions serves not only as an instrument for analysis, but prior to that, as standards for the delimitation of what we consider narratives. I can now formulate more precisely those characteristics that can be instrumental in specifying the corpus of narrative texts, the corpus for which this theory should be valid. Ideally, the characteristics of narrative text should be as follows:

1 Two types of 'speakers' utter the signs that constitute a narrative text; one does not play a role in the fabula whereas the other does. This difference exists even when the narrator and the actor are one and

the same person as, for example, in a narrative related in the first person. The narrator is the same person, but at another moment and in another situation than when she originally experienced the events.

2 We can distinguish three layers in a narrative text: the text, the story, and the fabula. Each of these layers can be described.

3 That with which the narrative text is concerned, the 'contents' it conveys to its readers, is a series of connected events caused or experienced by actors presented in a specific manner.

Plausible as this division seems – and I have found it very useful in practice – neither reading nor writing proceeds in this order. In fact, logically speaking, the reader first 'sees' the text, not the fabula. The fabula is really the result of the mental activity of reading, the interpretation by the reader, an interpretation influenced both by the initial encounter with the text and by the manipulations of the story. The fabula is a memory trace that remains after the reading is completed. And how writers proceed we simply cannot know. Writers work mostly alone, filmmakers are part of a team. Either way, they work in different manners. Nor do we need, or even want to know. Narrative, the object of study in this book, is a cultural phenomenon, one of the many cultural processes by which we live. It is the conditions of possibility of those processes that constitute the interest of narrative analysis; there lies the cultural relevance. To underscore this point more forcefully, I have reversed the more traditional order in which the three layers are presented.

Together, and keeping in mind that 'text' refers to units in all semiotic systems, the characteristics mentioned above produce a definition: a narrative text is a text in which all three characteristics are found. These characteristics are not exclusive to narratives. The third characteristic specifically also applies, for example, to dramatic texts. Yet, there are texts which display all three characteristics, but which nevertheless, on the basis of either tradition or intuition, people do not regard as narrative texts. This is true of many poems. *The Waste Land* by T.S. Eliot is one of the numerous examples. A poem such as this may be termed a narrative poem, and its narrative characteristics may also be narratologically described. That this does not often occur can be attributed to the fact that the poem displays other, more salient characteristics, such as poetic ones; Eliot's poem remains first a poem, and its narrative features are of but secondary importance. Evidently, the characteristics do not lead to an absolute specification of the corpus, and that's a good thing, too.

This in turn implies that a narrative theory facilitates description only of the narrative aspects of a text and not all the characteristics, even of a clearly narrative text. It is, therefore, as impossible as it is undesirable to specify a fixed corpus. This is an issue of *relevance*; the answer to the always-useful question 'so what?' We can only specify a corpus of texts in which the narrative characteristics are so dominant that their description may be considered relevant. Alternatively, we can use the theory to describe segments of non-narrative texts as well as the narrative aspects of any given text, such as, for example, the poem by Eliot. The relativity of such a specification is at least clearly established. Why bother with such analyses? A preliminary answer to that question of relevance is that narratives, or rather, the narrativity that makes artifacts narrative, grabs and holds the attention.

A number of descriptive concepts result from the development of the theory of such a narrative system. These concepts make possible a description of narrative texts *to the extent that they are narrative*. Because the theory to which these concepts pertain is a systematic one, it is in principle possible to give a complete description of a text, that is an account of all of the *narrative* characteristics of the text in question. However, the 'so what?' question applies here as well. Such a description would present the task of a lifetime and produce the most tedious, uninteresting kind of result. The analyst, therefore, will always make choices. Intuition often brings together a striking aspect of an artifact and a relevant theoretical element. Intuitively, on the basis of a careful reading of the text, as well as a careful attention to one's reader's response, one selects those elements of the theory which one thinks particularly relevant to the text. Those will be, I presume, the features that triggered your interest in the first place.

This partial description of the text helps make further assumptions about other aspects of the text. These assumptions can then be tested on the basis of other information. The textual description that results provides the basis for interpretation, from which, importantly, it cannot be distinguished. Common lore has it that it is possible on the basis of a description ('the text is so constructed') to attach a meaning to the text ('the text means this'). In reality, interpretation is involved every step of the way. Precisely for that reason a systematic theory is helpful, not to eliminate or bracket interpretation but to make it arguable. An interpretation is never anything more than a proposal ('I think that the text means this'). If a proposal is to be accepted, it must be well founded ('I think, on the basis of the data shown, that the text means this'). If a proposal is based on a precise description it can then be discussed, even if, in practice, the intuitive interpretation preceded even the first step of the analysis. The theory presented here is an instrument for making descriptions, and hence interpretations, discussable. *That*, not objectivity or certainty, 'being right' or 'proving wrong,' is the point.

Such discussions are possible and relevant because interpretation is both subjective and susceptible to cultural constraints. They define each reader as a cultural being; a participant in a continuous discussion about meaning. Endorsing that view entails an interest in framings – those constraints that make the process of interpretation of more general interest. This turns narrative analysis into an activity of *cultural analysis*. This is the case even if one's object of study is literary only. To underscore that point I will intersperse the literary and made-up examples with some non-linguistic ones, and also make remarks here and there about the cultural importance of the phenomena under scrutiny. These remarks, moreover, also emphasize the subjective nature of my own interpretations, and should be thus understood.

Subjectivity, understood as the crossing, in culture, of individual and social existence, also characterizes the concepts themselves. The provisional definitions given above, and the more elaborate ones that follow, have in common a special focus on *agency*. To talk about narrators, for example, is to impute agency to a subject of narration, even if this subject is not to be identified with the narrator. I will explain that focalizors, in the story, are the subjects of perception and interpretation. Actors, in the fabula, are the subjects of action. This attention paid to agency and, hence, to subjectivity is, indeed, the basic tenet of the theory presented in this book. It is not meant to claim exclusivity for this view but to insist on the complex manner in which narrative communicates. In the two decades since this book was first published, the need for such a view has become far from redundant.

I want to keep present the procedures of and responsibility for meaning in the face of more 'messy' philosophies of language which insist on the diverse provenance (Bakhtin) and ambiguous meanings (Derrida) of any utterance. Far from rejecting such philosophies, I find them useful to avoid overestimating the freedom of agency, which is such a dogma in the West. Yet, within a culture that functions within such 'messy' meaning-making, it is all the more important to take and assign responsibility for the choices we make. Cognitive and reception-oriented theories of language and narrative have persuasively argued that it is the reader who 'makes' the meaning. I am in fundamental agreement with both these positions. The point is not that meaning can be pinpointed in any simple way. But it is only once we know how a text is structured that the reader's share – and responsibility – for acting within those constraints can be clearly assessed.

In spite of two decades during which narratology went out of style, became hot again, and now appears a highly specialized occupation, I do not really think that the corpus of predominantly narrative texts and artifacts has been sufficiently explored with the help of narratology, or that the impact of narrative on cultural hotbeds of meaning-making has been clearly understood. On the contrary, most studies of narrative texts are weak precisely in that their authors fail to use adequate descriptive tools. Thus they fail to account for the subjectivity of their interpretations and to open these up for discussion. But the point I am making is that even if one assumes there have been enough narratological analyses of narrative texts, it is obvious that there have hardly been any narratological analyses of non-narrative texts, which undermines the very generic distinction on which the idea of 'narrative texts' is based. One may want to replace the approach with a different one, be it ideological, psychoanalytic, or rhetorical, but one may also, instead, want to mobilize narratological insights for other objects and approaches. Here, in contrast, narratology can help supply insights that the field where different objects are studied has traditionally not itself developed.

Remarks and Sources

On the irrelevance of formalist models, see Brooks (1984). See also my review article of Brooks, Stanzel, and Genette in *Poetics Today*, 1986, which discusses that irrelevancy claim. I contend, there, that Stanzel never took up the challenge of structuralism, that Genette did but then gave up, and that Brooks bypassed it. All three, then, failed to address the issues structuralism has raised, to the detriment of their own theories.

On Bakhtin, see Hirschkop and Shepherd (1989), and, of course, Bakhtin himself (1981). Peeren (2008) offers a discussion of Bakhtin's relevance for cultural analysis of popular culture (mainly television serials and films). My attempts to distinguish narrative from other discourses are not meant to turn narrative into a distinct 'thing' – to 'reify' it – but only to open narrative discourse, in whatever medium, up for analysis. I find the definition proposed by Cohan and Shires to lead to the opposite result. A definition such as 'the story is mediated by its telling' – its medium of communication – so that the two are insepa-rable – undeniable but so vague that it hardly helps the student inter-ested in specific narrative analysis (1988: 3). The best introduction to Derrida's thought remains Culler (1983).

Herman (2002) usuefully insists on interest as a guiding principle. His book is primarily anchored in classification. While often illuminat-ing, the approach through classification leads to an unnecessary cre-ation of new categories whenever analysis complicates the latter. This seems a loss to me; 'failure' of categories to 'fit' is important and best taken at face value. For more on the way readers construct stories and retain fabulas, see Herman, ed. (2003). A useful encyclopedia of narra-tive theory, primarily from a cognitive perspective, was edited by Her-man, Jahn, and Ryan (2005).

Finally, reviews of the second edition, especially Margolin (1998), have been very useful in further modifying both the tone and the actual concepts of the present book.

There are several specialized approaches to narratology that deserve mentioning. One is the psychological approach. This is a radicaliza-tion of the cognitive one, exclusively oriented to reception. I remain unconvinced, but a representative instance allows my readers to judge for themselves (Bortolussi and Dixon 2003). Another is feminist nar-ratology, which I find in itself a worthwhile endeavour, although not always elaborated systematically enough to help the practising analyst. See, for example, Mezei (ed.).

The insistance, in this third edition, on the cultural status of narra-tive is partially meant in response to Culler's resistance against cultural studies – a resistance that part of me shares but inflects, rather, into the development of 'cultural analysis' (Culler 2007; Bal ed. 1998).

1

Text: Words and Other Signs

1: Preliminary Remarks

A narrative text is a text in which a narrative agent tells a story. Earlier
I gave this as a definition of the textual layer. In this chapter, I further
explain the different aspects of this definition. The first question is that
of the identity and status of the narrative agent. Before we can begin
discussing this, however, I would like to place this concept in relation
to some neighbouring though different concepts. When, in this chapter,
I discuss the narrative agent, or narrator, I mean the (linguistic, visual,
cinematic) subject, a function and not a person, which expresses itself in
the language that constitutes the text. It hardly needs mentioning that
this agent is not the (biographical) author of the narrative. The narrator
of *Emma* is not Jane Austen. The historical person Jane Austen is not
without importance for literary history, but the circumstances of her
life are of no consequence to the specific discipline of narratology. In
order to keep this distinction in mind, I shall here and there refer to the
narrator as 'it,' however odd this may seem.

In his famous attack on the concept and authority of the author,
Foucault banishes four different concepts of authorship ('What Is an
Author?'). Not only does he question the psychological idea of the author, of the authorial intention, and of the historical author as 'origin'
of the work, but he also jettisons the last stronghold of the concept of
the author, the author-function as the centring of meaning. He does this
by demonstrating it to be a projection of a reader who needs semantic
centrality to deal with the work. Foucault's alternative is a radical pro-
liferation of meaning, where the author/work becomes a fluctuating
function always interacting with other functions in the larger discursive field.

So far so good; but is there a limit to these fluctuations? Or are we thus bound to an anything-goes attitude? I resist this, because it makes any future shift in power relations within the culture from now on invisible. My position here is that there *are* limits, but not limits that can be authenticated through appeal to the author, even when interpreting 'author' in the widest sense of the historical context. Instead, those limits are strategic, yet fundamental. They are fundamental, for any position that does not assess the political basis of the status quo cannot challenge the established cultural powers. This is so because, simply, these powers were established on political grounds. But once shifting, strategic limits are accepted as replacement for both 'natural' limits and Foucaldian 'anti-limits,' then these new boundaries will offer a starting-point. From that point it becomes possible to develop a politics of reading that draws its legitimacy from explicit political positions, not from any fictitious 'real' knowledge – let alone 'neutrality.' And once we acknowledge both the necessity and the strategic nature of limits to interpretation, we move from the question of the author back to the question of interpretation.

This is not to deny the importance of the author or artist as the historical subject who made the text. My concern to make this distinction is not to deny authorship but to emancipate both author and reader from the stronghold of a misconceived interpretive authority. This authority is ultimately a problem of censorship. Censorship of art, be it overtly political or subliminally social, is confirmed, strengthened, and perpetuated by censoring forms of interpretation. In a world where access to writing and other forms of artistic expression is made difficult – by the institutional censors of art – for all individuals not conforming to a self-asserting mainstream, making interpretation a privileged form of art-processing subjugates it to the same mechanisms of exclusion.

But there is more to it. True, the academic practice of interpretation, linked with journalism and other more popular forms of interpretation through a common ideology and often even through shared personnel, can be a form of censorship in itself. The margins built within art and the reigning concepts of beauty leave some space for the production of works that cannot be exhausted by mainstream response. Yet, the exclusions operating within the very activity of interpretation as a practice taught and learned can easily take care of all interpretations that might enhance the unsettling aspects of these not-so-mainstream works; of interpretations which make the works threatening. Masterful interpretations based on invisible assumptions can thus be given an authority that censors other views. But for the same reason, censorship *of* interpretation can be used to cover up censorship *by* interpretation.

A more open academic and educational policy can make room to include the views of those who respond to art from a less dominating social position. Such an opening up is an indispensable next step towards a better, more diverse and complex understanding of culture. In spite of its challenging and persuasive logic, we must place the authority of authorship within this dynamic. To put it overly simply: as soon as women began to speak, the subject of speech was no longer relevant; but also, as soon as women began to interpret, there was no more need for interpretation. In other words, the same threat is acutely present as the one that the 'death of the author' poses. This demonstrates precisely how the problematic of interpretation and the challenge to the authorial authority are related. The distinction between author and narrator, once a structuralist reification of textual subjectivity, continues to carry strategic weight in this sense. It helps to disentangle the different voices that speak in a text so as to make room for the reader's input in judging the relative persuasiveness of those voices.

In speaking of the narrator, I do not mean the so-called 'implied author,' either. This term was introduced by Wayne C. Booth (1961) in order to discuss and analyse the ideological and moral stances of a narrative text without having to refer directly to a biographical author. As such it preceded the generalized use of the term 'narrator.' There are three problems with this term. First, in Booth's use of the term, it denotes the totality of meanings that can be inferred from a text. Thus the implied author is the *result* of the investigation of the meaning of a text, and not the *source* of that meaning. Only after interpreting the text on the basis of a text description can the 'implied author' be inferred and discussed.

Second, therefore, the term mystifies and overwrites the reader's imput and is easily recuperated to grant the interpretation of one person, e.g., a teacher or critic, the authority of knowing 'what the author meant to say' and thereby relegates the reader again to the margins. Third, the notion of an implied author is, in this sense, not limited to narrative texts, but can be applied to any text. This is why the notion is not specific to narratology, which has as its objective the narrative aspects of a narrative text.

The notion of the narrator needs still further positioning, however. I do not mean a story-teller, a visible, fictive 'I' who interferes in his/her account as much as s/he likes, or even participates as a character in the action. Such an explicit narrator is a specific version of the narrator, one of the several different possibilities of manifestation. In this chapter, I shall rigorously keep to the definition of 'that agent which utters the (linguistic or other) signs which constitute the text.' Only if we confine ourselves to this definition can we avoid confusions which ultimately lead to an appropriation of authority, a blurring of textual nuances, and an invisibility of the power inequalities involved.

2: The Narrator

There are two reasons for beginning this chapter with the narrator. The narrator is the most central concept in the analysis of narrative texts. The identity of the narrator, the degree to which and the manner in which that identity is indicated in the text, and the choices that are implied lend the text its specific character. This topic is closely related to the notion of focalization, with which it has, traditionally, been identified. Narrator and focalization together determine the narrative situation. The focalizor, as this concept will be defined in chapter 2, is an aspect of the story this narrator tells. It is the represented 'colouring' of the fabula by a specific agent of perception, the holder of the 'point of view.' If we see focalization as part of narration, as is usually done, we fail to make a distinction between linguistic, visual, or auditive – hence, textual – agents and the purpose, the 'colouring,' the object, of their activity.

The fact that 'narration' tends to imply focalization is related to the notion that language shapes vision and world-view, rather than the other way around. As far as it implies that language can be isolated from its object only artificially, for the duration of the analysis, that idea makes sense. The separation into several layers is only temporarily meaningful, and has as its purpose a better insight into the functioning of the extremely complex meaning production of narrative texts. Distinguishing layers is meaningful analytically only. And doing so leads to the conclusion that 'seeing,' taken in the widest sense, constitutes the *object* of narrating.

This is, emphatically, not to say that the narrator should not be analysed in relation to the focalizing agent. On the contrary, precisely when the connection between these two agents is not self-evident, it becomes easier to gain insight into the complexity of the relationship between the three agents that function in the three layers – the narrator, the focalizor, the actor – and those moments at which they do or do not overlap in the shape of a single 'person.'

In Steven Spielberg's controversial 1993 film *Schindler's List* – an example that will recur throughout this book – the distinction is important. In the beginning, the actor Schindler is just one of the Nazis, socializing with them, taking advantage of the war and of the depletion of the Jews. But in order to do that he must deal with – that is, *see* – an individual Jew, the man named Stern. The filmic narrator has to show – cinema's major form of narration – what Schindler sees and what that seeing does to him. I didn't know the story when I went to see the film; I didn't know this awful man was going to change into a good man. There was no explication, no moment it happened inside him, but at some point he was a different man. How was this transformation *narrated*? Was there a conversion? If so, that is a Christian concept. True, Schindler was a Christian, although using the church to do business; but culturally he was. Yet, the reduction of conversion to a Christian meaning would obscure the narrative as well as (inter)cultural importance of that moment.

The distinction between narrator and focalizor is crucial here. For the 'conversion' scene implies an important statement on *vision:* conversion is defined as *seeing,* not in a positivistic or in a psychological but in a narratological sense; seeing differently, and seeing difference turns the fabula around, makes the character different. And in Jewish culture, as many a biblical text demonstrates, seeing primarily equals insight. The turn-around is, for Schindler, to see individuals instead of the devastating, dehumanizing bureaucracy of numbers. Schindler's moment of insight happens – as is visually told – when the filmic text 'tells' how he watches the destruction of the ghetto from the top of a hill, and from horseback. The scene emphasizes the seeing from top down, which is usually – in the visual discourse of Western culture –a mastering, colonizing gaze.. Later on, by another intervention of the narrator, this gaze is echoed in the gaze of Schindler's evil twin, Amon Goeth. Goeth *oversees* the camp from the balcony of his villa, which gives him the impulse to shoot inmates randomly.

These are two opposite extremes of what a top-down gaze can produce. It takes an agent of narration to (visually) 'tell' these two opposed reactions to a similar visual event. During this 'conversion' scene, Schindler sees the horror of what he has so far participated in, when he sees a little girl, whose red coat is the only element of colour in the film up to the ending. That scarce use of colour is a stylistic mark of the narration; the fact that Schindler sees it and acts upon that perception is an issue of focalization. That we see him seeing it results from (cinematic)

narration. Later at the holocaust one of the bodies on a cart is also coloured in this red; and again, Schindler's look follows it, perhaps her.
Thus, the narrator 'marries' Schindler's spiritual itinerary from evil to
good with the girl's itinerary from life to death. This matching is an act
of narration. Only through analysing this narration can we see that this
film, at least in these moments, does not glorify the former profiteer but
marks the fatal fact that his conversion is 'always-already' too late; that
sacrifice accompanies it.

The narrator's visual language works out this conjunction between
Schindler and the little girl in complex detail. Schindler's look becomes
an engaging look instead of a mastering gaze at the precise moment
when it detaches an individual from the machinery of massacre. The
little girl who runs around is detached from her parents – she seems
lost – and visually detached from the masses, from hell as backdrop.
Schindler's connection to her is her only 'place' in the narrative. Looking becomes in itself a way of saving – although, because of the narrative's avoiding of individualism as anecdotal, this girl will not survive
and never enters Schindler's factory.

Forms of Narration: 'I' and 'He' Are Both 'I'

Traditionally, narratives have been called, according to the 'voice' of
the narrator, 'first-person' or 'third-person' novels, with an exceptional
'second-person' experiment such as Michel Butor's *La modification*. To
what does the distinction between first-person and third-person novels
correspond? Let us first consider an example that will return at some
length in chapter 2: the beginning of Dutch naturalist novelist Louis
Couperus' *Of Old People*. There, a woman, Ottilie, hears the voice of her
estranged husband, Steyn.

a Steyn's deep bass resounded in the vestibule.

In this sentence we distinguish:

1 An event in an (in this case fictitious) fabula: the sounding of a voice
belonging to Steyn.
2 Someone who hears the voice resound, who is sensitive to the timbre
of that voice and to the specific (hollow) resonance that sounds acquire in a vestibule.
3 A speaking agent that names the event and its perception.

The speaking agent does not mention itself in the process. It might just as well have done so. Then we would have read: '(I narrate:) Steyn's deep bass resounded in the vestibule.' This does not change anything in the analysis. It does not make a difference to the status of the narration whether a narrator refers to itself or not. As soon as there is language, there is a speaker who utters it; as soon as those linguistic utterances constitute a narrative text, there is a narrator, a narrating subject. As soon as there are images that represent figures doing things, there is a form of narration going on. From a grammatical point of view, this narrating subject is always a 'first person.' In fact, the term 'third-person narrator' is absurd: a narrator is not a 'he' or 'she.' At best the narrator can narrate about someone else, a 'he' or 'she' – who might, incidentally, happen to be a narrator as well. Of course, this does not imply that the distinction between 'first-person' and 'third-person' narratives is itself invalid. Just compare the following sentences:

b I shall be twenty-one tomorrow.

c Elizabeth will be twenty-one tomorrow.

If what I said above is valid, we may rewrite both sentences as:

(I say:) I shall be twenty-one tomorrow.

(I say:) Elizabeth will be twenty-one tomorrow.

Both sentences are uttered by a speaking subject, an 'I': The difference rests in the object of the utterance. In b the 'I' speaks about itself. In c the 'I' speaks about someone else. When in a text the narrator never refers explicitly to itself as a character, we speak of an external narrator (EN). This term indicates that the narrating agent does not figure in the fabula as an actor. On the other hand, if the 'I' is to be identified with a character, hence, also an actor in the fabula, we speak of a character-bound narrator, a CN.

This difference between an EN and a CN, a narrator that tells about others and a narrator that tells about him- or herself – such a narrator is personified – entails a difference in the narrative rhetoric of 'truth.' A CN usually proclaims that it recounts true facts about her- or himself. 'It' pretends to be writing 'her' autobiography, even if the fabula is blatantly implausible, fantastic, absurd, metaphysical. Julio Cortázar's famous short story 'Axolotl' tells us 'in the first person' how the narrator changed into an axolotl, a kind of lizard. This form enables him to explore 'from the inside' what it means to be human. The narrative form sets up a confrontation between the limits of a sense of humanity confined to the individual and the recognition by others that defines it in poststructuralist thought. The narrative rhetoric of a CN is therefore here indicated by the addition:

(I narrate: (I state autobiographically:)) I felt a great anxiety that day.

Let me illustrate this with three examples involving children.

Compare the following passage from a children's book about a family accident in which the mother is so badly hurt that – after the quoted passage – she will die. The older daughter, who is about eight, narrates:

But this afternoon I hate it all. They don't know I dreamed about Mum, and why. What *do* they know? The same as I do? *Say* it then! I start yelling and calling names. Then I'm so ashamed that I creep away under the blankets. I hate everybody.

Arno Bohlmeijer, *Something Very Sorry*, 110

This moving story is actually a 'true,' that is, non-fictional account, written by the father, not the girl who is 'speaking' here. But the narrator emphatically claims to speak the truth, which is indicated by the emphasis on problems of access – 'what *do* they know?' – and the honesty with which she gives away her shame over her obnoxious behaviour. As a consequence, the reader not only believes her but understands her behaviour, better than she can herself.

Now, the following two passages come from an autobiographical book; yet the narrator has a different, though equally 'truthful' rhetoric:

We were sitting in a cornfield waiting for the sun to set. Mother, Daddy, and I and our guides, a man and a woman who had given us directions from the train station.

Susan Rubin Suleiman, *Budapest Diary*, 3

In the taxi to our hotel, all I could think about was that I was in a city where even the cabdrivers spoke Hungarian. Once he found out I spoke the language and had lived in Budapest, our driver started firing questions.   19

The first of these passages is the beginning of the book; the second opens the second chapter. The author is the same, Susan Rubin Suleiman (also a well-known literary critic). The narrators are different. From the language of the first passage we can assume the narrator is a child. The name 'Daddy' tells us that, as does the reference to the guides as 'a man and a woman,' without proper names. The information we get about the narrator implies much more, of course. The interpreter can speculate about the familial relationships suggested by the difference between 'Mother' and 'Daddy,' especially in light of the book's intriguing subtitle, 'In Search of the Motherbook.' The narrator of the second passage is an adult; or at least, someone whose knowledge of Hungarian was not obvious from the start ('Once he found out I spoke the language'). This anecdote tells us that the narrator was at first assumed to be a foreigner in Budapest.

The first passage, although not saying anything about language, suggests that the child narrator is in her own country, Hungary. As the narrator soon tells us, Hungarian was her mother tongue as a child, she lost it, and got it back as a 'foreign' language. In fact, the book is very much focused on this particular way of being 'in language.' The subtitle beautifully reflects this focus: 'Motherbook' is a literal translation of the Hungarian word for the arid administration of birth certificates. Given the narrator's double status as a former native and now foreign speaker, the word has the music of the childhood, in which, precisely, she is no more. The distinction between author and narrator is crucial for reading this book: the crucial issue that the story addresses is, precisely, the way language 'splits' the subject, a general idea in poststructuralism which is particularly dramatic in the case of this subject's relation to a language acquired, lost, and (partly) regained.

Yet another example of a child narrator shows that the autobiographical claim implied in CN narration can have vastly different implications.

> I drop the food and break into pieces she took my face away there is no one to want me to say my name ...
> ... I see her face which is mine. ... I have to have my face ... I follow her we are in the diamonds which are her earrings now my face is coming I have to have it I am looking for the join ... now I am her face my own face has left me ... I want to be the two of us ... I want the join.
> Toni Morrison, *Beloved*, 212–13

This narration of an experience is, at first sight, so strange that for that reason alone we do not doubt its veracity. The mixture of fusion with the mother and the fragmentation of the self, reminiscent of another tenet of the same psychoanalytic theory to which Suleiman's narrators related, speaks of the early infant's lack of a formed ego. This general idea is here inflected in the historical drama of slavery. The fragmentation and fusion that inhibit the formation of subjectivity are here used to represent the difficulty of remembering a traumatic past – that of slavery, in turn represented in the most painful of its experiences, the impossibility of mother-child relationships under such conditions. The difficulty of remembering that comes with trauma is, metaphorically, embodied in the difficulty of re-membering the body, the face.

These three examples of a CN (an 'I' identifiable as a character doing the narrating) imply a rhetoric of veracity. This rhetoric is not the privilege of CN narrators, however. The rhetoric of an EN can also be used to present a story about others as true. We may indicate this as follows:

(I narrate: (I testify:)) Elizabeth felt a great anxiety that day.

Unless otherwise indicated, there is no reason to doubt that the character did feel that anxiety. On the other hand, the rhetoric sometimes points to the presence of invention. Indications that the narrator is out to tell a fictive story and wants the readers to know it are, for instance, narrations of impossible or unknowable situations, or generic indications such as 'Once upon a time...,' which is often present at the beginning of a fairy tale, and subtitles such as 'A Novel' or 'A Winter's Tale.' These indications suggest fictionality. The fabula is fictitious, invented. An instance of the child's play of make-believe.

All Kinds of 'I's

Compare the following passages, of which only d is from Couperus' novel *Of Old People*.

  d Steyn's deep bass resounded in the vestibule.
    Come Jack, come dog, come along with your boss! Are you coming? The happy bark of the terrier resounded. Up and down on the stairs stormed his enthusiastic speed, as if tripping over his own paws.
    Oh, that voice of Steyn's! mama Ottilie hissed between her teeth, and she angrily turned the pages in her book.

e I sat quietly dozing in the room. But, again, I was not allowed to remain so. Hardly had I sat there five minutes when there it was again. Steyn's deep bass resounded in the vestibule. Oh, that voice of Steyn's!

f One day a gentleman, whom I shall, for simplicity's sake, call Steyn, went for a walk with his dog, while his wife sat dozing in the room. Steyn's deep bass resounded in the vestibule. She started at his voice, because she is very sensitive to sounds. Oh, that voice of Steyn's!

g Though Steyn assured me repeatedly that he only went out to walk his dog, his wife remained convinced that he kept a mistress. Every time he went out, she was irritated. One day it happened again. Steyn's deep bass resounded in the vestibule. Oh, that voice of Steyn's!

If we compare the relationship between the narrative 'I' and what is narrated in these four fragments, we can contrast d and f with e and g. The 'I,' the narrative subject in d and f, is not a character in the story it narrates, while the narrator of e and g is also a character. Looking at example a, we note that the sentence that this example consists of recurs unchanged in all four fragments. In each we have:

1 a speaking agent, which names the event and its perception
2 someone who hears the sound of that voice, and – it appears – is irritated
3 an event in a fabula: the sounding of Steyn's voice

In d, as we can say now that we have full information, the voice belongs to the character Steyn; the perception, i.e. the irritation, belongs to Steyn's wife Ottilie (a character-bound focalizor, or CF); and the speaking agent is an EN. Since we are dealing with a novel, we expect that the fabula is invented, but this is of minor importance here. Now we can interpret the sentence like this: (I narrate: (I invent: (Ottilie focalizes:))) Steyn's deep bass resounded in the vestibule. If we want to indicate briefly how the sentence works, we might also formulate it like this: EN [CF (Ottilie)–Steyn]. The narrator, the focalizor, and the actor are each of different identity: the narrator is EN, the focalizor is Ottilie, and the actor is Steyn.

In e we apparently have a narrator whose intention it is to relate the events of her own life in a story which will explain its eventual outcome (let us assume a divorce). We may interpret the sentence like this: (I narrate: (I state autobiographically in order to explain:)) Steyn's deep bass resounded in the vestibule. This sentence relates the event caused by the actor Steyn, its perception by the focalizor 'I,' and the narrative act by the narrator 'I'; both those 'I's are called Ottilie. Thus we have: CN (Ott.) [CF (Ott.)–Steyn]. Two of the three agents have the same name and the same identity.

In f the situation is different again. The word 'I' appears in the text. The narrator names itself. But it is not a character in the fabula. Still, it does more than just refer to its identity as an 'I.' A sentence like 'because she is very sensitive to sounds' presents itself as an explanation which might even denote partiality, though we cannot decide on the basis of this brief fragment. The sensitivity mentioned might constitute an accusation of Steyn, who takes insufficient account of it. On the other hand, it can be an accusation of Ottilie, who is hypersensitive. Let me, temporarily, choose the first interpretation. Then we have, as I will explain in the next chapter, a case of double focalization, that of the anonymous focalizor which may be located in the narrative agent, and that of the character to which it is partial: EF [CF (Ott.)]–Steyn, or, with an indication of the levels of focalization: EF1 [CF2 (Ott.)]–Steyn. The fact that the focalization cannot reside exclusively with the EN is apparent from the sentence that follows 'Steyn's deep bass resounded in the vestibule': Ottilie started at the sound of Steyn's voice. Supposing again that this fragment is taken from a novel, we take it as fictional. But the narrator may be in the process of explaining situations like the one disclosed in that novel in more general terms, hence the partiality signalled above. Thus we have: (I narrate (I invent with the intention to explain:)) Steyn's deep bass sounded in the vestibule.

I now take into account the fact that the narrator manifests itself in its text, refers to itself as 'I,' while also thinking of the fact that that 'I' is not a character, not an actor as in e. This I indicate by the addition of the term 'perceptible' or 'non-perceptible,' by which I mean perceptible (p) or non-perceptible (np) as specifically mentioned by the narrating agent in the text. The formula for that sentence might then be: EN(p) [EF1 [CF2 (Ott.)]–Steyn(p)]. Thus there is a partial coincidence of two of the three agents, while there are still three different identities at play. This form occurs quite frequently in older literature, such as Dostoievski, Tolstoy, Balzac, Dickens, and also *Don Quixote*. It often serves to state a truth claim – the best guarantee of fictionality. In the beginning of *Don Quix-ote* we read: 'But this does not much concern our story; enough that we do not depart by so much of an inch from the truth in the telling of it' (31). A bit later, the narrator claims to be the most truthful among his competitors by giving several versions of a fact (37). This goes so far as to turn the truth claim completely around: in chapter 5 a tale which is disqualified as coming from the kind of literature the novel consistently ridicules is thus framed by the EN(p):

> ... a tale familiar to children, not unknown to youth, and enjoyed and even believed by old men, though for all that no truer than the mira-cles of Mahomet.   53

In g the narrator is also an actor; there is reference to discussions be-tween the actor Steyn and the agent referring to him- or herself as 'I.' The actor 'I,' which, from the point of view of identity, coincides with the narrator, is, however, not important from the point of view of ac-tion. It stands apart, observes the events, and relates the story accord-ing to its point of view. A narrator of this type is a witness. The question whether the story it tells is invented can no longer be asked. The text is full of indications that the story must be considered 'true.' Of course, this does not prove that it is factually true; it merely speaks for the im-plied claim of the narrator. The interpretation of this sentence is:

> (I narrate: (I declare as witness:)) Steyn's deep bass resounded in the vestibule.

Since the narrator so clearly pretends to testify, it must also, suppos-edly, make clear how it got its information. In the first sentence of g it does so: its source, at that moment, is Steyn himself. With regard to the rest of the fragment we cannot tell. Perhaps Ottilie has told the narrator this anecdote. If that is so, this will, no doubt, be indicated somewhere in the text. If not, it seems self-evident to presuppose that the narrator/character-witness was present at the scene.

Let us suppose that this is the case. Then focalization is localized with the character-bound narrator who refers to herself and is, there-fore, perceptible in the text. In that case the formula is CN(p) [CF ('I')–Steyn(p)]. Now Ottilie has disappeared as an agent, and both narration and focalization rest with the CN(p), the anonymous witness who is yet an 'I.'

In these examples we have seen four different narrative situations. In d and f the narrator stood outside the fabula and in e and g it did not. In d the focalizor was a character. In f we considered a case of embedded focalization, since here we saw an infiltration of external agents into the story. In e the identification of the agents was closest: the narrator and the focalizor were both the character Ottilie. In g, finally, narrator and focalizor coincided; however, unlike e, not in the identity of one of the active actors, but in the identity of a witness. This position of the witness may be less crucial to the fabula, but can be key for the reader. Witnesses can convey compassion, irony, or other affective responses to the reader. They can also influence the veracity of the narrative. Hence, neither the quantitative presence nor the participation in the fabula a priori determine the importance of a particular type of narrator.

With these analyses, the fundamental distinction between a narrative 'I' that talks about itself and a narrative 'I' that speaks of others turns out too general. The implication of the narrator in one or both of the other layers is an aspect to consider. Sometimes the narrative 'I' exclusively narrates, as in d; it can also perceive, as in e, f, and g; and it can also act, as in e and g. When it acts, this action may remain limited to testimony, as in g. The traditional distinction between 'I'-narratives and 'he'-narratives is thus inadequate not only for terminological reasons. The difference between d and f would remain inarticulate because the infiltration of the 'I' into the story is neglected. In some narratives, the narrative situations analysed here – that is, the different relationships of the narrative 'I' to the object of narration – are constant within each narrative text. This means that one can immediately, already on the first page, see which is the narrative situation. But the narrative situation can also change. Displacements occur especially between d and f. A narrator may remain imperceptible for a long time, but suddenly begin to refer to itself, sometimes in such a subtle manner that the reader hardly notices. Yet, a sense of presence emerges – the presence of a witness.

However, focalization need not in every case always remain with the same agent. Technically it would be almost impossible to maintain such continuity. A spectacular example of a novel in which focalization rests from beginning to end with the CF, and narration with the EN(np), is Alain Robbe-Grillet's *La jalousie*. It is curious that precisely the consistency with which the technique is maintained has had the effect that almost all critics have termed that anonymous agent a specific character: a jealous husband. (Of course, the title has also been of influence here.) But more often, the narrative voice associates, then dissociates itself from, characters who are temporarily focalizing. This is precisely the reason for a consistent distinction between the two.

Second-Person Narrators?

Michel Butor's novel *La modification* (1957) is one of the few examples of a novel consistently written 'in the second person.' In the beginning, that grammatical form hampers the smooth narrative reading commonly associated with the genre. But fortunately for a compulsive reader of novels like myself, quite soon it is almost inevitable that the narrative takes over, and one can sit back and go along with the adventures of the protagonist on his train ride between Paris and Rome, between his wife and his lover.

The narrative thrust of this novel seems to depend on the fact that the second person cannot be sustained; without much effort, the reader 'translates' it into first-person format, which enables her to read on and process the text into a story. The 'you' cannot be subsumed by the reader's position, nor can it be construed as the addressee of apostrophe, as in lyrical poetry. The 'you' is simply an 'I' in disguise, a 'first person' narrator talking to himself; the novel is a 'first-person' narrative with a formal twist to it that does not engage the entire narrative situation, as one would expect it should.

Although the normalizing effect of narrative reading at the expense of second-personhood cannot be sensed in a short quotation, I submit that the following passage, for all its brevity, already fails to sustain the second-personhood which is its overt narrative mode:

> If you were afraid of missing the train to whose movement and sound you are now already accustomed again, it is not because you woke up later than you planned this morning, since, to the contrary, your first movement upon opening your eyes was to extend your arm to prevent the alarm from going off, while dawn was beginning to sculpt the disordered sheets of your bed, the sheets which emerged from the dark like defeated phantoms trampled on that soft and warm floor from which you tried to tear yourself away.

This passage has all the appearance of a so-called interior monologue, that equally artificial mode of narration 'in the first person' – with a character-bound narrator – that seeks to eliminate reference to the first-person voice in favour of a silent, 'pure' first-person focalizor.

There is a reason for this easing-back into the traditional narrative from which the author sought to estrange his readers. This relapse is a consequence of Butor's failure to take seriously what the second person is: to be, to act out, the essence of language. Only when speech is addressed to a second person can language fulfil its mission to communicate. This is the nature of words called *deixis*: words that only have meaning in the context in which they are uttered, such as 'I' and 'you,' 'yesterday,' 'here' or 'there.' According to French linguist Emile Benveniste, who gave currency to the importance of deixis, the 'essence' of language lies in deixis, not reference, because what matters in language is not the world 'about' which subjects communicate, but the constitution of the subjectivity required to communicate in the first place. This idea illustrates beautifully the crossing of individual and social others that I alleged to make my case for the cultural importance of narrative.

The pronouns 'I' and 'you,' as opposed to 'she,' 'he,' 'they' and the like, are empty in themselves. They do not refer outside of the situation in which they are uttered. Each utterance is performed by an 'I' and addressed to a 'you.' This second person is crucial, for it is that subject that confirms the 'I' as a speaker. Conversely, the 'you' becomes an 'I' as soon as the perspective shifts. It is only as (potential) 'I' that the 'you' him- or herself has the subjectivity to act, hence, to confirm the subjectivity of the previous 'I.'

What is lacking, in *La modification*, is that key feature of deixis: the reversibility, the exchange, of the first and second person. Not only is the 'you' a clearly distinct, even semantically dense individual doing certain things, but the other people in his life, hence, in the fabula, are consistently described in the third person. The 'you' is cut off from the others, or cuts them off, so that, rather than mutually confirming one another's subjectivity, the figure of this 'you' lapses into an autistic monologism. The pronoun 'you' becomes a reminder of the alienation, that recession of subjectivity, rather than a fulfilment of it. As a consequence, the 'you' can never be identified with the reader, nor is the reader the 'you''s symmetrical counterpart, the 'I': There is simply no 'you' here whose turn-taking will make the written 'you' into an 'I.' I contend, therefore, that Butor has based his novel on a misconception of deixis. To extend this conclusion further, second-person narrators are not only logically impossible but also not manageable for a reader. It is the latter who is narrative's 'second person.'

3: Non-Narrative Comments

Not every sentence in a narrative text can be called 'narrative' according to the definitions presented in this book. Sometimes it is worthwhile analysing the alternation between narration and non-narrative comments. Often, it is in such comments that ideological statements are made. This is not to say that the rest of the narrative is 'innocent' of ideology, on the contrary. The reason for examining these alternations is precisely to measure the difference between the text's overt ideology, as stated in such comments, and its more hidden or naturalized ideology, as embodied in the narrative representations.

   The following excerpt from an old-fashioned Dutch children's book, *Danny Goes Shopping* by L. Roggeveen, presents a fairly obvious case. It shows that the commentary of the external narrator may far exceed the function of narrating.

1 Danny is barely able to hear him above the music.
2 What is the matter? he thinks.
3 Wide-eyed, he looks about him.
4 Then he understands everything!
5 There they come, arm in arm, with happy faces: Mr Alexander and Miss Ann!
6 Mr Alexander is a poet.
7 In his life, he has already written many rhymes.
8 He has written a poem about Danny, one about currant bread; one about the singing of the nightingale in the silent wood; and more than seven about Miss Ann!
9 Why did Miss Ann get so many poems?
10 Well, that is not difficult to guess!
11 Because Mr Alexander loves Miss Ann so much!
12 And, fortunately, Miss Ann loves Mr Alexander just as much!
13 What do two people who love each other do?
14 Well, that also is not difficult to guess!
15 They get married! Of course! They did in the past, they do so now, and they always will!

16 Mr Alexander and Miss Ann act just like all other people.
17 And today is their wedding day!
18 The mayor is waiting for the pair in the town hall.

Intuitively, I summarize the fabula of this page as follows: Danny watches the arrival of a bridal pair. Focusing on the actors and their actions, I would summarize what Danny sees as: the bridal pair arrives, the mayor is waiting. A lot disappears in this summary. Analysing what exactly helps to distinguish between narrative and non-narrative parts of the text.

In lines 9 through 15 no events are presented. In addition, we are also not exclusively confronted with objects from the fabula. Lines 9 through 12 convey the idea that Mr Alexander and Miss Ann love each other. The two actors are described in their relationship to each other, or rather, the collective actor 'bridal pair' is described as consisting of two people who 'love each other.' But in doing so, we neglect the word 'fortunately' in line 12. This word communicates an opinion. The opinion given here relates to the balance ('just as much') between the two actors. Apparently, a balance of this kind is evaluated favourably. This word cannot be termed descriptive, because it refers to something of a more general, more public and cultural bearing than the fabula. Parts of the text referring to something general are best called argumentative. Argumentative textual passages do not refer to an element (process or object) of the fabula, but to an external topic. From this definition, it appears that the term 'argumentative' should be taken in the widest sense. Not only opinions but also declarations on the factual state of the world fall under this definition: for instance, sentences like 'water always boils at 100 degrees,' or 'Poland lies behind the Iron Curtain.' Sentences of this type also communicate no more than a vision of reality. High in the mountains, or using another method of scaling the thermometer, water boils at a different 'temperature' (i.e. different representation of temperature).

That the second example does not denote a fact but an opinion is evident when we change the sentences into 'Poland lies in Eastern Europe,' or 'Bonn lies behind the Iron Curtain,' and whereas the sentence could still appear factual when I first wrote this book, it has now become a 'dated' sentence that is no longer true even if one still holds on to the opinion it expresses. Because the division between opinions and facts is so difficult to draw, it makes sense to consider 'argumentative' any statement that refers to something of general knowledge outside the fabula.

The word 'fortunately' formed part of a sentence that is, for the rest, descriptive. Analysing the story line by line, I term lines 9–12 descriptive; they describe elements of the fabula. Lines 13–15, however, do not contain any reference to elements of the fabula that could be described. Here we only see the representation of opinions about behaviour: people who love each other marry; this is what is usually done, and is as it should be. This opinion is represented in a certain form. This form, the game of question and answer in a mock dialogue, had already started in line 2. The form conceivably has a convincing effect: the opinion is not presented as a personal one, but as something self-evident. This catechism is extended to convince the reader that she has known the 'truth' all along. The exclamation marks and additions like 'of course' pursue the same goal. This kind of ideological drill may not be so common any longer in contemporary children's fiction, but in subtler forms it is not absent at all.

In the next line, the actors are linked to the public opinion through mention of their conformism. They are merely described in that sentence. Only in the last sentence is a presentation of an event narrated. A new actor appears, the mayor. He is confronted with another actor, the bridal pair. This confrontation has a temporal aspect that will be explained in the next chapter. Though the act of the mayor is durative, not circumscribed in time, it appears from the lines following those of our quoted passage that waiting must, nevertheless, be seen as an event. The mayor gets angry because he has to wait, and takes action. It would be naïve to suppose that only argumentative parts of the text communicate ideology. This happens equally in descriptive and narrative parts of the text; but the manner in which it happens is different. In addition, the example shows that the discursive form – here, the catechistic style – itself has ideological implications. What matters most is not the ideology of marriage as the universal form of 'acting' upon love, but the presentation of it in a form of 'teaching,' itself of a particular kind, the drill.

The argumentative parts of the text often give explicit information about the ideology of a text. It is, however, quite possible that such explicit statements are treated ironically in other parts of the text, or are contradicted by descriptive or narrative parts of the text to such an extent that the reader must distance herself from them. If we want to evaluate the ideological tenor of a text, an analysis of the relationship between these three textual forms within the totality of the entire text is a crucial element.

The following example demonstrates the relevance of the search for narrativity and the identification of the narrator even within apparently non-narrative discourse. Physicist and philosopher of science Evelyn Fox Keller has conducted two studies of the connections between language and science. The first was about the way scientific inventions and ideas are presented to the larger public. The study focused on the word 'secret' as in 'the secret of life.' The second study was about the language in which biology continues to build on evolutionary theory. A central concept in that work was the term 'competition,' traditionally related to 'struggle for life' and 'survival of the fittest.' The price to pay for this attention to competition was a lack of attention to collaboration, an evidently indispensable element in the sexual reproduction of organisms. One doesn't need to be a biologist to see that this privileging of one term over another has potential consequences for the further development of the theory itself.

In the first study, the issue was the use of metaphors which one can still maintain to be 'innocent,' 'just language': rhetorical. It concerned the discourse the developers of DNA used to present the importance of their research to the public. That discourse was filled with words carrying a long tradition. Thus the initial molecule was called mother-molecule, and nature was constantly referred to as a woman; the unknown that it was the project to understand was 'the secret of life,' which had to be found, if necessary by means of violence. And Keller interpreted this discourse as follows:

> And if we ask, whose secret life has historically been, and from whom has it been secret, the answer is clear: Life has traditionally been seen as the secret of women, a secret *from* men. By virtue of their ability to bear children, it is women who have been perceived as holding the secret of life.   4

I focus on the metaphor in that word 'secret,' which sounds so common and ordinary. Whereas the word 'secret' in combination with 'life' or 'nature' has indeed become quite usual, the word is here a substitute for something else, not a single term but, I will argue, a narrative.

What is unknown, as the negating prefix suggests, can be known. The subject 'of' that knowing is the researcher. What is secret can also be known. But here, the subject is not quite the researcher. The word 'secret' implies an action, hence, a subject of withholding. If there is a secret, then somebody is keeping it. This fits into the network of gendered language in which nature and life are made feminine. And it implicitly tells a story in which secrecy is an act. 'Secret' as metaphor for the unknown establishes an opposition between two subjects: the researcher who wants to know the secret and 'woman' who withholds it. This opposition is easily turned into hostility, as the well-known metaphor of philosopher Francis Bacon shows, who wanted to put nature on the rack to torture 'her' secrets out of 'her.'

But this gendering of the unknown comes with a second aspect of the word 'secret' which is of an altogether different nature. A secret that must be found out implies a process in which that finding out takes place. The series of events involved in that process can be considered a fabula. That narrative is 'told' by the user of the metaphor; the male scientist's spokesman is its narrator. The narration is subjective in the precise sense of emanating from a subject. The word tells the narrative in the version of – from the perspective of – the subject of 'unknowing' who feels excluded by the lack of knowledge and experiences it as an action by an 'insider,' the subject of knowing and withholding. That subject is the narrator's opponent. This interpretation of metaphor as mini-narrative yields insight, not into what the speaker 'means,' but into what a cultural community considers acceptable interpretations; so acceptable that they are not considered metaphorical at all; and certainly not narrative. It requires analysis – cultural analysis – to follow up on the question of cultural interaction involved here. This is a case of ideology in ordinary language that becomes visible through narratological analysis. The argumentative nature of the metaphor becomes apparent as soon as we consider the metaphor an implied narrative. This is one example of how narratological analysis inherently serves political or ideological critique. It demonstrates, therefore, that all approaches that isolate ideology from structure, or reject structural analysis because it is not political, are missing an important point of narrative theory.

4: Description

Description is a privileged site of focalization, and as such it has great impact on the ideological and aesthetic effect of the text. But it is also a particular textual form, indispensable, indeed, omni-present in narrative. In this section description will be analysed as a textual form; in chapter 2 the concept of focalization will be added.

Delimitation

I had characterized lines 9–12 of the page from *Danny Goes Shopping* as descriptive. Rather than recounting events, they qualify the characters. Although descriptive passages would appear to be of marginal importance in narrative texts, they are, in fact, both practically and logically necessary. Practically, they help the imagined world of the fabula become visible and concrete. Logically, fabula elements need to be described so that their functions make sense. Narratology, therefore, must take these segments of the text into account.

> a Bob Assingham was distinguished altogether by a leanness of person, a leanness quite distinct from physical laxity, which might have been determined, on the part of superior powers, by views of transport and accommodation, and which in fact verged on the abnormal.   Henry James, *The Golden Bowl*

This excerpt is clearly a description. Mostly, things are less straightforward. Just try to define what a description is. Is the following fragment, which not only describes objects and people but also accounts for the passage of a certain stretch of time, descriptive?

> b Presently he told her the motion of the boat upon the stream was lulling him to rest. How green the banks were now, how bright the flowers growing on them, and how tall the rushes! Now the boat was out at sea, but gliding smoothly on. And now there was a shore before him.   Charles Dickens, *Dombey and Son*

This passage is a description, for it ascribes features to objects: the banks are green, the flowers are bright, the bushes tall. I will, therefore, define a description as a textual fragment in which features are attributed to objects. This aspect of attribution is the *descriptive function*. We consider a fragment as descriptive when this function is dominant. Thus, example a is predominantly descriptive, while b is a mixture of description and narration.

Within the realistic tradition, description has always been considered problematic. In the *Republic*, Plato tried to rewrite fragments of Homer so that they would be 'truly' narrative. The first elements to be discarded were the descriptions. Even Homer himself attempted to avoid, or at least to disguise, descriptions by making them narrative. Achilles' shield is described as it is in the process of being made, Agamemnon's armour as he puts it on. In the nineteenth-century realistic novel, descriptions were at least narratively motivated if they were not made narrative. And despite its efforts to avoid representation, the *nouveau roman* has continued to follow this tradition.

Description Contested

In order to motivate my readers to take an interest in description, I begin with detailed analysis of a single instance of it. In Djuna Barnes' modernist novel *Nightwood*, the following passage arrests the reader's imagination as it multiplies entrances to vision. In this chapter, the passage helps us understand what descriptive discourse is and does.

> On the second landing of the hotel (...) a door was standing open, exposing a red carpeted floor, and at the further end two narrow windows overlooked the square.
>
> On a bed, surrounded by a confusion of potted plants, exotic palms and cut flowers, faintly oversung by the notes of unseen birds, which seemed to have been forgotten – left without the usual silencing cover, which, like cloaks on funeral urns, are cast over their cages at night by good housewives – half flung off the support of the cushions from which, in a moment of threatened consciousness she had turned her head, lay the young woman, heavy and disheveled. Her legs, in white flannel trousers, were spread as in a dance, the thick lacquered pumps looking too lively for the arrested step. Her hands, long and beautiful, lay on either side of her face.
>
> The perfume that her body exhaled was of the quality of that earth-flesh, fungi, which smells of captured dampness and yet is so dry, overcast with the odor of oil and amber, which is an inner malady of the sea, making her seem as if she had invaded a sleep incautious and entire. Her flesh was the texture of plant life, and beneath it one sensed a frame, broad, porous and sleepworn, as if sleep were a decay fishing her beneath the visible surface. About her head there was an effulgence as of phosphorus glowing about the circumference of a body of water – as if her life lay through her in ungainly luminous deteriorations – the troubling structure of the born somnambule, who lives in two worlds – meet of child and desperado.
>
> Like a painting by the *douanier* Rousseau, she seemed to lie in a jungle trapped in a drawing room (in the apprehension of which the

walls have made their escape), thrown in among the carnivorous flowers as their ration; the set, the property of an unseen *dompteur*, half lord, half promoter, over which one expects to hear the strains of an orchestra of wood-wind render a serenade which will popularize the wilderness.   Barnes 56

The narrator describes a visual event. Felix Volkbein sees Robin Vote. An aristocrat in search of a wife meets the most fugitive human being, and the story of *Nightwood* can begin. Form-wise, this piece presents itself as a classical novelistic description. It comprises an introductory frame, a clear subject-object split, and a detailing of both the perception of the object and the elements constituting it. An external narrator utters the words. But the passage also turns away from description, through its deployment of metaphor, its decentring evocation of endless other things – sea, forest, mushrooms, painting, circus ('unseen *dompteur*,' a key ambiance for the man Felix, framer of this description by his act of perception), music – and its narrativity. The reader is warned: 'the thick lacquered pumps looking too lively for the arrested step' counter rational knowledge. At the same time, 'arrested' foregrounds the descriptive nature of the passage; the way it stops narrative in its tracks.

This passage also ruptures linearity through its anticipatory foresight, turning from the metaphor-announcing 'as if' to the referent, which escapes the focalizor and will continue to escape him forever: 'the born somnambule,' who cannot be a wife to him, or a lover to anyone, 'meet of child and desperado.' Through a rhetoric ranging from expansion to the description of a non-existent painting (called *ekphrasis*), from disorder to distraction, and from deceleration to intensification of the moment, this description contains, in a nutshell, the history, the theory, and the criticism of description.

'On the second landing,' 'On the bed': these phrases literalize the realistic framing so characteristic of the modernist novel's predecessors. The former narrativizes the focalizor, Felix, whose vision of Robin is the narrative referent of the description; what, in the next section, I will term 'motivation.' He goes up, then looks down. As I will discuss in the next chapter, the focalization establishes the link of perception between subject and object. Ascending in body, the focalizor descends in vision. Presenting the future object of obsessive pursuit – and the subject of obsessive withdrawal – as lying on a bed, the passage presents itself not only as a view from above, but also as a traditional painting. The frame comprises the paraphernalia of the late nineteenth-century artist's studio – 'potted plants, exotic palms and cut flowers' – and the subliminal orientalism inherent in it. The fake fairy atmosphere of that site of representation is further expanded by 'faintly oversung by the notes of unseen birds,' a clause that thickens the subjectivism with senses other than vision, with sound, for example (soon, smell will be added), while enhancing the limited view.

The intensification of the focalizor's perception, together with the narrative expansion of the moment, prepares the reader for a heightened sense of suspense, giving anticipatory importance to what will come. And here she is, the image of an obelisk in a Matisse painting: 'half flung off the support of the cushions from which, in a moment of threatened consciousness she had turned her head, *lay the young woman*, heavy and disheveled.' Half flung: as a spectacle of arrested intimate movement, unsuitable for the public gaze, so that the man looking down on her is caught up in the inevitably voyeuristic position. Passive, with the door open, the young woman 'asks for it.' And, although the two people involved in this description are soon to marry and procreate, it seems predictable that in terms of *relationship*, their case is hopeless.

This description of Robin Vote, the central character of *Nightwood*, foregrounds quite precisely what it is that has made description such a bone of contention, so subject to paradox, such an object of contempt. It also demonstrates subjectivity and chance as the two critical responses to realist fiction, whose traps these two states of mind constitute. Moreover, it recalls the dual status of ekphrasis as interruptive and constitutive of narrativity. This convoluted and self-undermining love story begins when one of Robin's prospective lovers, Felix, chances upon her in a hotel room, where he goes because someone told him to. This description, therefore, is a beginning. It is also a prediction of an end. Thus it comprises the time of the novel, including the body of its fabula, which is none other than the repetition of the failure to relate that is staged here. Description, thus, is both narrative's 'other' and an integral part of it.

Is the comparison 'like a painting by the *douanier* Rousseau' a decorative, expansive, or specifying metaphor that clarifies the vision so that it can become visible for the reading viewers? Earlier, the woman was already described as 'earth-flesh, fungi, which smells of captured dampness,' so that the painted jungles follow, logically and aesthetically, rather than flesh out what is there on stage. If this description is ekphrasitic, does the ekphrasis produce the woman, or the woman the ekphrasis? While the reader caught by focalization goes along with Felix, adopting his perceptual apparatus, including sight, sound, and smell, our narrative goodwill is put to the test when the focalizor loses his power in favour of the awakening text, departing from the Sleeping Beauty to turn him into a generalized 'one.' This is the narrator's word; its direction for reading. The description neither presents nor explains the character for the narrative. Instead it produces the former *as the latter*, seducing the realistic reader into getting lost in the modernist jungle. This is why modernist novels appear difficult.

Much easier is the well-known strategy used, for example, by Thomas Hardy in his 1891 novel, *Tess of the d'Urbervilles*. There the heroine's moods and states correspond, almost point by point, with the brightness or darkness of the environment in which the character evolves. Colours appear to 'stand for' – be a sign of – states of mind, which easily translate into metaphorical colours and shades. Almost inevitably, the convergence of the visible features of the character and her environment produces a prose in which description mingles with the narration of events. Hardy's novel seems to get away with a kind of descriptive exuberance that rhetoricians and, later, theorists would somehow find problematic – in other words, worth attacking or defending. I think it is because of the habit of scholars to reiterate the same examples from a limited corpus that the gap between critical writings on the novel and narrative theory is wider than necessary.

To the contemporary literary sensibility, the gap between a criticism that applauds description and a narrative theory that marginalizes it appears to come from the experience of reading versus the logic of structure. Structuralism is useful only when kept in its modest place: as a trigger for discussion, a measure for comparision; not as a truth that makes its overflow invisible.

Like Cervantes, these novels both deploy and de-naturalize description. Whereas Cervantes' anti-hero is declared 'mad' for seeing what is not there – for seeing an army in a cloud of dust produced by a herd of sheep – and Zola & Co boasted the referential existence of their described objects, modernism, with its dual philosophy of subjectivity and chance, is well placed to demonstrate an altogether different status for description.

The cited passage from *Nightwood* makes the complexity abundantly clear. The introductory frame represents the difficulty of keeping that frame within its own bounds. In this way framing is put on the table.

The passage posits itself as ostentatiously far from naturalizing the description through character-bound focalization. Binding each element to a larger whole, which is *not a woman* but a domain of sense-perception, a painter's studio, a painting, and an object that refuses to stay still, respectively, descriptive discourse comments on the coherence within narrative as an altogether different kind of order.

This is quite unsettling for those used to realist narrative. In the case of a person, for example, the description would move from head to foot and from the eyes to the rest of the face. This is the order from top to bottom combined with the move from centre to periphery. For landscapes, the order might be from foreground to background, vague to clear, left to right. Alternately, the description could run through the different senses involved in the perception of the object. The famous opening of Balzac's *Le père Goriot* follows the long shot zooming into a close-up, a move that, as it turns out, follows the steps of the character. And, as this fellow, Eugène, enters the rooming house, the sense of sight is complemented with the sense of smell. This ordered and neatly hierarchized expansion is parodied in Barnes' novel, where smell intervenes too early and practically takes over. This strategy results in a motivation that absorbs descriptions within the narrative.

Motivation

Working intuitively from the premise that descriptions interrupt the line of the fabula – a premise that, as we have just seen, is somewhat problematic – the ways in which descriptions are inserted characterize the rhetorical strategy of the narrator. In realistic narrative, insertion necessitates motivation. If, as Zola argued, the novel should be objective, this notion of objectivity necessitates naturalization – that is, making those interruptions known as descriptions seem self-evident or necessary, so that the inflections of the presentation, the attribution of qualities, and the ideological machinations remain invisible. This so-called objectivity is, in fact, a form of subjectivity in disguise. This is most conspicuous when the meaning of the narrative resides in the reader's identification with the psychology of a character. This happens when characters are given the function of authenticating the narrative contents. If 'truth,' or even probability, is no longer a sufficient criterion to make narrative meaningful, only motivation can suggest probability, thus making the contents believable, plausible. That is why motivation is an aspect of realist narrative rhetoric.

On the basis of the theory of narrative presented in this book, we can distinguish three types of motivation. Motivation is brought about by speaking, looking, or acting – the three forms of narrative agency distinguished here. The most effective, the most frequent, and the least noticeable form is motivation via looking. Motivation is, then, a function of focalization. A character sees an object. The description is the reproduction of what the character sees. Looking at something requires time, and, in this fashion, the description is incorporated into the time lapse caused by the interruption. But an act of looking must also have its exterior motivation. There must be enough light so that the character is able to observe the object. Hence, there is a window, an open door, an angle of vision which also have to be described and therefore motivated. Furthermore, the character must have both the time to look and a reason to look at an object. Hence the curious characters, the men of leisure, the unemployed, and the Sunday strollers.

Given the fundamental arbitrariness of the elements of the fictional world, there is, equally fundamentally, no end to the need for motivation. This predicament of realistic fiction has been mocked by later writers such as Nathalie Sarraute and Alain Robbe-Grillet in the French *nouveau roman*. The less conspicuous this motivation is, the more easily it can be terminated. In the following fragment, for example, the motivation is easily integrated into the description itself (emphasis added):

> When they had washed they lay and *waited* again. There were fifteen beds in the tall, narrow room. The walls were painted grey. The windows were long but high up, *so that you could see* only the topmost branches of the trees in the grounds outside. *Through the glass* the sky had no colour.
>
>   Jean Rhys, 'Outside the Machine,' *Tigers Are Better-Looking*

The sentence immediately preceding the description ('they lay and waited again') gives sufficient motivation for the act of looking. Hospital patients, particularly after their morning wash, have an ocean of time ahead of them. This is a subjective motivation. Not only is the act of looking itself motivated, but also the contents of what the women see. And this is indicated by 'so that you could see,' by the boundaries of the visible area. This exterior motivation is doubled up. The window motivates the fact that the women are able to see anything at all of what is happening outside the hospital. But also, the restricted quality of the field of vision is emphasized: 'Through the glass the sky had no colour.' This lack of colour has its own thematic meaning, so that even in this aspect the description is fully integrated into the text.

When a character not only looks but also describes what it sees, a certain shift in motivation occurs, although in principle all of the motivational demands mentioned remain valid. The act of speaking necessitates a listener – the 'you' to whom the 'I' speaks. The character-bound speaker must possess knowledge which the character-bound listener does not have but would like to have. The listener can, for example, be blind, or young, or amateurish; curious, in need of information, or threatened. There is yet a third form of motivation, which resembles Homeric description. On the level of the fabula, the actor carries out an action with an object. The description is then made fully narrative. An example of this is the scene in Zola's *La bête humaine* in which the compulsive killer, Jacques, polishes (strokes) every individual component of his beloved locomotive.

Motivation occurs at the level of text when the character itself describes an object, as a CN; at the level of story when the glance or vision of the character supplies the motivation; and at the level of fabula when the actor carries out an action with an object. One clear illustration of the latter form, and one which also demonstrates that a distinction between descriptive and narrative is no longer possible within this form, is the following 'description' of a dead man:

> Then they went into Jose Arcadio Buendia's room, shook him with all their might, screamed in his ear, and held a little mirror in front of his nose, but they weren't able to wake him.
>
> Gabriel García Márquez, *One Hundred Years of Solitude*

Examples of the second type, motivation via focalization, are numerous. An illustration of the first type is the description of the Linton family as given by young Heathcliff in *Wuthering Heights*. He is forced to give this description because Nelly Dean has made him responsible for his escapades with Cathy and for the fact that he has returned alone.

In narrative visual images and in film, motivation also plays a part. Attempts to make paintings fit the expectations of what the object should look like indicate a concern for descriptive plausibility. Raphael's famous 1504 painting *Betrothal of the Virgin*, at the Pinacoteca di Brera in Milan, is often quoted as an example of geometrical perspective, a realist rhetoric enhanced by the progressive dimunition of the tile as a consequence of the recession into space. This recession is an indispensable tool in the construction of a perspectival space which positions the viewer as the master overseeing the world in which the fabula of the betrothal takes place. In this way the work is the pictorial equivalent of a narrative told by an imperceptible, external narrator, an EN(np). In order to integrate this blatant effort, which appoints the viewer as the ideal realistic reader, the painting's narrator has carefully populated this descriptive space with figures who, engaged in actions that enhance the painting's narrativity, at the same time motivate the description of space by their diminishing size.

In literature as well as in visual art, such conventions of motivation have been criticized and challenged. In postmodern literature the motivation of descriptions is sometimes exaggerated to the point of collapse, in a motivational madness, or made blatantly incoherent. In film, a medium that is plagued by an excess of realistic effects, the opposite of motivation is often necessary. This is not only the case in postmodern challenges to realism. In modernist literature, the emphasis on the subject's access to the world tends to blow up motivation to the point of completely subordinating the described element for which it was invoked. And in early cinema, the recent invention of the medium was still such a marvel in itself that the registration of the visible world was more important than the often tenuous fabula that was set in it. For example, the earliest specimens of the Western were not at all primarily stories of suspenseful adventures, but resembled rather a kind of travelogue, with the camera mounted on the back of a train to register the landscape, as a form of visual tourism – called 'phantom rides.' The fabula was a rather meagre pretext to take the viewer on a trip. Even in the more or less realistic cinema that is currently predominant, many strategies have been developed which counter the unsuitable realistic effects the medium tends to entail. *Schindler's List* is a case in point.

Let me preface the following example briefly. It is by now a common view that the horror of the Holocaust cannot be represented; yet as time goes by, the need to make sure it is remembered becomes more and more acute. Film is an expository medium: its narrative mode is 'showing.' Its power to affect is based on showing. Films on the Holocaust have not been very successful in avoiding the pitfalls of representation. They either use the tragedy as a backdrop, sideways (*Sophie's Choice*), or sentimentalize it through individual identification (the TV series 'Holocaust'). It cannot, ever, be adequately – realistically – represented, and I contend that Spielberg didn't try. The reason for the severe criticism of his film is, I think, that critics assumed he did. Instead, however, he 'touched' it, established a relationship with it based on continuity. He explores ways to do so through a medium that can hardly avoid the pornographic effects of showing torture, shame, and sadism.

To at least complicate that effect, the film's narrator deploys a cinematic discourse that counters the effects of realism. For example, when showing victims it uses quick takes, avoiding the grazing gaze of mastery and sadism. Also, the visual images struggle with emphatic musical accompaniment, which sometimes even takes over, monitoring transitions from the story. This monitoring is necessary because the film represents a fabula that interweaves the lives of a number of individuals, to the history of mass events. The film text deploys excessive close-ups that confine, make faces hard to see, and thereby avoid a pleasant visual experience. The use of black-and-white, often misunderstood as historical pretension, can also be seen as part of this anti-realistic style that de-naturalizes what we see, even as it also evokes the connotation 'history.' By alternating 'telling' and 'showing' – making us sympathize with the predicaments of a few families and individuals, but alternating those moments with broad historical evocations that remind viewers of the world-wide scale of the disaster – the narrator keeps sentimentalizing identification at bay. The combination of emphatic symbolization and constructedness contributes to the narrator's rhetoric, which aims at representing not 'it' (the horror of the Holocaust) but the index that touches (it): the girl Danka's hand.

One anti-realist strategy in the film is a 'poetic of doublets'; rhyming, repetition, symmetrical reversals. It allows real historical and mythical biblical allusions to develop together, intertwined. This strategy undermines the tendency of the anecdotal to take over and impose realism as sentimentalism, the tendency of individual stories to overrule the historical tragedy. Yet it manages to individualize the Jews. Carefully the same characters are made to appear in the mini-stories of daily life, so that they are real persons, but their stories are framed by history. The strategy of doublets demonstrates the parallel development of good and evil (Schindler versus Goeth) within the evil party, as two possibilities. Goeth sometimes almost looks like Schindler; when Goeth looks at himself in the mirror he doubles himself, just for a brief moment, into a good and an evil person. All these strategies are forms of motivation that, instead of supporting realism, counter it.

Motivation is a way of making the relationship between elements explicit. Precisely because these relationships are not self-evident in fictional texts, they can never be motivated enough. And, for this reason, motivation is, in the final analysis, arbitrary.

A Rhetoric of Description

To enable the arbitrary to pass for inevitable or even 'natural,' writers appeal to rhetoric. This is particularly the case for descriptions because their arbitrary motivation is in need of masking. This is why I discuss the intertwinement of rhetoric in narrative in this section, although it is not at all limited to description. Descriptions consist of a theme (e.g., 'house'), which is the object described, and a series of sub-themes (e.g., 'door,' 'roof,' 'room'), which are the components of the object. Taken together, the sub-themes constitute the nomenclature. They may or may not be accompanied by predicates (e.g., 'pretty,' 'green,' 'large'). These predicates are qualifying when they indicate a characteristic of the object ('pretty'); they are functional when they indicate a function, action, or possible use ('habitable for six people'). Metaphors and comparisons can occur on any level. A metaphor can replace the theme or accompany it. The same holds for the sub-themes. The inclusive relation from theme to sub-theme is synecdochical (a part stands for the whole); the relation between the sub-themes is contiguous (one thing follows, or is adjacent to, another). Both relations can be termed metonymical. Between theme or sub-theme compared and the predicates that replace them in metaphor, or specify them in comparison, the relation is termed metaphorical. On the basis of these two possible rhetorical relations, we can roughly differentiate six types of description.

1: The Referential, Encyclopaedic Description
In principle, there are no figures of speech in this type of description. The selection of components is based upon the contiguity of the elements of the contents. This means that the presence of some elements implies the absence of others. The missing detail can be filled in by the reader. General characteristics imply specific characteristics, unless the latter represent the former. The objective is to convey knowledge. The encyclopaedia is a model of this type of description.

2: The Referential-Rhetorical Description
The tourist guidebook rather than the encyclopaedia is the model for this second type of description. The units are now combined on the

basis of both the contiguity of the components and their thematic function. The latter is evaluative. The objective is both to convey knowledge and to persuade. Persuasion occurs via the wording (a pleasing rhythm, a style that reflects the value of the object to be described, for example a luxurious style to describe the Champs-Elysées), and via the contents; persuasion also occurs via the choice of traditionally valued subthemes, and by the addition of evaluative predicates. Even when a number of metaphors are included in such a description, the construction of the text continues to follow the principle of contiguity.

3: Metaphoric Metonymy
Here again, contiguity is the dominating principle of construction. But, in this case, metaphors are made of each individual component. Various compared elements may, in fact, be omitted altogether. Only the comparing elements are found in the text which, as a result, is of a very metaphoric nature. However, there is no relation of contiguity among the components of the comparison. Such a relation exists only among the implicit components of the compared elements. Superficially, this type of description would make an incoherent impression upon the reader. That such is not the case indicates that the reader is engaged in a filling-in activity.

4: The Systematized Metaphor
This description is one large metaphor. The elements of the comparison and those of the compared objects are systematically related to one another. Each series is built upon the principle of contiguity. The series balance each other. The question as to which of the two series dominates the meaning cannot be answered without taking the context into consideration. Also included in this category are descriptions in which elements of the two series imply each other.

5: The Metonymic Metaphor
The description is one large metaphor. The elements are contiguously related to each other. They form a coherent description which, taken as a whole, is the comparison of an object which is compared to it. This relationship can remain implicit, in which case this type of description, when taken out of its context, cannot be distinguished from one of the other types. An explicit comparing element results in a Homeric comparison.

6: The Series of Metaphors

This description consists of a metaphor which is expanded without continually referring to the compared element. The metaphor is repeatedly 'adjusted,' creating the impression that the compared element is elusive and indescribable. This rhetorical categorization of description on the basis of its tropes has been used to characterize narrative in different historical periods or styles.

5: Levels of Narration

In the fragments d to g of our discussion of Couperus' *Of Old People* (pp. 24–5), there was one phrase that remained unchanged throughout: 'Oh, that voice of Steyn's!' This phrase shows several characteristics of emotive language use – that is, the use of language which aims at self-expression of the speaker with regard to that about which it speaks. The element of this phrase that most strikingly indicates an emotive function is the word 'Oh.' The exclamation mark is a graphic representation of an emotionally laden intonation. Moreover, the grammatical peculiarity that this 'sentence' lacks a verb enforces its emotional effect.

Who is expressing this emotion? In other words, who says: 'mama Ottilie hissed'? The verb 'hiss' is in this sense a declarative verb, comparable to 'say' but colouring that verb. Declarative verbs indicating that someone is about to speak are, in a narrative text, signs of a change in level in the narrative text. Another speaker enters the scene. In d the EN temporarily yields the floor to Ottilie. The character Ottilie thus becomes a speaker at the second level, which I indicate as CN2. Note, however, that the use of CN2 is not entirely convincing. Though Ottilie, at least temporarily, speaks, she does not narrate: what she says is not a story. Nevertheless, I shall use this indication because it makes clear that the character is a speaker, just like the narrator. What that narrator says is another matter, to which I shall return in the subsection 'Relations between Primary and Embedded Texts,' later in this chapter. CN2, then, refers to a character that is 'quoted' by the narrator of the first level, whether that speaker is an EN1 or a CN1. CN2 is a speaker of the second level.

But what about that phrase in the fragments e, f, and g? It is on purpose that I have broken off the quotation in such a way that we cannot see who speaks. The declarative verb is missing. In e there are two possibilities:

e.i Oh, that voice of Steyn's, I hissed between my teeth.

e.ii Oh, that voice of Steyn's! I could not bear it any longer.

In e.i there is a declarative verb to indicate that what precedes is direct discourse, an embedded sentence. The speaker of the first level yields to the speaker of the second level. CN1 ('I') 'quotes' CN2 ('I'). Just as in d, the emotive sentence is an embedded sentence, a sentence within a sentence, which can be represented by the use of brackets: CN1 [CN2]. The character in both cases is called Ottilie. But narratologically speaking, it is not the same Ottilie. CN1 only relates after the fact (in the narrative 'now,' albeit in the past tense) what CN2 said earlier ('then,' the past of the narrative 'now'). As a linguistic act, the emotive phrase forms part of the text. In another version of the same story, for instance, it might be represented thus: 'Ottilie expressed her irritation at the voice of Steyn.' Direct discourse or direct speech, an embedded sentence, is the object of a language act. Thus it is, in principle, an event like so many other events.

In e.ii the emotive sentence belongs to the text of CN1. Though the emotion which is communicated does form part of the text, the expression of it does not. In a summary of the fabula we would read: 'Ottilie was irritated by Steyn's voice.' Not the act of verbal expression of the irritation but the irritation itself is, in principle, an event.

Fragment f contains the same possibilities:

f.i Oh, that voice of Steyn's! Ottilie hissed between her teeth.

f.ii Oh, that voice of Steyn's! I understood how Ottilie could not bear it any longer.

In f.i the EN1 yields the word to the CN2 (Ottilie). Thus we have an ordinary embedded sentence, as we might find in any narrative text. The sequel given to the emotive phrase in f.ii is of a piece with the interpretation of f given above, where I assumed that the EN(p) [EF] was on Ottilie's side. The words of the emotive phrase are thus ascribed to the EN(p), and the first level is maintained.

Still, something has changed in this fragment. Through the addition into the narrative text of so clearly an emotive sentence of the first level, the EN's voice becomes much more perceptible than it already was.

It suggests, in this emotive expression, that the EN has heard Steyn's voice, and that 'it' has been irritated by it too. If this agent has heard the voice, he or she was, implicitly, present as an actor at the scene. That is why f and the variant f.ii have the same structure as g. The narrative 'I' has become, by implication, a testifying actor. The reader will not be surprised therefore when a narrative situation with a CN-witness presents itself in the text. This is one of the cases in which a superficial, general characterization of the narrative situation tends to be unsatisfactory. The EN1 may any minute start speaking on the second level as CN2, or do something else which makes it into an actor.

There is no reason to dwell on g. The possibilities are identical to those of f. Considering the narrative situation of g, it would seem obvious that either Ottilie speaks the emotive sentence as CN2, or the CN-witness speaks it as CN1. In the subsection 'The Focalized Object' in chapter 2, I will propose a distinction between perceptible and non-perceptible focalized objects. The same distinction must be made for the object of the narrative act. In the analysis of examples e through g, we only took into account the possibility that the character-speaker, the CN2, utters the words in fact. It does, however, also frequently occur that words, put in direct speech, are merely thought. Thus f might also have the following variant:

f.iii Oh, that voice of Steyn's! Ottilie thought.

What the CN2 has narrated is not perceptible, because other actors who may happen to be present cannot hear the text. When an utterance which is narrated at the second level is not perceptible, this is also an indication of fictionality, an indication that the narrated story is invented. If the narrator's realistic rhetoric seeks to keep up the pretence that it relates true facts, it can never represent the thoughts of actors other than itself. This variant, then, only contradicts the pretence 'I state autobiographically' or 'I testify' when a CN1 ('I') quotes a CN2 (another actor), while the verb is not declarative, but a synonym of 'to think.' This distinction is of importance in order to gain insight into the balance of power between the characters. When a character does not hear what another character thinks, and readers do receive information concerning these thoughts, readers may easily come to expect too much of the first character. They may, for instance, expect that the character will take feelings, only formulated in thought, into account, in this case that Steyn will speak less loudly because his voice upsets Ottilie. But Steyn cannot know that it does, in this case, because he is outside the room; in another case, perhaps, because the irritation would not be expressed in words.

This inequality has been put to strategic use, for example, in the French novel *The Cat* by Colette. There, a young couple's first months of marriage are presented as an inexorable decline of the relationship. Systematically, the thoughts of the man, who judges his wife mercilessly, are 'quoted,' often without the attributive verb that would make clear that the thoughts are not uttered out loud. The woman, in contrast, is only quoted when speaking, mostly to her husband. As a result, the criticisms the man holds against his wife are told to the reader over her head, so to speak. She does not have a clue that he is so dissatisfied; nor does she get access to his negative responses to what she says to him.

Intermediate Forms: Indirect Speech and Free Indirect Speech

Why does the way in which example f.ii is phrased entail a change in narrative situation? Analysing the sentence, I have emphasized the signs of emotive function. I did this because, with this emotive function, the narrator refers to itself. If in a statement the feelings of the speaker are expressed, the statement is about the speaker. We might also say that such an expression is comparable to (I narrate:) I shall be twenty-one tomorrow, and not to (I narrate:) Elizabeth will be twenty-one tomorrow. Even if the narrator does not explicitly refer to itself, still, the 'I' narrates about itself. This means that an actor with the same identity as the narrator forms part of the fabula. Signs of emotive functioning are, therefore, also signs of self-reference. There are more signs of this kind. I would even speak of two different language situations here: language about the contact between speaker and hearer, and language about others.

This distinction into two language situations, a personal and an impersonal one, may help us understand this and comparable phenomena. In f.ii we have seen different pieces of evidence that the narrator is involved with its object. Its language is personal in that it refers to the position of the narrator itself. In doing so, it places itself on the same level as that about which it is speaking in the same statement. Thus it has made itself into a virtual (possible, still unrealized) actor. We may say that, in this case, narrative levels begin to intertwine or even merge. The impersonal language situation which we found in example f.ii is invaded. The personal language situation intrudes, but not, as in f.i, on the second level. When an actor in a story begins to speak, she does so, in principle, in a personal language situation, in contact with another actor. In the basic narrative situation, speech is only possible on one narrative level in the personal language situation. At first sight this happens when the narrator addresses herself explicitly, or implicitly, to the reader; at the second level, when an actor speaks to another actor (this may be the speaking actor himself). In f.ii we find a 'mixture' of the two narrative levels, which is called text interference.

The two narrative situations are to be distinguished on the basis of references in the text to personal or impersonal language situations. These references can be taken as signals, as signs indicating: 'this is a(n) (im)personal language situation.' These signals are often related to the following forms:

		personal	*impersonal*
1	personal pronouns	I/you	he/she
2	grammatical person	first and second person	third person
3	tense	not all past tenses are possible	all past tenses
4	*deixis:* indicative pronouns	this, these	that/those
	adverbs of place	here/there	in that place
	adverbs of time	today, tomorrow	that day, the day after
5	emotive words and aspects	Oh!	(absent)
6	conative words and aspects: address, command, question [format; can't fix it]	please	(absent)
7	modal verbs and adverbs which indicate uncertainty in the speaker	perhaps	(absent)

When the signals of the personal language situation refer to the language situation of the narrator, we are dealing with a perceptible narrator (N1(p)). When the signals refer to the language situation of the actors, and a clear change of level has been indicated by means of a declarative verb, a colon, a dash, or quotation marks, we speak of a personal language situation at the second level (CN2). This situation can be called dramatic: just as on the stage, actors communicate through speech in a personal language situation. When, however, the signals refer to a personal language situation in which the actors participate without previously stepping down from their narrative level, then we have text interference. This was the case in f.ii. The n1(p) stepped across, so to speak, to the second level. But that was just one possibility. The inverse occurs more often. Then the words of the actors are represented at the first level, so that the narrator adopts the actor's discourse.

The most common form of this is indirect discourse. Here the narrator represents the words of the actor as it is supposed to have uttered them. Compare the following examples:

h Elizabeth said: 'I think I shall be able to find time to go out with you tomorrow night.'

i Elizabeth said that she might be able to find time to go out with him tomorrow night.

j Elizabeth said that she would probably have time to go out with him tomorrow night.

k Elizabeth said that she would probably have time to go out with him the following night.

In i, j, and k the contents of Elizabeth's words are represented in an equally adequate manner. The words themselves are represented with maximum accuracy in i, with less accuracy in j, and still less in k. It is impossible and irrelevant to reconstruct 'the 'original' direct speech from indirect discourse. Comparing the examples, however, it is as if i represents the allegedly spoken words more 'accurately' than j, and j than k. We do not need h to come to this conclusion. In i we read 'she might be able to,' where the modal indication of uncertainty 'might' has been combined with a subject-oriented positive verb, 'be able to find.' 'Tomorrow' is a deictic adverb of time. In j the modal form is still present, but less strongly, in 'would probably.' The adverb is less emphatic about personal uncertainty than the expression 'might be able.' In j we also find the deictic adverb 'tomorrow night.' In k only the weak modal value of 'probably' is a trace of the personal language situation. In i, j, and k, we find, compared to h, a number of signs of the impersonal language situation, because the sentence is in indirect discourse. The personal pronoun 'I' has been changed into 'she'; the verb is now in the third person, and not in the first; and the present future has been changed into a past future. On the basis of this analysis, it makes sense to look out for three characteristics which distinguish these forms:

1 Indirect discourse is narrated at a higher level than the level at which the words in the fabula are supposed to have been spoken.
2 The narrator's text explicitly indicates that the words of an actor are narrated by means of a declarative verb and a conjunction, or a substitute for it.
3 The words of the actor appear to have been rendered with maximum precision and elaboration.

The first characteristic distinguishes indirect discourse from direct discourse. The second characteristic distinguishes indirect discourse from a mode of representation which is even more indirect. This is most frequently termed free indirect discourse, but also 'free indirect style' or 'reported discourse.' I call it free indirect discourse. The third characteristic distinguishes (free) indirect discourse from narrator's text. This last distinction is the one that gives us most problems in the practice of analysis. That is because the third characteristic is relative.

When characteristic 2 of indirect discourse is left out, and characteristic 3 is present, the result is free indirect discourse. This is a form of interference between narrator's text and actor's text. Signals of the personal language situation of the actor and of the (im)personal language situation of the narrator cross, without explicit reference to this. Thus we have:

l Elizabeth might be able to go out with him tomorrow.

'Tomorrow' and 'might' indicate the personal language situation of the actor Elizabeth, while the other signals suggest the impersonal language situation: third person, past tense.

Precisely because the second characteristic of indirect discourse is lacking – the explicit sign that there is indirect discourse – it is not always clear whether we have to do with indirect discourse or ordinary, 'pure' narrator's text. This is so because the third characteristic is relative. That is why we only distinguish free indirect discourse from the narrator's text when there are positive indications that there is indeed representation of words of an actor. Such indications are:

1 The signals of a personal language situation, referring to an actor.
2 A strikingly personal style, attributable to an actor.
3 More details about what has been said than is necessary for the
  course of the fabula.

To demonstrate this I shall represent one event – Elizabeth seeks a confrontation with John – in various forms.

direct speech	m	Elizabeth said: 'I refuse to go on living like this.'
indirect speech	n.i	Elizabeth said that she refused to go on living like that.
	n.ii	Elizabeth said that she would not go on living like that.
free indirect discourse	o.i	Elizabeth would be damned if she'd go on living like this
	o.ii	Elizabeth would not go on living like this.
narrator's text	p.i	Elizabeth did not want to go on living in the manner disclosed
	p.ii	Elizabeth had had it.

In the analysis of these sentences I assume that the verb 'to refuse' fits
the usage of the actor Elizabeth, and not the narrator. Of course, without a context, such an assumption is meaningless.

   The direct discourse in m seems unproblematic. We read the precise
text as it was supposedly uttered by the actor, and the indications of
the changes in level are explicit. As soon as the actor's text is given by
the narrator in the following sentences, changes occur. In n.i, the actor's
text is represented as precisely as possible. As far as contents are concerned, this is also true for n.ii. But the style which – we may assume
– is clearly recognizable as the personal style of the irritated actor refers
to a personal language situation of the actor, involved in a quarrel. The
difference between n.i and n.ii on the one hand, and o.i and o.ii on the
other, lies in the presence or absence of a declarative verb with a con-

junction. In o.ii the actor's text has been represented with less precision than in o.i.

These examples are utterly artificial. Of course, in studying narrative texts, we never have such comparable combinations at hand. But even without comparison, we may say that o.i is strongly inflected by the actor's text, and o.ii by the narrator's text. Still I also sense free indirect discourse in o.ii, because the adjunct 'like this' signals a personal language situation of the actor. The presence of these words also distinguishes o.ii from p.i. In p.i I have used the heavy-handed expression 'in the manner disclosed' in order to avoid a deictic element. But even if I had chosen 'in that manner,' 'that' would refer to what had been stated earlier, hence to the language situation of the narrator, and not the actor. In p.i and ii we have a narrator's text. We cannot distinguish any signal of the actor's personal language situation. We have no reason to take p.i as the representation of certain spoken words. Finally, p.ii is the purest form of the narrator's text. The content is presented as an act, a verbal act of the actor. The words in which the refusal is uttered are not mentioned at all.

Indirect discourse, free indirect discourse, and the narrator's text in which language acts are narrated are all forms in which the words of an actor are narrated at first level. The degree to which, in this series, justice is done to the text of the actor decreases; on the other hand, the degree to which the speaking of the actor is seen as an act gradually increases. The interference of narrator's text and actor's text may, therefore, occur in widely varying proportions. At the first level, the actor's text is given minimal reflection in indirect discourse, sometimes the narrator's text dominates (o.ii), then again the actor's text (o.i). In the narrator's text the words of the actor are not represented as text, but as an act. In that case we no longer speak of text interference.

Relations between Primary and Embedded Texts

When there is text interference, narrator's text and actor's text are so closely related that a distinction into narrative levels can no longer be made. The relationship between the narrative levels has exceeded the boundary of maximum intensity. When the texts do not interfere but are clearly separate, there may still be a difference in the degree to which the embedded actor's text and the primary narrator's text are related. In this section, I discuss a number of possible relationships between texts. I systematically term the narrator's text 'primary,' without implying a value judgment; neither (temporal) priority nor (qualitative) primacy is implied. It only means that the connection is one of levels in the technical sense. In the end, the narrative text constitutes a whole, into which, from the narrator's text, other texts are embedded. The dependence of the actor's text with regard to the narrator's text should be seen as the dependence of a subordinate clause to a main clause. According to this principle, narrator's text and actor's text are not of equal status. The hierarchical position of the texts is indicated by the fundamental principle of level. The relations between narrator's text and actor's text may be different in kind and intensity. Quantitative aspect is of influence here: the more sentences frame the actor's text, the stronger is the dependence.

Embedded Narrative Texts

A first difference resides in the nature of the embedded text. When the criteria for narrativity have been met, the embedded text may also be considered as a narrative text. This is most obvious in so-called frame narratives: narrative texts in which at the second or third level a complete story is told. The classic example is the story cycle of the *Arabian Nights*. Here we find narration at several levels. The primary narrative presents the story of Scheherazade, threatened with death by her husband, the king. Only if she succeeds in fascinating him with her stories will she survive the night, night after night. Every night she tells a story; in that story new stories are embedded, so that we have the construction: Scheherazade tells A that B tells that C tells, etc., sometimes until the eighth degree.

Relations between Primary Fabula and Embedded Text

When the embedded text presents a complete story with an elaborate fabula, we gradually forget the fabula of the primary narrative. In the case of *Arabian Nights*, this forgetting is a sign that Scheherazade's goal has been accomplished. As long as we forget that her life is at stake, the king will too, and that was her purpose. In that case, the apparently loose relationship between primary and embedded text is relevant to the development of the primary fabula. The narrative act of the actor-narrator Scheherazade which produces the embedded text is an important event – even *the* event – in the fabula of the primary text. The relationship between the primary text and the narrative subject lies in the relationship between the primary fabula and the embedded narrative act. Summarizing the primary fabula we might also say: 'That night Scheherazade enchanted the king.' From this summary it is immediately clear what the symbolic function of the act of narration is. That interpretation is endorsed by the motive for the threat: the infidelity of a previous wife of the king. To the king and to Scheherazade narrating means life, in two different senses.

In Morrison's *Beloved*, a much more complex narrative, this principle – narration gives life – is also dramatized. In a much-quoted metanarrative phrase, the primary narrator says that 'the two did the best they could to create what really happened' (78), and indeed, Beloved's existence as a subject must be 'created' by story-telling. This story-telling must be performed by the primary narrator because, precisely, Beloved herself lacks the subjectivity that is required for the act of narration.

Relations between Primary Fabula and Embedded Fabula

Another possible relationship between the two texts presents itself when the two fabulas are related to each other. This structure has two possible meanings. Either the embedded story explains the primary story, or it resembles the primary story. In the first case the relationship is made explicit by the actor narrating the embedded story; in the second the explanation is usually left to the reader, or merely hinted at, in the fabula.

Explanation
Here, it depends on the relationship between the two which fabula the reader sees as more important. It may very well be the embedded one. Often the primary fabula is hardly more than the occasion for a perceptible, character-bound narrator to narrate a story. The primary fabula may, for instance, be presented as a situation in which the necessary change cannot be made, because ... Then the embedded narrative follows. A stereotypical example: a boy asks a girl to marry him. She loves him, and would rise on the social scale by marrying him. Still she cannot accept him. The reason is [that in the past, she has been seduced by a ruthless villain with the usual consequences. Since that time she carries the stain of her contact with a perfidious man who took advantage of her innocence. He seduced her ...]. The girl retires to a nunnery, and the boy soon forgets her. This structure is, in fact, extremely widespread.

The embedded text may take up the larger part of a book, as sometimes happens in cautionary tales of this type. The primary fabula is minimal here, because the number of events is small: proposal – exposition – rejection. In this example, the embedded story explains the primary fabula. The relationship between the fabulas was merely explanatory. The situation was unchangeable. The fact that the woman tells her story is of no influence on the outcome of the primary fabula.

Explanation and Determination
In other cases, however, an explanation of the starting situation may also lead to change. For instance, if the young man had been very moved by the sad account of his beloved's past, and recognized her innocence, he might have come to the conclusion that he wished to forget the past. Thus he would 'give her a second chance.' The function of the embedded fabula is then no longer merely explanatory. The exposition influences the primary fabula. Consequently the structure of narrative levels becomes more than a mere story-telling device; it is part of the narrative's poetics, and needs to be understood for the narrative to be fully appreciated.

This is particularly important in a novel like *Beloved*, where the secondary narrators' joint efforts slowly narrate Beloved into life. As the meta-narrative phrase quoted earlier ('the two did the best they could to create what really happened,' 78) has already suggested, narration is an act of creation. In this sense the narrative aligns the power of narration with the divine creation as recounted in the biblical book of Genesis, which is also primarily a speech act. Incidentally – or not so incidentally – this attention to the relations between narrative levels in *Beloved* also solves the dilemma of this novel's critics: does Beloved, the reborn girl who was murdered as a baby, 'really' exist, or is she a supernatural phenomenon? The novel gives 'evidence' of both possibilities. If we take the relation between primary and secondary narrator seriously, however – but without a priori deciding that the primary level is more important or more 'truthful' than the secondary – the question becomes moot. The point of the narrative is, precisely, the creative power of story-telling itself, as a life-giving act.

In proportion to the degree of intrinsic interest of the fabula in the primary, as well as in the embedded, text, the tie between the two texts will be more intense, and the explanation more functional. The previous fictitious example of a banal love story is extreme in one respect, both *Beloved* and *Of Old People* are extreme in another. In *Of Old People*, the embedded texts relate bit by bit the story of the events in 'the Indies,' which explain a number of events in the primary fabula. In this case, the relationship between the texts is so intense because the embedded fabula, the 'Thing,' the murder in the Indies, is always presented only in part. Moreover, the functioning of the CN2 (Harold) is also curious. Sometimes he narrates the story of CN2 (Harold), the older man who remembers things, then again he tells the story of CN3 (Little Harold), the boy who witnessed without understanding. Views of the past as seen then are presented, intermingled with images of the past interpreted with the insight of the present. Within this subtext, a double, or subtly varying, focalization is narrated. This, in turn, relates to the events in the primary fabula, the slow, inevitable encroachment of the past upon the present. The influence of the explanatory sub-fabula, in all its doubleness, is of decisive importance.

When the embedded text is, however, restricted to a minimum, its importance for the primary story diminishes. A sentence like 'I shall kill you at dawn to prevent you from deceiving me, because my first wife betrayed me' (*Arabian Nights*) contains an example of a minimal, declarative, embedded narrative text.

Resemblance
The fabulas resemble one another. If they resembled each other completely, we would have identical texts. In that case, the primary text would quote itself. Resemblance, however, can never be identity, even if, as in the example of Borges below, the entire thrust of the narrator is to establish such identity. Therefore, we speak of stronger and weaker, not absolute resemblance. Even in passport photographs, taken with the express intention to show resemblance to the person portrayed, degrees of likeness vary.

When can we speak of resemblance between two different fabulas? A simple and relative solution is this: we speak of resemblance when two fabulas can be paraphrased in such a way that the summaries have one or more striking elements in common. The degree of resemblance is determined by the number of terms the summaries share. An embedded text that presents a story which, according to this criterion, resembles the primary fabula may be taken as a sign of the primary fabula.

Consider the famous story by Jorge Luis Borges, 'Pierre Menard, Author of the *Quixote*.' The story is a paradigmatic example of postmodern literature that questions the foundations of its own art. Pierre Menard is a deceased poet who had verbally transcribed portions of

Cervantes' *Don Quixote*. The narrator states that, although verbally identical to Cervantes' text, the transcription by Menard is 'almost infinitely richer.' He then goes on to demonstrate how that is possible by comparing a half-sentence. I will quote a rather long stretch of Borges' text:

[Cervantes] wrote (part one, chapter nine):

> ... truth, whose mother is history, rival of time, depository of deeds, witness of the past, exemplar and adviser to the present, and the future's counsellor.

Written in the seventeenth century, written by the 'lay genius' Cervantes, this enumeration is a mere rhetorical praise of history. Menard, on the other [hand], writes:

> ... truth, whose mother is history, rival of time, depository of deeds, witness of the past, exemplar and adviser to the present, and the future's counsellor.

> History, the *mother* of truth: the idea is astounding. Menard, a contemporary of William James, does not define history as an inquiry into reality but as its origin. Historical truth, for him, is not what has happened; it is what we judge to have happened. The final phrases – *exemplar and adviser to the present, and the future's counsellor* – are brazenly pragmatic.
> The contrast in style is also vivid. The archaic style of Menard – quite foreign, after all – suffers from a certain affectation. Not so that of his forerunner, who handles with ease the current Spanish of his time. 69

Borges' Menard has, the narrator says towards the end, 'enriched, by a new technique, the halting and rudimentary art of reading: this new technique is that of the deliberate anachronism and the erroneous attribution' (71).

What is the point, for Borges' primary narrator's rhetoric, of such 'copying'? The issue is time, and history. Of course, what this fictional story proposes is not that we all start to copy historical works in order to update them. But there is an important point to make about the reversal Borges' narrator operates, without really saying so, between writing and reading. Writing, and by extension, painting or making a film, is an act of reading, and reading is a manner of rewriting or repainting. And such acts, as German philosopher Walter Benjamin knew, don't occur in 'empty' time but in a time filled by the present. In the present, social agents, subjects with more or less easy access to the codes that direct the cultural integration of images, confront images and see mirrors held up to them. How to read – that is, how to give meaning to messages one vaguely senses but fails to analyse when only dogmatically restricted methods are consecrated as 'historical' or 'visual' enough – seems to me a valuable contribution of narratorial experiment to the understanding of art and literature; art, not as a fixed collection of enshrined objects, but as an ongoing, live process. For some, even life-saving, for others just enlivening; for us all, part of life.

This phenomenon (the embedded text presenting a story that resembles the primary fabula) is comparable to infinite regress. In French the term is 'mise en abyme.' This term derives from heraldry, where the phenomenon occurs in pictorial representation. In literature, however, we have to do with infinite regress in the medium of language. It would be wrong, therefore, to overstress the analogy to graphic representation, since in language mise en abyme occurs in a less 'ideal' form. What is put into the perspective of infinite regress is not the totality of an image, but only a part of the text, or a certain aspect. To avoid needless complications, I suggest we use the term 'mirror-text' for 'mise en abyme.'

An Indication to the Reader

When the primary fabula and the embedded fabula can be paraphrased in such a manner that both paraphrases have one or more elements in common, the subtext is a sign of the primary text. The place of the embedded text – the mirror-text – in the primary text determines its function for the reader. When the mirror-text occurs near the beginning, the reader may, on the basis of the mirror-text, predict the end of the primary fabula. In order to maintain suspense, the resemblance is often veiled. The embedded text will only be interpreted as mirror-text and 'give away' the outcome when the reader is able to capture the partial resemblance through abstraction. That abstract resemblance, however, is usually only captured after the end, when we know the outcome. Thus suspense is maintained, but the prefiguring effect of the mirror-text is lost.

The reverse also occurs: the fabula of the embedded text does not veil its resemblance to the primary fabula. The foreshadowing effect is preserved at the expense of suspense. This does not always imply that suspense is entirely lost. Another kind of suspense may arise. From the kind in which both reader and character are equally in the dark, we have stepped up to a second kind: the reader knows, but the character does not, how the fabula will end. The question that the reader raises is not 'How does it end?' but 'Will the character discover in time?' We can never be sure of this, because resemblance is never perfect. Until the end, there is always the possibility that the embedded fabula resembles the primary one apart from the ending.

When a mirror-text has been added more towards the end of the primary text, suspense presents itself less emphatically. The course of the fabula is then largely familiar, the function of the mirror-text is no longer predictive, but retrospective. A simple repetition of the primary fabula in a mirror-text would not be as interesting. Its function is mostly to enhance significance. The paraphrase of the primary and of the embedded text that we have made in order to infer resemblance will have a more general significance. This more general sense – a human being always loses against a bureaucracy, or, even more abstractly, 'no one escapes fate' – lifts the whole narration on to another level. Kafka's novels do this. The mirror-text serves as directions for use: the embedded story contains a suggestion how the text should be read. Even in this case, the embedded text functions as a sign to the reader.

An Indication to the Actor

Just now I have hinted at the possibility that the actor her- or himself may also interpret the mirror-text as a sign. In this way she may find out the course of the fabula in which she is herself engaged. Thus the actor can influence the fabula's outcome. She can take fate into her own hands. This happens, for instance, in Poe's story 'The Fall of the House of Usher.' The actor who relates the story in which he himself figures saves his life through the correct interpretation of the signs that are presented to him. In the embedded text, which is read out loud, there is mention of a fall. This word 'fall' and the concept 'house' have two meanings. Fall refers of course to the reduction of a house to ruins, but also to the end of a family line. The Usher family will fall with the death of its last descendant, and the castle will fall down. This is what the CN ('I'-witness) realizes. Because he has the insight that double meanings should be taken seriously, the actor is able to interpret the embedded fabula as a mirror of what is about to happen. That is why he can save himself. He flees, and behind him he sees the castle fall down. Thus he can be a witness and relate this curious story.

This mirror-text is interesting for yet other reasons. The actor's realization that double meanings should be taken seriously is itself a sign. It is a 'prescription' for the reading of literature. The embedded text, which is double in meaning, consists of a piece of literature. This text, interpreted in the widest sense, suggests: 'Literature has (at least) a double meaning, or it is not literature.' Thus this embedded text also implies a poetics, a declaration of principle with regard to the ideas about literature that have been embodied in the events in this text. Just as for the actor-witness the right interpretation of the doubleness of the meaning of the embedded text was a matter of life or death, so the double interpretation of the relationship between primary and embedded text is a matter of life and death, to be or not to be, for literature. As is so often the case, the title of the text, through its use of puns, has already given an indication of these meanings. But, at the same time, this title seems deceptively simple. It needs the whole story to disclose the multiplicity of its meanings.

Non-Narrative Embedded Texts

By far the majority of embedded texts are non-narrative. No story is related in them. The content of an embedded text may be anything, from assertions about things in general, discussions between actors, descriptions, to confidences, and the like. The most predominant form is dialogue. Dialogues between two or more actors may even make up the larger part of the entire text. Dialogue is a form in which the actors themselves, and not the primary narrator, utter language. The total of the sentences spoken by the actors produces meaning in those parts of the text. Such embedded texts share that characteristic with dramatic texts. In dramatic texts the whole text consists of the utterances of actors who together, in their interaction, produce meaning. Except, of course, the stage directions in the paratext. The dialogues embedded in a narrative text are dramatic in kind. The more dialogue a narrative text contains, the more dramatic that text is. Hence the relative nature of the definition of a corpus.

Of course, the same applies to other modes and genres. In some dramatic texts a narrator appears, albeit as a (meta-narrative) figure with actor status in his own right, as happens often in the plays of Bertolt Brecht. The statement 'The more dialogue, the more drama,' however, is a simplification, since not only quantity matters here. The 'purity' of the dialogues also influences the degree to which a text may be experienced as dramatic. When between each utterance of an actor the primary narrator intervenes with additions like 'Elizabeth said,' or even more elaborate commentary, the hierarchical relationship between N1 and N2 remains clearly visible. When the clauses follow each other without intervention by the N1, we are likely to forget that we are dealing with an embedded dialogue.

When the embedded text is spoken – or 'thought' – by one actor, it is a soliloquy or monologue. The content of a monologue can, again, be practically anything. There is no intrinsic difference between an embedded monologue and other language use. Embedded passages contain confidences, descriptions, reflections, self-reflections, whatever one wishes. This is the reason I will not discuss the monologue further here.

I began this chapter with the thesis that all utterances, hence, also all narratives, imply a speaker. In the course of the chapter it has also become apparent that all speakers address an interlocutor; that 'I' can only be 'I' if there is a 'you' who allows it. As if to make the case against a purist narratology, *Arabian Nights,* that canonical instance of narrative, dramatizes this situation in an intensive and complex way. Scheherazade's interlocutor is primarily the king, who lets her live as long as her stories keep him engaged. As in Morrison's *Beloved*, story-telling is presented as life-giving, life-saving. But there is a second interlocutor, Scheherazade's sister Dinarzade, who hides under the royal bed. She is the one who keeps the narrative clock, so to speak; she wakes the couple to request the continuation of the story-telling. Narratively speaking, the two interlocutors exist on the same level. But dramatically, in this typically dramatic situation, the one act of story-telling addresses two very different realms. Scheherazade is the speaker, the narrator in the one – telling stories to the king – and the dramatic dialogist on the other – giving her sister encoded instructions.

It would take a complete text theory to discuss all kinds of embedded texts. For dramatic embedded texts, the theory of drama, and a general semiotic theory are better sources. To give an idea of the way narratology here spills over into semiotics, here is one example. Imagine overhearing the following dialogue in a hospital's consultation room:

'Ever had scarlet fever as a child?' 'No, doctor.' 'German measles?' 'No, doctor.' 'Ra ... Rickets?' 'Eh ... no, doctor. 'Do you know what rickets is?' 'Well, no, doctor.' Why do you say "no" then?' 'I was afraid that you would ask further questions if I said "yes."' 'But you can also say "I don't know," can't you?' 'Is that allowed, doctor?' 'How many times have you been pregnant before?' 'I don't know, doctor.' 'You don't know?!!' 'Yes I do, doctor. Eight times.' 'Eight?' 'No no, doctor, eleven.' 'Are you absolutely sure?' 'To tell you the truth, no ... eh ... doctor.' 'But you must be able to tell me how many children you have exactly?' 'Oh dear, professor, you look so intimidating.' 'I am not a professor. I am a training resident.' 'Really ... my friend was also delivered by a training resident. She had some very good laughs with him.' 'No wonder. I bet your friend knew exactly how often she had been pregnant.' 'Or, that resident was not as intimidating and less precise. ... Good, now you are laughing. What a relief. You were just glaring at that paper from behind those glasses. To be exact, I have seven children, and I've had two miscarriages and one was still-born. Is that clear enough for you to do the counting?' 'And, eh ... your last period, could you guess, approximately, no need to be precise, about which month, which week it was perhaps? Before the vacation or after?' 'The 28th of June.' 'The 28th of June?!!' 'Absolutely, the 28th of June. A woman does know those things, you know.'

The exchange of signs between the two people pursuing the same goal, adequate medical treatment, is very unsuccessful in the beginning. The resident uses normal English words, and if the patient is reasonably educated and English-speaking, there should be no problem. Yet, there is. The accompanying signs preclude communication at the expense of both parties. The doctor gives signs of various kinds which the woman interprets as intimidating: his impatience when she hesitates, the rebuff when she gives an inadequate answer, and his looking at the papers instead of at his interlocutor; his firing off question after question, leaving no room for hesitation; the whole setting in his office, and the social context of power that pertains to it. These signs, subliminal in various degrees, are not intended by the speaker, but are nevertheless decisive. As such, they are part of the primary narrator's rhetoric, even if not a single word uttered by this primary narrator occurs in the text. This speaker does not want to produce the sign-events that have this negative effect. But he or she could not help their occurrence.

The theory of speech acts is relevant here, too. What is meant as a question, an open request for information, becomes, in the eyes of the intimidated woman, an order. This confuses her, and prevents her from responding adequately. The result is the total linguistic incapacitation of the woman: she cannot answer any question any more. To see this woman as stupid, uneducated, unable to cope, or shy is one way of interpreting her behaviour. But that would be a pretty rude, unsophisticated response, unworthy of the competent sign-user. To think with the doctor that it is utterly stupid not to know how many times you have been pregnant is missing the various possibilities in the question. Did he mean the number of medically acknowledged pregnancies, the number of deliveries, or the number of actual living children? For a woman for whom each of these possible questions yields a different answer, the question is hard enough and some time to think should be granted her; but the situation of intimidation does not let her. This exchange in fact shows that in some ways, the doctor, who does not realize this, is no more competent at communication than the woman. His question is unwittingly ambiguous.

The kinds of signs the doctor intends to send out – questions clear enough to yield clear answers – do not match the interpretations the addressee makes of them. She sees them either as orders or as unanswerable. This situation could go on forever, and the interview would turn out to be useless. The woman manages to reverse the situation, however, by breaking through the false relation of authority, and restores communication. Exchange of information becomes possible. Now that the sign (question) is no more interfered with by the subliminal sign (order) and by the other contextual signs, it can be answered. No trace remains of the impression of incompetence.

The dialogue was, in fact, a short story by Hanna Verweg, entitled 'Anamnesis' and published in 1984 in a Dutch newspaper. The title is the only utterance of the primary narrator. It is highly relevant: it is a word that not all readers know; I, for one, did not. It is certainly not a word expected in a small newspaper column. As a consequence, the word is intimidating. It makes the reader insecure. As the sole stuff of the primary narration, it is a mirror-image of what is going to be the story's point. Unlike the fellow patient overhearing that dialogue who may respond by identifying with the patient – if she is next – or by proudly taking her distance and looking down on her – if she has been more successful – the reader intimidated by a difficult word is likely to sympathize with the woman immediately, warmed up as s/he is by the title at the doctor's expense. There is, then, a continuity between the narrator, who is also the first speaker of the story, the woman-speaker in the embedded story, and the reader at the other end.

This example also allows me to raise the issue of the narratee, the receiver of the narrated text. In this case it is particularly important to realize that the interpretation of signs is dependent upon the subjects who use them. The narrator of the piece could tell the story in this way because he or she had, for whatever reasons, sympathy for the intimidated woman. The narrator's reticence, which turns the narrative into a virtually dramatic text, is part of that sympathy: the narrator turns the narration over to the embedded speakers, presumably to empower the woman to get to make her victorious point herself. The addressee of the text – the narratee – is strongly suggested to invest sympathy in the same figure, but a training resident who reads the story before setting off to her first practice may very well put her sympathy elsewhere.

The narratee, as much as narrator, is an abstract function rather than a person. Actual readers will have different responses. Women readers are likely to better understand the final exchange, and probably be more strongly gratified by the role-reversal at the end than most men readers will, but this division according to gender lines does not – heaven forbid! – hold for every single person. Each person brings to the signs her or his own baggage. This theoretical point is part of the meta-narrative thrust of the text. For, the story itself shows that roles are not fixed. It displays how the initial incapacity to get the message is changed into adequate semiotic behaviour which includes, aside from the information requested, a surplus to it, a subtle and humorous message, a view on gender boundaries and a sign of restored self-confidence. In the original Dutch text, the resident is clearly male; in English, the language does not show he is male, but the traditionally male role s/he takes on suggests as much. And the author, signing the narrative with a woman's name, turns out to be a man.

When the embedded text itself is not discussed in greater detail, little can be said about its relationship to the primary one. In every case, the relationship tends to be determined by two factors. Sometimes, explicit commentary on the embedded text which influences our reading of that text is given by the N1. That commentary may be disguised when the embedded text is only hinted at by implication. 'Anamnesis' is an extreme example of this. Also, the relationship between the two contents determines the relationship.

The contents of the embedded text sometimes link with those of the primary one, sometimes it is even its natural sequel. At other times it is perhaps completely divorced from the primary text; or it has an explanatory function; it is similar to the primary text; it contradicts or contravenes it. In each case, the relationship is different. It is, therefore, impossible to just suppose that, as a general rule, the assertions of either a narrator or an actor carry the meaning of the whole text. Given the technically hierarchical relation between the two texts, one negative word of the N1 would, in principle, be sufficient to radically change the meaning of the whole. That this cannot possibly be maintained is a statement on the limit of the relevance of such technical structures.

This recognition offers an opportunity to establish the interface between the rather technical, structural theory presented in this book and a different approach, which seems to compete with it but is rather, in my view, complementary to it. The clash in 'Anamnesis' between the (man)resident and the (woman)patient dramatized the misunderstanding, the non-communication, which occurs when two people seem to 'speak different languages.' According to the theory of the Soviet philosopher of language Mikhail Bakhtin, who wrote – probably under different names – in the 1930s, this is a general feature of language. He developed the notion that language use – or rather, discourse – is always an intertwining of different discourses coming from a variety of backgrounds. This principle is known as the dialogic principle. What Bakhtinians call dialogue, however, is better understood as a metaphor that underscores the heterogeneity of discourse. In fact, 'heteroglossia,' literally 'multilinguism,' is another key term in Bakhtin's work.

The most widespread term Bakhtin's work offered is 'intertextuality.' This term refers to the quotation, in a text, of another text. Such quotations are not always marked as such; in fact, according to the philosophy of language Bakhtin proposed, any discourse is always already a patchwork of quotations. No narrative text makes this more dramatically clear than Cervantes' *Don Quixote,* with a hero – or anti-hero – who goes mad from his reading and can only speak in quotations. These quotations are cleverly dramatized, reversed, and ridiculed passages from sources one can actually trace. I like to reserve the term 'intertextuality' for such traceable cases.

On the other hand, since discourse is for Bakhtin always a mix of different discourses, there are many instances where tracing actual sources makes no sense whatsoever. In 'Anamnesis,' for example, the resident and the woman 'speak different languages' in the sense that they each have their own points of departure, assumptions, manners of speaking, and also, things they do not say because they seem self-evident. In this text the discrepancy is clearly marked by the different speakers who each speak in their own discourse. But if a single narrative voice speaks a mix of different discourses, the more suitable term is 'interdiscursivity.' Kathy Acker's postmodern novels are good examples of an ironic use of interdiscursivity. They consist of a variety of textual modes (dramatic dialogue, prose narrative as well as poetry), narrative modes (character-bound narrator as well as external narrator), genres (autobiography, art and political criticism, travel literature, pornographic literature), media (words, images), and typographic styles.

But in spite of current interest and extensive use of interdiscursivity, the phenomenon is by no means limited to contemporary culture. Again, *Don Quixote* remains a paradigmatic if not founding case. And in her 'loa' (a kind of dramatized preface) to her play *El Narciso Divino*, the Mexican baroque author Sor Juana Inés de la Cruz has an allegorical representative of the native population called 'America' not only speak in what was perceived as the language of the 'other' but also in the discourse of Native religion. This was a smart political gesture: under the pretext of showing how Native people ended up converting to Christianity, this play, meant to be performed at the Spanish court, confronted the Spaniards with the existence of a religious discourse different from their own, but which was in many ways congenial to Christianity.

Nor is interdiscursivity always so self-consciously deployed. In one of the oldest texts of the Western tradition, the biblical book of Judges, I have seen cases of interdiscursivity that could point to the seams where the text is patched together. The daughter of Jephthah, in Judges 11, uses a discourse that could be remnants of a different tradition, oriented to a women's culture. In my study of this text I call such remnants 'wandering rocks,' in reference to the ice age.

Bakhtin's legacy has a strong liberating potential. The very notion that language is not unified provides access to bits and pieces of culturally different environments within a single text. It makes readers aware of the limited importance of the individual author and the impossibility of completely repressing ideological and social others. To realize that any text is a patchwork of different strata, bearing traces of different communities and of the contestations between them, is an essential insight. The analysis of 'Anamnesis' demonstrates this clearly. The idea of a discursive plurality also makes it easier to envision a narratological analysis of a mixed-media work such as film, or even of entirely visual works. I will discuss this issue a bit more in chapter 2.

In 'Amamnesis' the heterogeneity of the discourses spoken by the two embedded speakers produces the clash between them. So far, the theory presented here is compatible with Bakhtin; in fact, a Bakhtinian view suffices to notice this. But for two reasons I will not incorporate this view. First, although Bakhtin did put forward claims about the specifically heteroglossic nature of the novel, he did not refer to narrative as a discursive mode but to the novel as a historical genre. Second and more important, on the basis of 'Anamnesis' I would like to maintain that a Bakhtinian perspective does not fully account for the narratological particularity of this story. The technical distinction in narrative levels is necessary to account for the great impact of the minimally speaking primary narrator. And it is basically this organizing voice that makes the clash work to promote one position over the other – the woman over the resident – even though readers will respond according to their own cultural position. By setting the stage for the reader's own sense of being left out, intimidated, the two speakers, who are technically equal, are assigned different opportunities to gain the reader's sympathy. Whereas a Bakhtinian view is very useful to keep in mind, I prefer to complement it with a more technical narratological view for this reason.

The examples analysed in this chapter not only demonstrate that an analysis of the text as such helps to gain access to a complex narrative text. They also help to historicize narratological analysis, as we saw particularly clearly in the section on description. The meta-narrative and ironic commentaries implied by the relation between embedded and overall text underscore the idea that postmodernism has a special preference for the use of mirror-text. Thus, another preconception can be eliminated: that structural analysis is ahistorical.

6: Remarks and Sources

I have limited myself in the choice of topics for this chapter. Only the status of the narrative agent and its relationship to what is narrated have been discussed. This restriction is the effect of the decision, already put forth in the introduction, to limit our subject matter. Narratology studies narrative texts only in so far as they are narrative; in other words, in their narrativity. In particular, the topic of this chapter, the text, is also studied elsewhere in several other aspects. Linguistically oriented disciplines such as stylistics, but also grammar, syntax, and semantics, are important for different kinds of investigations of the text, but I have left them out deliberately here. Side trips to other disciplines would inevitably have interfered with the systematic organization of this study.

Nevertheless, the connections with related disciplines have made themselves felt at several points. The distinction between direct, indirect, and free indirect discourse, which I have discussed here because it concerns the status of the narrative agent with regard to the object of narration, is one of the classic topics of linguistics. The delimitation of the subject of discussion, however, cannot be more than preliminary. I wish to mention one competing theory of free indirect speech that explicitly rejects the thesis that all narrative utterences can be attributed to a narrator. Ann Banfield's alternative theory considers such speeches as 'sentences without speaker,' even 'unspeakable sentences' (1982; for a philosophical underpinning, 2000). Strong as this theory is in itself, I cannot accept its implied elimination of responsibility.

Wayne C. Booth introduced the concept of the implied author (1961). The confusion between pragmatics and semantics that has arisen around this concept is especially noticeable in the work of Booth's followers, who are numerous. A clear discussion of this problem can be found in Pelc (1971), also a useful discussion of dialogue.

I entirely refrain from using another concept from classical narrative theory, the 'omniscient narrator.' I find it both phantasmagoric and ideologically manipulative to even suppose such a possibility. See Culler (2007) for a definitive critique of that concept and its cognates.

Benveniste (1966) made the distinction between personal and impersonal use of language, for which he used the terms 'histoire' and 'discours.' Because these terms have given rise to confusion, I have avoided them there. Benveniste's work, translated into English (1971), remains of fundamental importance. Silverman (1983) offers a wonderful discussion of the usefulness of this theory (among others, many also relevant here) for the subject of this chapter and for film. Her later book (1996) pursues this direction.

Ideology and, subsequently, the politics of narrative are difficult to pin down. I would not wish to isolate that aspect from the narrative structure in which it functions, as such narratologists as Bertens (2001) and Cohan and Shires (1988) tend to do.

About the difference between 'pure' narration and non-narrative commentary, see Genette (1969), which has appeared in English as 'Boundaries of Narrative.' There are many different views of free indirect discourse. A clear survey is offered by McHale (1978). Rather unsystematic is Lanser (1981). Perry (1979) labels the phenomenon 'combined discourse.' On text interference, see Doležel (1973).

Dällenbach (1977) wrote an interesting book about mirror-texts. A critical discussion and systematization is offered in Bal (1991). See also Jefferson (1983).

There is a long article (1972) and a subsequent book (1981) by Hamon about description. The typology of motivation is based on this article. The six types of description are largely inspired by Lodge (1977). Motivation as a strategy is best explained in Culler (1975). The phenomenon is also called 'naturalization.' On motivation in postmodern fiction, see Van Alphen (1988); for a good survey on the concept of postmodernism, Van Alphen (1989). For a in-depth theory of description, see Bal (2004). The example of early Westerns as travelogues is from Verhoeff (2006), who took part of her clue from Musser (1984). The concept of authentication is discussed in a very useful article by Doležel (1980).

The concept of the narratee is attached to the name of Prince, who decisively integrated it in his book on narratology (1983). A sample of Bakhtin's own writing is offered in Bakhtin (1981). As mentioned, Peeren (2008) makes Bakhtin's ideas available for the analysis of popular culture, especially film and televison. Todorov's introduction to Bakhtin's work is also useful (1984). On the current interest in intertextuality and interdiscursivity as a more general cultural phenomenon such as 'recycling,' see Moser (1981).

For *Don Quixote* I have used the accessible Penguin edition, tr. J.M. Cohen (Harmondsworth 1950). Sor Juana's 'loa' was published as Sor Juana Inés de la Cruz 'Loa para el auto sacramental *El Divino Narciso*' 3–21 (1995); *El Divino Narciso*, 21–97. *Obras completas de Sor Juana Ines de la Cruz*. Vol. 3, *Autos y Loas*. Edited, with preface and notes by Alfonso Mendez Plancarte (Mexico: Fondo de Cultura Económica). Borges' 'Pierre Menard, Author of the *Quixote*' is in *Labyrinths* (Harmondsworth: Penguin, 1962), 62–71.

The example of the family accident comes from Arno Bohlmeijer, *Something Very Sorry*, Boston: Houghton Mifflin Company, 1996. The comments on *Beloved* are an implicit response to Shlomith Rimmon-Kenan (1996). Page numbers refer to Toni Morrison, *Beloved* (New York: Signet, 1987).

The example of second-person narrative is from Michel Butor, *La modification* (Paris: Les Editions de Minuit, 1957); translation mine. The most important study of this text is Françoise van Rossum-Guyon's *Critique du roman. Essai sur 'La Modification' de Michel Butor* (Paris: Gallimard, 1970), a book-length study which is also a theoretical discussion of narrative structure, but within an earlier, more or less pre-structuralist framework. On second-person narrative, including Butor's novel, see Kakandas (1996), who is much more positive about the success of Butor's experiment than I am. In another important article (1993) she develops second-person narrative specifically in the context of postmodernism.

The passages from *Budapest Diary* are from Susan Rubin Suleiman, *Budapest Diary: In Search of the Motherbook* (Lincoln and London: University of Nebraska Press, 1996). On the poetics of apostrophe, see Culler (1981), and on the political implications, Johnson (1987).

The example 'Anamnesis' was borrowed from my more extensive analysis (1994). The Evelyn Fox Keller example is from *Secrets of Life, Secrets of Death* (New York: Routledge, 1992). I borrowed the example of the camera mounted on trains from Verhoeff (2006).

The idea that artists emulate their predecessors in their 'wilful misreadings' has been put forward by Bloom (1973). It was criticized as well as applied to visual art by Bryson (1984). A femnist critique and revision is offered by Lord (1999). For *Arabian Nights*, see the excellent discussion in Khanna (2008).

2

Story: Aspects

1: Preliminary Remarks

I have called those features that distinguish the structured story from, on the one hand, the narration and on the other, the fabula, *aspects*. With this term I indicate that the story – the middle of the three layers I distinguish in the narrative text – does not consist of material different from that of either the text or the fabula, but that this material is looked at from a certain, specific angle. If one regards the text primarily as the product of the use of a medium, and the fabula primarily as the product of imagination, the story could be regarded as the result of an ordering. As mentioned, this distinction is of a theoretical nature only. Let me reiterate that the aim of textual analysis is not to account for the process of writing, but for the conditions of the process of reception. The distinction emphatically does not imply that the one layer exists before the other.

The question that underlies the story is different. How is it that a narrative text comes across to the reader in a certain manner? Why do we find the same fabula beautiful when presented by one writer and trite when presented by another? Why is it so difficult in a simplified edition of a classic, or of a masterpiece of world literature, to preserve the effect of the original? How can Jane Campion's film *Portrait of a Lady* (1996), while 'faithful' to the fabula of Henry James' novel by the same title, be so utterly different, not only in 'text' – this is obviously inevitable – but also in focus, interest, ideology?

For one thing, this difference comes from the working of the text itself. Describing a woman as beautiful, spirited, ambitious, and naïve is necessarily different from 'showing' a beautiful face and figure, combined with actions that 'demonstrate' her character. Even from one written text to another – indeed, from one version to another – the effect changes with any alteration in the author's use of language. But that is not the only reason. The effect will be at least equally dependent on the way the material, the fabula, has been handled. This is why many translations of texts – which necessarily lose a substantial part of the original effect of the use of language, but less of the technical aspects of the story – sometimes seem to relate more closely to a first reader's reading experience than do adaptations, school editions, film versions, and so on, which tend to interfere more deeply with the ordering of the material.

The best-known principle of ordering, and perhaps easiest to grasp, is the presentation of events in an order different from their chronological order. In the tradition of the theory of literature, this aspect has survived from the distinction between *fabula* and *suzjet* as used by the Russian formalists. I begin therefore with the ordering of events. Characters – individualized actors – are here discussed in the more traditional sense; in the next chapter they will be treated in their relation to the events of the fabula. An analysis of the relations between the various actors in the fabula as abstract units is indispensable, in addition to an investigation of individual features such as looks, character, psychological qualities, and past. When those relations are clear, it is easier to distinguish between those relations and the relations between the reader and the characters in the story, and the flows of sympathy and antipathy between the characters and from the reader to the individual characters. For the reader's view of characters and events will be accounted for with the help of the concepts presented in this chapter.

Manipulation originally meant simply 'handling,' 'treatment,' and even though its modern sense has shifted to include more unfavourable connotations, the original meaning is still synonymous with 'operation.' The fabula is 'treated,' and the reader is being manipulated by this treatment. I would like to suspend the negative connotations of manipulation, also in this second sense. It is basically at this level that suspense and pleasure are provoked, and that ideology is inscribed. Such manipulation takes place not only in that actors are 'turned into' specific characters, placed into specific spaces with mutual symbolic and circumstantial relations. The prime means of manipulation that has taken up an ever more important place in the literature of the last two centuries is what is traditionally known as perspective. The point of view from which the elements of the fabula are being presented is often of decisive importance for the meaning the reader will assign to the fabula. This concept plays a part in the most everyday situations. A conflict is best judged by letting each party give its own version of the events, its own story. Any treatment can be reduced to the point of view from which the image of the fabula and the (fictitious) world where it takes place are constructed. Perspective, then, is the technical aspect, the placing of the point of view in a specific agent.

If the first aspect that will be dealt with (deviations from chronology) is first and foremost a technical feature of the story – in most cases contributing only indirectly to the shaping of meaning – this chapter ends with an aspect (perspective, here called focalization) which has far more influence on meaning. The order in which the various aspects will be dealt with can also be explained in that sense: though all aspects point to narrative techniques, in most cases the importance of those various techniques for the shaping of meaning will become more significant as we go along.

2: Time

In one sense, time is a given, a self-evident for the time-based arts to which it even gives its name – narrative, theatre, film, video, dance, music, to name but the most obvious ones. These arts unfold in time. In appearance, but in appearance only, other art forms, such as photography, painting, drawing, sculpture, and architecture, produce immutable, still artifacts. This division is built on the illusion that processing these still artifacts can be done in a blink. I do not endorse that illusion, and have argued elsewhere that still artifacts also 'take time.' But for our purposes here, it is not the obvious time-consuming nature of the media that helps us analyse the story. It is, instead, the many ways in which narratives complicate this apparently self-evident temporality that are of interest.

The time that regulates our lives, by means of clocks, schedules, and other means of uniforming lives, is so incorporated, interiorized, or naturalized that it is difficult to imagine that there are conflicts built into it. The *day-to-day time* of schedules does not match the long-term sense of time we learn mainly from history. *Monumental time* is a temporality that denies even that *historical time*; it aspires to eternity. On the other side of this tension, the small time of moments and the variations of intensity of experience cross through the regulated time of the day's occupations. These tensions are different according to one's life. Mothers with small children live in a rhythm that is stricter than that of the other parent, if present, or of mothers of older children. The routine of small acts of care determines the experience of time where even sleep is no longer continuous. We could call it *micro time*.

To realize this thickness of time, just imagine the life of an undocumented immigrant. The moment of border crossing occurs after a long journey. The heightened danger intensifies that moment, even if it can take days to actually cross. Once on the other side, inside the new country, the immigrant's inner clock starts ticking. The justification for the departure, the loss of the affective base of family and friends, is to make money to help out at home. But as long as documents such as residency and work permits are not forthcoming, much of his or her time is spent waiting. This produces a kind of social schizophrenia, which makes the migrant always hasty and always stagnating at the same time; and always in a different experience of time from the residents of the host country. Then, if and when the long-awaited documents finally arrive, the hoped-for relief is slow in coming. The time lost is also a loss of the opportunity to learn the new language, acquire work skills, and make new friends. People in such situations are condemned to live in the present. As a consequence, the memories of their past that should sustain them are in fact put on ice. This living in an enforced presentism is a symptom of disenfranchisement.

Once we realize this, the thickness of time becomes impressively complex. Looking at temporality in *Arabian Nights* is rewarding, for example. The king, who kills all virgins at the end of the night, is a slave to day-to-day time. He suffers from chronophobia, the fear that time is the enemy's gain, as much as from gynophobia, the fear that women have a life and desires of their own and hence, a subjectivity. What Scheherazade does in response to the king's disease is stealing time, or borrowing it. But how can you borrow something, or steal it, that has no owner? She needs to make things very complicated to circumvent this drawback. She does so by seducing the king into the different temporality of her stories. This temporality is itself complex. It comprehends at the very least the time of telling, the time of the events, and the suspense of time wheren these two do not match up. She borrows time, that is, from narrative, not from the king.

These different conceptions of time and the issues pertaining to them must here be streamlined. I present only three forms of temporality that emerge specifically from the three-tiered narrativity that underlies this book's theoretical principles. While the characterizations of different temporal experiences outlined above remain a useful interpretive backdrop, below I sketch the technical devices narratives deploy to produce such experiences for their readers.

3: Sequential Ordering

In these subsections, the relations are being explored which hold between the order of events in the story and their chronological sequence in the fabula. The latter sequence is a theoretical construction, which we can make on the basis of the laws of everyday logic which govern common reality. According to that logic one cannot arrive in a place before one has set out to go there. In a story that is possible, however.

> a John rang the neighbours' doorbell. He had so irresistibly felt the need to stand eye to eye with a human being that he had not been able to remain behind the sewing machine.

This is a quite ordinary passage, which no one would be surprised to come across in a narrative text. But anyone knows that in 'reality' (fictitious or not), the sequence of events must have been the other way round: first John must have felt the desire to go and see someone; then he acted accordingly and went to ring the doorbell. The reader assumes this, but such assumptions are narrative effects; they do not imply that there exists, or has ever existed, such a series of events, in that order.

Data are needed for such a confrontation between the ordering of events in the story and their sequence in the fabula. The latter will be deducible from explicit data or from indirect indications. In a, for example, the tenses of the verbs in the text indicate the sequence of events: simple past for the later event; past perfect for the preceding events. But even without such indications in the text there is information that, with our sense of everyday logic, we can combine in such a way that we can say, 'The ringing of that doorbell is likely to be the result of the occurrence of the desire.'

It is not always possible or relevant to reconstruct the chronological sequence. In many experimental modern novels, we find, for instance, that these matters are intentionally confused, the chronological relations expressly concealed. In such a case the chronological chaos we note is often still quite meaningful. The films of Alejandro González Iñárritu, for example – *Amores Perros* (2001), *21 Grams* (2003) and *Babel* (2006) – deliberately confuse the chronology so as to build an impossible simultaneity. Thus he creates in *Babel*, for example, a truly global world, but one that is not unified. Such a chaotic temporality can even be concealed behind apparent chronology, as in Gabriel García Márquez' *One Hundred Years of Solitude* and Marguerite Duras' *L'après-midi de Monsieur Andesmas.*

In other respects, these two novels are totally different. The significance, therefore, which can be attached to this astonishing game with chronology is equally different. The effect of García Márquez' novel is to let people, generations, social contexts succeed each other in rapid turmoil in the course of a hundred years which seem to contain a history of mankind, to terminate in the absurd failure of (communal) life. Duras simply makes a man wait three hours for his daughter, and presents in those three hours the vision of a growing despair through a mixture of inertia and chronological chaos, indolence and the effort to endure that indolence – one of the tragic aspects of the aging person, who has to continue living while, in fact, he is already dead. In neither novel is it easy to grasp the deviations in sequential ordering; both seem strictly chronological. Here, too, the 'failure' of an analysis done with the aid of a systematic concept is a significant result in itself. The analysis is not based on application of a concept that is, like a master-code, beyond questioning, but rather a confrontation between theoretical concept and narrative text that is mutually illuminating. On the other hand, it sometimes remains desirable that chronological relations be investigated when indications of chronological sequence can be found. At least one argument for the relevance of such an investigation can be given.

As against various other art forms – architecture, visual arts – a written linguistic text is linear. One word follows another, one sentence follows another; and when one has finished the book, one has sometimes forgotten the beginning. In a narrative text, it is even possible to speak of a double linearity: that of the text, the series of sentences, and that of the fabula, the series of events. Moreover, narrative texts are usually fairly long, longer than most poems, which is why one usually reads them straight through, not retracing one's steps as one tends to do in the case of poems. There are various *ways* of breaking such linearity, forcing the reader to read more intensively. Deviations in sequential ordering may contribute to intense reading; later on, some other means will be discussed. If deviations in sequential ordering correspond with conventions, they will not stand out. They can, however, be so intricate as to exact the greatest exertions in following the story. In order not to lose the thread it is necessary to keep an eye on the sequential ordering, and the very effort forces one to reflect also on other elements and aspects. Playing with sequential ordering is not just a literary convention; it is also a means of drawing attention to certain things, to emphasize, to bring about aesthetic or psychological effects, to show various interpretations of an event, to indicate the subtle difference between expectation and realization, and much else besides. Interestingly, it is literary narrative's way of achieving a density that is akin to the simultaneity often claimed for visual images as distinct from literature.

To give an example of the emulation of literary narrative with the still image: in Morrison's *Beloved*, Denver often dwells on memories of events she cannot in any realistic sense have witnessed, including her own birth, about which she has been told so many stories. These not only provide her with memories she needs to build up her sense of self – because, as I mentioned before, story-telling is a gift of life – but also *paint* for her a picture: 'easily she stepped into the told story that lay before her eyes on the path she followed away from the window' (29). The play with sequence, although too complex to trace, calls attention to itself, because it contributes to the important wavering in the novel between supernatural and 'real' existence – a wavering that is, among other things, a metaphor for the bond between history and present, group and individuals.

Not all narratives are so complex; or, for that matter, so gripping. Turns of phrase such as

b Little could I then foresee

c Only yesterday I was thinking

point for instance in their own way at different interpretations of events. In b speaks, let's say, a disillusioned old man looking back on the mistakes he made in his youth; in c someone may have recently discovered some important data on the grounds of which she has changed her opinion. These are mere guesses about fictitious examples that might be explained in different ways. Often, the misapprehensions of actors who are not in possession of the right information are 'afterwards' cleared up and explained in this way on the level of story. But the issue of chronology is not a tool to decide literary quality. Narratology helps understanding, not evaluation. Nor is there a direct relation between chronological play and intellectual complexity. In the children's book *Something Very Sorry*, already mentioned, the child whose voice is the narrator needs the chronological deviations to convey the sense of loss in the character:

> I'm in the hospital.
> The others are also injured. That's why they don't come to take me home.
> Doctors and nurses keep coming in to examine me. They tell me what happened – we crashed into a tree. It was a serious accident. These words stick in my head.   7

The movement back and forth from present to past to present is the story's basic rhythm. The girl's slowly returning memories of the accident alternate with her experiences in the hospital and the happy past before the car crash. These delicate alternations contribute to the story in a very meaningful way: they provide insight into the broken sense of self of the traumatized child in a modulation that makes the reader experience it with her on an emotional level as well.

Differences between the arrangement in the story and the chronology of the fabula are chronological deviations or anachronies. There is no question of anything abnormal, but of something specific, something in which one text may differ from another. Practically all novels contain anachrony, even in emphatically chronological ones, such as Dutch writer Gerard van het Reve's *The Evenings* – despite the apparent chronological ordering. Deviations from chronology tend to be more drastic when the fabula is more complex. Sometimes this seems to be the result of the need to explain much in a complicated fabula. The explanation often takes the form of reference to the past. Also the difficulty of bringing the many different threads of a fabula together to form a coherent unity may create the need to refer back or point ahead. In particular, the 'classic' novel, after the model of the nineteenth-century realistic novel, makes much use of this possibility. A conventional construction of a novel is the beginning in medias res, which immerses the reader in the middle of the fabula. From this point she is referred back to the past, and from then on the story carries on more or less chronologically through to the end. Anachrony in itself, then, is by no means unusual.

In popular romances and other popular fiction one encounters all kinds of variants of this form. However, anachrony can be used as a means for the realization of specific literary effects. I discuss three aspects of chronological deviation successively: direction, distance, and span.

Direction

Seen from that moment in the fabula which is being presented when
the anachrony intervenes, the event presented in the anachrony lies either in the past or in the future. For the first category I use the term
retroversion; for the second, anticipation. I avoid the more common
terms 'flashback' and 'flash-forward' because of their vagueness and
psychological connotations. An example of a complete anachrony is the
beginning of Homer's *Iliad*:

> d Sing, Goddess, the anger of Peleus' son Achilles and its devasta-
> tion, which put pains thousandfold upon the Achaians, hurled in
> their multitudes to the house of Hades strong souls of heroes, but
> gave their bodies to be the delicate feasting of dogs, of all birds,
> and the will of Zeus was accomplished since that time when first
> there stood in division of conflict Atreus' son the lord of men and
> brilliant Achilles.
>
> What god was it then set them together in bitter collision? Zeus'
> son and Leto's, Apollo, who in anger at the king drove the foul
> pestilence along the host, and the people perished, since Atreus'
> son had dishonoured Chryses, priest of Apollo, when he came be-
> side the fast ships of the Achaians to ransom back his daughter,
> carrying gifts beyond count and holding in his hands wound on a
> staff of gold the ribbons of Apollo who strikes from afar, and sup-
> plicated all the Achaians but above all Atreus' two sons, the mar-
> shals of the people: 'Sons of Atreus and you other strong-greaved
> Achaians, to you may the gods grant who have their homes on Ol-
> ympus Priam's city to be plundered and a fair homecoming there-
> after, but may you give me back my own daughter and take the
> ransom, giving honour to Zeus' son who strikes from afar, Apollo.'
>
> book 1, p. 59

The first object presented here is the grudge of Achilles. Subsequently
we are told about the distress of the Achaeans, which resulted from it.
Then the dispute between Achilles and Agamemnon is treated, which,
as the direct cause of Achilles' anger, should precede it. The disease
(the plague) is, in turn, the cause of the dispute, and the insult to Chrys-
es was its cause in turn. We indicate the five units presented with A, B,
C, D, E in the order in which they are presented in the story.

Chronologically, their positions are 4, 5, 3, 2, 1, so that the anachronies can be represented by the formula A4-B5-C3-D2-E1. Clearly, with

the exception of the beginning, they form a direct return to the past. This beginning of the *Iliad* fits the convention that prescribes that one indicates what the story will be about. The apparently endless series of causes and effects shows, moreover, how strongly the vicissitudes of human beings are determined by powers beyond them. And at the same time the reader is, already at the beginning, presented with a summary of the book's contents: the summary which the muse is asked to sing is what the reader will hear.

Another example, from a modern story this time, shows an entirely different sequential ordering:

e   A I saw that he could not take it. With a haggard face he looked at what was left of Massuro. He wanted a reason – otherwise, where was he? And the only thing that could pass for a reason, with a great deal of good (and occult) faith, was fear. B But there was no fear. Massuro hadn't known what fear was. C I knew Massuro well, in a manner of speaking. D So I shall tell it to you as if you were a friend, Gentlemen, although it's a mystery to me what you will do with the information when you have it.

E Two years ago, when he was posted to my section at Potapego, I happened to be standing jabbering to the village headman. The truck from Kaukenau arrived, and out of the cab stepped a swarthy, heavily built fellow with a big head, round eyes and thick lips. F Then, suddenly, I saw his name in the Major's letter before me again. G 'Heintje Massuro!'

Harry Mulisch, 'What Happened to Sergeant Massuro?' 126

The capital letters indicate the various chronological parts into which the fragment can be divided.

Chronologically, all parts but one precede the story-time proper, the moment when the I-narrator, reporting the events, addresses the Dutch authorities, the War Department, with the words: 'it is a calm man who is writing this to you – a man with the calm that comes to the surface when hope has fled.' I would infer here that we are going to be presented with some kind of fantastic story which has ended unhappily. In A the speaker is in contact with a medical officer – rather an emotional sort of contact, as far as we can judge. No wonder, since there is between them the 'remains' of a human body, the body of Massuro, who has gradually turned into stone, in a mysterious manner. B treats the possible fears of Massuro, who has already died in A.

So, in the fabula, B precedes A. C covers a longer period, let us say from the renewed acquaintance between Massuro and the speaker, and the beginning of the sinister events, whether or not caused by the fears mentioned in B. In D we return to the story's present: the I is writing his report to the department. E recalls the moment at which the renewed acquaintance in New Guinea took place, and thus immediately precedes C, or rather E introduces the beginning of C. F lies even further back in the past: the speaker recalls the moment when, before the arrival of Massuro, he sees his name mentioned in a letter. Indicating the various parts with capital letters, and their chronological position with figures, the following formula ensues: A5-B4-C3-D6-E2-F1-G2.

The fragment began with a haggard look and confusion, it ends in the placidity of a renewed meeting with the man – 'Heintje Massuro!' – where the contrast between the familiarity of the Dutch boy's name and the exotic surname is striking – something like the contrast between 'Chuck' and 'Charles,' not unlike Suleiman's 'Mother' and 'Daddy.' In view of the mysterious events which happened to the man in question, this contrast, combined with the conflicting circumstances of the actors (a conflict which is already present in the colonial name of the place, Dutch New Guinea), is by no means accidental. The chronological sequence of events, so clearly violated here, is broadly maintained from this passage onwards. But this confused beginning has already given us a picture of the confusion which underlies the fabula as a whole.

Nuances of Anachrony

I have ignored one thing in this analysis. The chronological deviations are not all of the same order. F, for instance, takes place in the 'consciousness' of the first-person actor. In fact, the event is not the seeing of the name, but the remembering of the seeing. Note that again, there is a coincidence of anachronical complexity and an emulation with visual perception. In that sense the fragment is not a chronological deviation, and it belongs to E ('Then'). In many texts, however, one finds this type of 'unreal' anachrony almost exclusively. The so-called 'stream-of-consciousness' literature, for instance, limits itself to the reproduction of the contents of consciousness, and would, therefore, not be subject to the analysis of chronology at all. In order to solve this problem, and also in order to be able to indicate in other texts the difference between such 'false' anachronies and others – such as E above – the addition of subjective and objective is introduced. A subjective anachrony, then, is an anachrony which can be only be regarded as such if the 'contents of consciousness' lie in the past or the future; not the past of being 'conscious,' the moment of thinking itself.

A similar problem occurs when a retroversion or anticipation is presented as direct discourse. Properly speaking, here too there is no question of a real anachrony. The moment of speech is simply part of the (chronological) story; only in the contents are past or future mentioned. Example a, for example, could continue as follows:

f   Sobbing, John sat on his neighbour's couch, pouring out his woes. 'I didn't know, when I married Mary five years ago, that she would sacrifice everything to her work, did I? That I would be no more to her than a cheap servant, always at hand to pour her a drink and fetch her an ashtray?'

The outburst itself chronologically follows the ringing of the doorbell in a. But the substance of John's lament has to do with the past, his marriage five years ago, as well as the entire period from his wedding to the present moment.

This issue of narrative levels has been treated in the previous chapter. Here, we need only note that the above constitutes a retroversion of the second degree, since speech takes place on the second level. Similarly, the anachrony through which the child in *Something Very Sorry* realizes how she ended up in the hospital – 'They tell me what happened – we crashed into a tree' – is bound up with an instance of free indirect discourse, introduced by the anachronizing 'what happened' and preceded by the attributive indication of the speakers: 'they tell me.'

A third issue concerns the position of the narrative units we have distinguished with respect to each other. Which time should we consider the primary story-time: that is, the time in relation to which the other units may be called anticipations? Obviously, the answer to this question is relative. In e, I labelled the time in which the speaker writes the letter primary. With respect to this primary time, all the events which actually constitute the contents of the fabula, the gradual fossilization of Sergeant Massuro, are retroversions. If the rest of the story were now to be presented chronologically, it would be pointless to note in each sentence that we are concerned with fabula-time 2, the period of renewed acquaintance until the death of Massuro.

There are texts, moreover, in which the relationship between story and fabula is so complex that a thorough analysis would be useless. In such cases, a rough indication of the different time units suffices, while interesting or complex fragments can be studied in detail. This is the method which Genette has used in his analysis of Proust's *A la recherche du temps perdu*, a novel which spans more than four thousand pages. The question which time can be appointed as primary is in itself not particularly significant; what is relevant is to place various time units in relation to each other. In Mulisch's text, for instance, it is also possible to take 2, the time of renewed acquaintance, as the starting-point and consequently to view all references to periods 3 up to and including 6, the writing of the letter to the Ministry of War, as anticipation.

The decision which time segment is primary can become a highly charged question. An example is Patrick Chamoiseau's *Texaco*, set in Martinique, an intricate narrative that some critics have called an epic. In this text a 'primary' story line in which an urban planner comes to the neighbourhood of Texaco in order to erase it is, first, interrupted by the secondary story told by Marie Sophie, who provides the place that was about to be erased with a past that makes the erasure impossible. As a result, the urban planner 'converts' and becomes the saviour of the site. Which line of the fábula comes chronologically first is clear: the past, embedded one. But this embedded fabula takes over and becomes the main one that rearranges the rest of the fabula set in the present. The point is not to decide this unambiguously, but, on the contrary, to acknowledge the important effect of the irresolvable conflict between the technical subordination of the past and its power to change the present.

Finally, a fourth interesting complication. Sometimes anachronies are embedded in each other, intertwined to such an extent that it becomes just too difficult to analyse them. Such is the case already, in fact, with the second-degree retroversion in f: 'when I married her five years ago.' The contents of John's words are a retroversion: the words 'I didn't know ... did I' belong to it, but that which follows, the substance of the knowing, is, with respect to 'five years ago,' in its turn a (subjective) anticipation; a situation which is borne out clearly by the form of the verb itself, 'would sacrifice.'

I have raised these issues mainly to dispel the illusion that such a sequential analysis is simple, but also to indicate the myriad possibilities of variation available if we wish to experience the structural 'thickness' of a story compared to its fabula – a thickness to which the analysis of narrative levels and narratorial voices alone cannot do justice.

One final problem, however, is in some cases insoluble. Once again example e serves to demonstrate it. There I stated that c covers the pe-

riod between the renewed acquaintance of the I-speaker with Massuro
and the latter's death. That this is the period concerned seems probable
in view of the fact that it is during this segment of time that the events
occurred which the speaker must relate. However, when we continue
to read Mulisch's text, it becomes clear that the two actors also 'kind
of' knew each other in the past. Consequently, it is no longer possible
to determine whether c refers to the period in New Guinea alone, or
whether the time that they knew each other in Holland is also included.
To use a term derived from linguistics, we could here refer to chronological homonymy.

In the same way that, in certain contexts, it is impossible to ascertain
whether the word *bank* refers to a financial institution or the side of a
river, so too in this case it is impossible to determine which period in
the fabula is being referred to. And just as it is possible to use puns to
achieve certain effects (confusion, humour, a sense of the absurd), so
too chronological homonymy may be purposefully employed for the
same effect. In the case of Massuro, we have already been confronted with traces of confusion between the periods in Holland and New
Guinea. This is why in such cases I recommend acknowledging the
achrony rather than developing yet another category, as if classifying
rids us of the problem.

Distance

By 'distance' I mean that an event presented in anachrony is separated
by an interval, large or small, from the 'present'; that is, from the moment in the development of the fabula with which the story is concerned at the time the anachrony interrupts it. The arrival of Massuro
in Potapego occurs, as is indicated, two years prior to the writing of the
letter. The other time units are more difficult to pinpoint, although we
do know that A should be placed after the death of Massuro and shortly
before the writing of the letter, since the doctor's examination and the
writing of the letter are both part of the administrative winding-up of
the extraordinary decease, the certification of the cause of death, a process which is usually carried out as speedily as possible. Somewhat later
in the text we notice that this period covers six days.

In Butor's *La modification* the distance is much greater. The primary
story-time is the train journey from Paris to Rome. The subjective retroversions to the past, and the broken marriage of the man making that
journey, span a distance of years. Facts from the 'present,' things ob-

served during the journey, are associated with facts stored in his memory. Clearly, all the flashbacks in this narrative are subjective.

On the basis of 'distance' we may distinguish two kinds of anachrony. Whenever a retroversion takes place completely outside the time span of the primary fabula, we refer to an external analepsis, an external retroversion. This is the case in *La modification*, if we take only the return journey to be the primary fabula. If the retroversion occurs within the time span of the primary fabula, then we refer to an internal analepsis, an internal retroversion. If the retroversion begins outside the primary time span and ends within it, we refer to a mixed retroversion. Fragment A from example e becomes an internal retroversion if we take as our primary time span the period running from the renewed acquaintance until the 'present,' the writing of the letter. If, however, we view only the writing of the letter as the primary fabula, all retroversions become external.

It seems to make more sense to opt for the solution that helps to account for the greatest number of phenomena. Consequently, in this case, our choice must fall on the first one. Thus, we establish as our primary time span the period between the meeting and the writing. If then, as I proposed, we view fragment c as a chronological homonymy, this retroversion becomes a mixed one: starting before the meeting in Potapego, it continues until the death of Massuro. Although I have only given examples of retroversions, the same applies to anticipations – but these occur much less frequently. With respect to the latter, too, three possibilities can be discerned: external, internal, and mixed.

Functions

External retroversions generally provide indications about the antecedents, the past of the actors concerned, in so far as that past can be relevant for the interpretation of events. I have already suggested that in *La modification* the subjective retroversions explained the man's dissatisfaction with his wife and his nervousness about the confrontation with his mistress. The very fact that these are subjective retroversions increases, in this case, the explanatory function: dissatisfaction is subjective, after all. This, incidentally, demonstrates the potentially political importance of such narratological aspects.

At one point in 'What Happened to Sergeant Massuro?' an anecdote is recalled about the schooldays of the two actors, their first meeting, the mutual feelings of friendship that neither of the two ever expressed.

This anecdote elucidates the odd, sober relationship between the two men in New Guinea, which, in its turn, is an explanation of the narrator's inability to explain Massuro's strange death, while he so positively denies that fear was the cause. More and more, it becomes likely that a colonial problematic underlies this story. All of this corresponds to the other facts we have discovered in this text. Because of all these aspects the peculiar atmosphere of menacing mystery in this text becomes more and more obvious. The genre of the fantastic, I am beginning to sense, serves the purpose of a colonial perspective.

Internal retroversions often (partly) overlap with the primary narrative, they may 'overtake' it. They do not do so when the information communicated by the internal retroversion is new, when it is a sidetrack of the fabula. Such is the case when information is given about a newly introduced actor, who 'during' the events of the primary fabula has been concerned with other things which afterwards turn out to have been of importance.

If the contents of an internal retroversion overlap that of the primary fabula, then the retroversion usually serves as compensation for a gap in the story. This occurs because the information was not yet complete. There may, for instance, be a gap in chronological succession. When we are told, in one chapter of a novel, that the heroine is pregnant and, at the beginning of the next chapter, we find ourselves in the baby's room, by now in use, the information about the delivery is missing. In Victorian novels such a gap in the flow of information, such an ellipsis, will, for 'decency's' sake, not have been filled. The ellipsis – a form to which I will return shortly – can also be maintained for more specific reasons that characterize the story. In Flaubert's *Madame Bovary*, the end of the first part – 'When they left Tostes, Madame Bovary was pregnant' – through skipping the conception and enhancing this skipping by the rapidity of the narrator's sentence, underlines the great disappointment of Emma's marriage, specifically its sexual poverty. A less economical narrator might erase such ellipses by means of internal retroversion.

In addition to this complementary function, internal retroversions can have yet another function. When they do not fill up an ellipsis or paralipsis – i.e. lack of information concerning a sidetrack – but instead elaborate on information already given, they seem to be a repetition. The repetition of a previously described event usually serves to change, or add to, the emphasis on the meaning of that event. The same event is presented as more, or less, pleasant, innocent, or important than we had previously believed it to be. It is thus both identical and different:

the fabula elements are the same, but their meaning has changed. The past receives a different significance.

In Proust, such internal retroversions form a part of the famous and specifically Proustian interruption of the linearity in searching for, and recovering, the elusive past. But in much simpler literature too, frequent use is made of possibilities such as these. Detective novels and all kinds of texts that are constructed around mysteries, masquerades, and puzzles adopt this technique as an important structural device.

Span

The term 'span' indicates the stretch of time covered by an anachrony. Like its distance, the span of an anachrony may vary greatly. If a letter states

h Last year, I went to Indonesia for a month.

the span of the retroversion is a month, while its distance is a year. In Couperus' *Of Old People* all the allusions to the murder in 'the Indies' are subjective (when the old people again call the scene to mind) or they are second-degree (when they talk about it) external retroversions with a distance of sixty years, and a span that varies from a quarter of an hour to one night to, at times, a few days.

The anachrony is either incomplete or complete. A retroversion, for instance, is incomplete if after a (short) span a forward jump is made once again. Disconnected information is thus given about a section of the past, or, in the case of an anticipation, of the future. In *Of Old People* the retroversions concerning the murder are incomplete, as they are in any detective novel. Only when all the consequences of the murder – in *Of Old People* the anxiety which has remained with them – are discussed up until the 'present' is the retroversion complete. Only then has the entire development of the retroversion, from its starting-point to its conclusion, been presented. All the antecedents have thus been completely recalled. This occurs quite frequently in the tradition of beginning in medias res, where the narrative begins in the middle of the fabula and the preceding events are then recalled in their totality. This is a special kind of anachrony: the distance and the span cover each other exactly; the retroversion ends where it began.

A classical example of an incomplete anachrony is the retroversion in which the origin of Ulysses' scar is explained in the nineteenth book of the *Odyssey*. When Ulysses, still incognito, appears in his own house and the servant who had nursed him when he was a baby washes his feet according to the custom of hospitality, she recognizes him by his scar. She begins to cry out for joy, but Ulysses stops her. At that moment, the story is interrupted by a lengthy explanation of the way in which the young Ulysses had come by the scar. After this extensive retroversion, the chronological narrative is resumed; Ulysses is still trying to silence his servant. The distance of this retroversion is many years; the span is a few days – the infliction of the wound and its healing.

There is yet another way of considering anachronies in terms of their spans; distinguishing between punctual and durative anachronies. These terms have been borrowed from the linguistic distinction of time-aspects of verb tenses. Punctual corresponds to the preterite in English and Spanish, the passé simple in French, and the aorist in Greek. Durative indicates that the action takes longer. In French and Spanish the imperfect is used to indicate a durative aspect, in English it is expressed by the use of the progressive form. Punctual is used in this paragraph to indicate that only one instant from the past or the future is evoked, the moment that the wound was inflicted on Ulysses. Durative means that a somewhat longer period is involved, the days of convalescence that followed.

Often, a punctual anachrony recalls a brief but significant event; that significance then justifies the anachrony, despite its short span. Durative anachronies tend to sketch a situation which may or may not be the result of an event that is recalled in a punctual anachrony. Sometimes this distinction covers that between incomplete and complete anachronies, as in the case in example f. The presentation of the marriage between Mary and John is both punctual and incomplete. That which follows, the situation of John, who, after the romantic honeymoon period, feels neglected by his ambitious wife, is both durative and complete.

But durative and complete do not by any means always coincide. In *Of Old People* the memory of the murder is itself a (subjective) punctual retroversion; that of the period following it, the uneasiness and the feeling of guilt, the doctor's blackmail, is a (subjective) durative, but incomplete, retroversion. These possibilities can characterize the author's narrative 'style' and may even give insight into his or her view of life. Frequent use of punctual anachrony sometimes makes for a business-like style; systematic combinations of punctual and durative retroversions can create – or at least add to – the impression that the story is developing according to clear, causative laws: a certain event causes a situation to emerge which makes another event possible, and so on. If durative retroversions are dominant, then the reader quickly receives the impression that nothing particularly spectacular is happening. The narrative appears to be a succession of inevitable situations.

In *A la recherche du temps perdu* Marcel Proust made particularly powerful use of the possibilities offered by these two forms. Quite frequently he began a retroversion in a punctual manner, writing something like 'This reminded me of the day I entered ...' and then developed the retroversion at such length that it ended up like a durative, almost descriptive passage. The opposite also happens with great frequency in the same novel: a durative retroversion ('I used to visit my aunt every Sunday') gets fleshed out in such detail that it becomes inevitably punctual. The detailed account makes it simply too hard to believe that such events would all happen every Sunday. In this risky play with time, Proust announces the postmodernist experimental novel half a century beforehand. The tone for this play is set at the very beginning of the book with its famous opening line, 'Longtemps je me suis couché bonne heure' (For a long time I used to go to bed early).

Anticipations

Everything I have discussed so far concerning anachrony is, in principle, applicable both to retroversions and to anticipations. It is no coincidence, however, that almost all the examples used have been retroversions. Anticipations occur much less frequently. They are mostly restricted to a single (frequently covert) allusion to the outcome of the fabula – an outcome which one must know, in order to recognize (in retrospect) the anticipations for what they are. They may serve to generate tension or to express a fatalistic vision of life.

One more or less traditional form of anticipation is the summary at the beginning. The rest of the story gives the explanation of the outcome presented at the beginning. This type of anticipation can suggest a sense of fatalism, or predestination: nothing can be done, we can only watch the progression towards the final result, in the hope that next time we recognize the writing on the wall. This type robs the narrative of suspense, at least a certain kind of suspense. The suspense generated by the question 'How is it going to end?' disappears; we already know how it is going to end.

However, another kind of suspense, or rather a tension which keeps the reader engaged, may take its place, prompting questions like 'How could it have happened like this?,' with such variants as 'How could the hero(ine) have been so stupid?' or 'How could society allow such a thing to happen?' or 'How did the hero(ine) find out about this?' and so on, according to the direction in which the conventions of the genre steer the reader. Narratives with a CN (so-called 'first-person novels') are most suitable for references to the future. A narrative whose narrator claims to be presenting his own past can easily contain allusions to the future, which, in relation to the story-time, is 'the present' or may even already be the past. A sentence like

i Little could I then suspect that ten years later I would again run into the man who is now my husband.

contains such an anticipation. In relation to the time of the fabula ('then') this sentence is an anticipation ('ten years later'), but in relation to the story-time ('now') it is a retroversion, although the distance of the retroversion is smaller than that of the retroversion in which (in the form of an anticipation) it has been embedded. Whether such a sentence is regarded as an anticipation or as a retroversion is of little importance; what matters is both the fact that there are three distinct moments involved, and the question of how they are related to each other.

Anticipations, too, can be grouped as internal or external, and here, too, uncertainty can be effective. In *La modification*, Cécile's visit to Paris is constantly being evoked. By the end of the story we still do not know whether that visit will ever take place. That uncertainty fits in with the overall defensiveness of the man who is running away from the situation and does not really want to know it. The allusions to Cécile's moving house, all subjective anticipations, cannot be classified as internal or external, although they appear to me to be internal. Internal anticipations frequently complement a future ellipsis or paralipsis: things are made clear now, so that later on they can be skipped, or only mentioned in passing. Conversely, such anticipations may have a connecting or an accentuating function when they constitute nothing more than the marker 'I shall be coming back to this.' Such is the case in this book, for instance, whenever I am compelled to touch briefly upon a subject that I would rather discuss in detail later.

A highly effective use of anticipation is the so-called iterative anticipation. In an iterative anticipation an event is presented as the first in a series. Such an anticipation often begins in the following way:

j Then the prime minister appeared on the screen, a spectacle that would weigh on our spirits every Friday from now on.

Subsequently, the spectacle in question is presented in full detail and the reader is to view each particularity as an example of something that will occur again and again in the future. The fuller such a report, the less credible its iterative character, for it is unlikely that the same actions could be performed in exactly the same way every week, right down to the smallest detail.

In such a case, one is apt to forget quickly that the event was the first of a series, and with its iterative character its anticipatory aspect dissolves. One obvious technical advantage of this form is that it offers a good opportunity for showing the scene through the eyes of an inquisitive newcomer, which makes its detailed character immediately more plausible. Precisely this combination of iterativity and the uniqueness of the first time gives this form its special possibilities. As I mentioned, Proust makes a characteristic use of this figure.

The novel that has already come up, Duras' *L'après-midi de Monsieur Andesmas,* is constructed for the most part around the tension between the promise, made just before the beginning of the fabula presented, and the fulfilment of that promise, just after the end of the fabula. Both the anticipation of the promised return of Monsieur Andesmas' daughter and the uncertainty concerning the distance of that anticipation determine the importance of the events in the story, which ultimately consist of various phases of waiting. This temporal play produces an emotional suspense that I feel to be the very 'stuff' of this novel.

Of some anticipations the realization is certain, of others, it is not. This distinction undergoes adaptation, however, when the terms *announcement* and *hint* are employed. Announcements are explicit. Attention is drawn to the fact that we are now concerned with something that will only take place later on. Adverbs such as 'later' and verbs such as 'expect' or 'promise' are used in the text or may be logically added to it. Hints, in contrast, are implicit. A hint is simply a germ, of which the germinating force can only be seen later. The clues in a detective novel have as their primary mission to function as hints. In such cases, a good story takes care to keep the knowledge from the reader, to prevent the understanding that these hints are anticipations; if not, the puzzle will be solved prematurely. On the other hand, it must remain possible for the attentive reader to glimpse their anticipatory nature. It is this possibility that initiates the game between story and reader.

Announcements work against suspense; hints increase it, because the trained readers of detective fiction will be asking themselves constantly whether a certain detail is an anticipation or not. This curiosity can then be manipulated by means of false hints: details that create the suggestion of being clues, but turn out in the end to have been only details after all. A good example of the above is offered in Hawthorne's *The Blithedale Romance*. There, the impulses are often not really false, but turn out to be irrelevant.

Achrony

In the preceding sections I have assumed that it is possible to determine, with more or less precision, the direction, the distance, and the span of a deviation in chronology. Sometimes, however, although we may see clearly that we are dealing with a deviation, either the information cannot be sorted out, or there is too little of it to define the deviation further. I call such a deviation an achrony, a deviation of time that cannot be analysed any further.

Various kinds of deviations resembling achrony occur. One of them has already been discussed briefly in connection with complications of direction. That was the form anticipation-within-retroversion, referring forward within a back-reference. This form does not always lead to achrony. Example f seems clearly an anticipation from within a retroversion and together forms a complex and complete second-degree retroversion. However, when an anticipation from within a retroversion brings us back once again into the 'present,' direction is no longer relevant. If a continuation of f were to read:

k When she asked me to marry her, she promised she would be home every evening, that she would have a lot of time for me.

a future which would have to be the 'present' is being evoked from within the past. This expected 'present' stands in shrill contrast to the realized 'present': instead of running home after work, Mary rings up more and more often to say that urgent business will keep her a few more hours.

As far as the passing of time is concerned, the situation predicted in k should have been realized by now. But reality has turned out differently, as if to give the lie to overconfidence in anticipations. Such an anticipation-within-retroversion, which verges on achrony, can effectuate a confrontation between an expected and a realized 'present.' In that capacity it may even contribute to an implied meta-narrative commentary, e.g., by emphasizing the fictionality of the fabula.

A second possibility is the opposite form, the retroversion-within anticipation. This occurs, for instance, when we are told beforehand how circumstances in the 'present' will be presented to us. The meaning of an event can only be made known later, and the coming of that revelation is announced 'now':

1 Later, John would understand that he had wrongly interpreted Mary's absence.

The revelation of John's mistake will come later, but 'now' it is being foreshadowed. At the moment of revelation reference is made to a mistake made in the past; but in relation to the future, that past is the 'present' evoked by means of a retroversion-within-anticipation.

A third anachrony that comes close to achrony may occur when an anticipation in relation to the fabula turns out to be a retroversion in the story. An event which has yet to take place chronologically has already been presented, e.g., in embedded speech, in the story. Then an allusion is made to it which is an anticipation with respect to the fabula, but a retroversion with respect to the story (Later John understood that ...).

In addition to these three forms, which are difficult to pinpoint because of their complex structure and, consequently, come close to achronies, there are two more possibilities for definite 'achrony': that is, deviations which are impossible to analyse because of lack of information. To begin with, an achrony is sometimes 'undated,' when it does not indicate anything about its direction, distance, or span. One example:

m I have never seen him without his wig.

Here a relationship of sorts with the past is given. In a pinch, this sentence could be seen as a complete retroversion of indeterminate distance. In fact, however, nothing indicates whether the span is restricted to the past or not; in any case, it includes the 'present' if nothing establishes that the situation comes to an end. A second possibility lies in the grouping of events on the grounds of other than chronological criteria, without any mention of chronological sequence.

Proust sometimes presents a whole series of events, all of which have occurred in the same place. Spatial connections thus replace chronological ones. As I will argue later on, this is a significant feature of Proust's narrative style that cannot easily be analysed on the level of either the text or of the fabula. Proust, like other modernists such as Virginia Woolf, makes his story particularly visual. If such a series were to be constructed solely according to spatial or any other criteria (association, for instance), the text would no longer fit my definition of narrative. But if such a series occurs in a narrative in which chronological connections are indicated everywhere else, we are dealing, in any case, with an achrony. With this last form of achrony we have exhausted the possibilities for structuring the chronological flow within a story into a specific sequence. Here, the linearity of the fabula and the linearity of its presentation to the reader no longer have any correspondence at all.

4: Rhythm

Background

Rhythm is as striking as it is elusive. Much as narrative media, especially film, work with rhythm, the analysis of it has not been successful at all. Investigations into the relationship between the amount of time covered by the events of a fabula and the amount of time involved in presenting those events are already old. In the 1920s Percy Lubbock wrote his *Craft of Fiction*, in which he made a distinction between a summarizing, accelerating presentation and a broad, scenic one. Twenty years later in Germany, Günther Müller wrote a number of extensive studies on this subject. Students applied Müller's principles to a large number of texts.

But narrative rhythm, although quite characteristic and effective, will remain the most elusive aspect. What are we to take as a measure of the speed of presentation, the rhythm? Let's assume that it is possible to calculate, at least approximately, the time covered by the events. Yet the problem is with what kind of time this time of the fabula should be compared. Is it the time taken up by the writing of the narrative? Not only is it impossible to discover what period of time was involved in writing but also this time is of little importance for the effect of the text on the reader. Should we take as a standard of measurement the time it takes to read the narrative? This varies. Suppose that a rough average reading-time per novel could be calculated. This reading-time would then, in principle, be comparable to the time covered by the performance of a play or piece of music, even though this performance-time does not vary with each receiver (listener or spectator) but with each performance. The end product of these calculations remains dubious; and then relevance still has to be argued, to say nothing of the problems involved in working them out. For the moment, I suggest that the so-called time of telling (this is the term Müller and his followers employ) is not available to us, and that, therefore, the comparison between two times is impossible.

Nevertheless we can estimate the speed with which the various events are presented. Just as speed in traffic is gauged by juxtaposing the amount of time involved with the distance covered (she is doing sixty: she is travelling sixty kilometres in one hour), so too the amount of time covered by the fabula can be juxtaposed with the amount of space in the text each event requires: the number of pages, lines, or words. This is the solution Müller and his followers have chosen.

Every analysis is continuously preoccupied with demonstrating its own relevance; and there is no point in initiating a detailed calculation of temporal relationships unless some degree of relevance can be predicted. Hence, such an analysis should not simply aim at precise calculation of the number of words or lines per event; the amount of text set aside for each event only indicates something about how the attention is *patterned*. The attention paid to the various elements gives us a picture of the vision on the fabula communicated to the reader. That is why I discuss this subject here and not in chapter 1. The attention paid to each element can only be analysed in relation to the attention for the other elements.

Overall Rhythm

Once a survey has been drawn up of the amount of time covered by the various events or series of events, episodes, it becomes possible to use these data to determine the general rhythm. Let us take as an example a complete life-story of the kind frequently written in the nineteenth century. The fabula contains the birth of the hero, his childhood, adolescence, military service, first love, the period of social ambition, decline, and death. It is possible to determine the number of pages devoted to each episode. Often, this simple exercise alone will make clear that certain episodes are given more attention than others. Childhood, for instance, is often summarized quickly, while 'first love' is dwelt upon in much more detail. On the other hand, the novel may also reflect an even division of attention. In Dickens' *Dombey and Son*, for instance, the story begins with the birth of Paul Dombey. At that time, his father is forty-eight years old. After approximately one-third of the story Paul dies, at about the age of twelve. The story continues until Dombey's old age, so that, as far as rhythm is concerned, Paul's death takes place 'at the right moment,' for Dombey then has twenty-odd more years to live.

Whether or not the attention is spread more or less evenly across the fabula, there will always be an alternation of sorts between extensive and summarizing presentation. This alternation is generally viewed as the most important characteristic of the narrative genre; be that as it may, it is clearly an important marker. Lubbock already made a distinction between these two forms, the scene and the summary. It has been noted, and rightly so, that this relative contrast should be pushed through to its limit. On the one hand, we can distinguish the ellipsis, an omission in the story of a section of the fabula. When a certain part of the time covered by the fabula is given absolutely no attention at all, the amount of TF (time of the fabula) is infinitely larger than the TS (story-time). On the other hand, we can distinguish the pause, when an element that takes no fabula-time (so an object, not a process) is presented in detail. TF is then infinitely smaller than TS. This is the case in descriptive or argumentative fragments.

Both summary and slow-down are to be viewed relatively, in relation to each other. The easiest way to set up such a comparison is to establish a kind of norm tempo, a zero-line. Real isochrony, a complete coincidence of TF and TS, cannot occur in language. We can, however, assume that a dialogue without commentary takes as long in TF as it does in TS. The dialogue, and in principle every scene, every detailed presentation of an event with a claim to isochrony, thus functions as a point of comparison. By scene I here mean a segment of text in which TF = TS. In total, five different tempi would thus become distinguishable:

$$
\begin{array}{llll}
\text{ellipsis} & TF = n \quad TS = 0 \quad \text{thus} & TF > \infty \, TS \\
\text{summary} & & TF > TS \\
\text{scene} & & TF < \, \simeq \, TS \\
\text{slow-down} & & TF < TS \\
\text{pause} & TF = 0 \quad TS = n \quad \text{thus} & TF < \infty \, TS
\end{array}
$$

Here > means longer than
      < means shorter than
      ∞ means infinite
      ≃ means is ± equal

Every narrative can be divided into segments corresponding to one of these five tempi. In the following sections I shall discuss a number of characteristics of each tempo.

Ellipsis

An ellipsis cannot be perceived: according to the definition, nothing is indicated in the story about the amount of fabula-time involved. If nothing is indicated, we cannot know what should have been indicated either. All we can do, sometimes, is logically deduce on the basis of information or filling in that something has been omitted. Note that this kind of deduction is based on realistic reading, which may be predominant, but not always meaningful. That which has been omitted – the contents of the ellipsis – need not be unimportant; on the contrary, the event about which nothing is said may have been so painful that it is being elided for precisely that reason, such as the conception of Madame Bovary's child. Or the event is so difficult to put into words that it is preferable to maintain complete silence about it. Another possibility, which I have already mentioned, is the situation in which, though the event has taken place, the actor wants to deny that fact. By keeping silent about it, he attempts to undo it. Thus the ellipsis is used for magical purposes, as an exorcism. This is one reading of the ellipsis central in Robbe-Grillet's *Le voyeur*.

How are we to become aware of these ellipses, which can, apparently, be so important that it seems worth the trouble to look for them? To begin with, our attention is sometimes directed towards an elided event because of a retroversion. We know that something must have happened, and sometimes we know approximately where, but usually it is difficult to indicate the exact location.

Sometimes, however, an ellipsis is indicated. Mention is made of the time that has been skipped. If a text reads:

a When I was back in New York after two years

we know exactly how much time has been left out. It is even clearer when an ellipsis is mentioned in a separate sentence:

b Two years passed.

In fact, this is no longer an ellipsis, but could be called a minimal summary, or rather, a summary with maximum speed: two years in one sentence.

Such a pseudo-ellipsis, or mini-summary, can be expanded with a brief specification concerning its contents:

  c Two years of bitter poverty passed.

The pseudo-ellipsis is beginning to look more and more like a summary. Whether we still regard the next sentence as a pseudo-ellipsis or whether we now label it a summary simply depends on how far we wish to go: the borderline between these two tempi is flexible.

  d Two years of bitter poverty passed, in which she lost two children, became unemployed, and was evicted from her home because she could not pay the rent.

Summary

This last example shows how pointless it is to set up an absolute dividing line; in fact, it is fairly clear that we should refer to it as a summary. In example c the content-specification indicated a situation. None of the events of those two elided years are mentioned, even though according to the realistic reading game, it is unlikely that no events took place at all. In d, however, various events are presented, at least three, but probably four or more. Let's say that the children died one after the other and that loss then counts as two events. The unpaid rent implies a good many events, the landlord's visits, the woman's desperation and its expression, her attempts to find money and the failure of those attempts. The woman is evicted. What then? At that moment in the fabula, the situation changes. Consequently, the rhythm of the narrative changes. A slower tempo is adopted, the next event – a meeting? an inheritance? a discovery? – must alter the situation radically. Consequently, this key event receives all the attention.

The so-called 'dramatic climaxes,' events which have a strong influence on the course of the fabula – the turning-points, moments at which a situation changes, a line is broken – are presented extensively in scenes, while insignificant events – insignificant in the sense that they do not greatly influence the course of the fabula – are quickly summarized. This can be phrased the other way around: it is because they get more narrative time that events take on major importance. The opening of Dickens' *Oliver Twist*, a classical example of a realistic novel, exhibits something like this rhythm. Oliver's birth is presented extensively: three pages. Then, at the age of nine months, the hero is sent to a charitable institution. The situation there is sketched in a page and a half, and suddenly Oliver is nine and is taken away: three pages.

The rhythm of Flaubert's *Madame Bovary* is very different. Many events, which one could expect to have been presented as dramatic climaxes, are summarized rapidly, whereas routine events – for instance, situations that recur every week – are presented extensively. This reversal of the traditional rhythm is very well suited to a fabula that reflects boredom, the emptiness of a person's existence. In this sense the novel is realist; rhythm matches content. But the reversal of the expected rhythm can also initiate reflection of the non-realist poetics of this novel. It can even qualify as (proto) postmodern as a result. To a very great degree, the originality of Flaubert's work is determined by this double-edged technique.

As should be clear, the summary is a suitable instrument for presenting and, for the reader, for gleaning background information, or for connecting various scenes. The place of the summary in a story depends strongly on the type of fabula involved: a crisis-fabula will require much less summarizing than a developing fabula (see 'Duration').

Scene

In longer narratives such as novels, the scene is, by definition, in the majority. Although traditionally an even alternation between summary and scene used to be the aim, in order neither to overtire the readers with too rapid a tempo nor to bore them with one that was too slow, in the course of time a development has made itself felt towards rejection of that stereotypical pattern. In *Madame Bovary* the scenes frequently present an event in extenso as an example of a whole series of such events. Every Thursday the heroine went to Rouen to visit her lover: thus a long scene follows, in which such a visit is presented in detail. The effect of this technique is to dull the newness of the event, to indicate that daily routine has once again re-established itself in Emma's life, at exactly that moment which was intended to demonstrate her efforts to break out of that routine. A hopeless enterprise, we therefore conclude. Proust, who was greatly inspired by Flaubert, also showed a preference for scenes. But in his work they function somewhat differently. In *A la recherche du temps perdu* scenes are often the first in a series of similar scenes. This transforms them into anticipations. The curiosity, the intensity of the sensations of a 'first time' justify, in these instances, the lavishness of the presentation.

In a scene the duration of the fabula and that of the story are roughly the same. Such coincidence cannot be qualified with any other adverb than 'roughly.' Most scenes are full of retroversions, anticipations, non-narrative fragments such as general observations, or atemporal sections such as descriptions. This is understandable once we realize that a truly synchronic scene, in which the duration of the fabula coincided completely with that of the presentation in the story, would be unreadable. The dead moments in a conversation, the nonsensical or unfinished remarks, are omitted. In the eighteenth century, Sterne's *Tristram Shandy* explored and mocked the impossibility of describing 'real' time. Even a writer who is trying to give precisely these aspects of a conversation their due – like Marguerite Duras – is forced to abridge them considerably, on pain of unreadability.

If a writer wishes to fill out a scene, she will automatically employ more attention-grabbing material – material that can also serve to connect the preceding and the following chapters. Thus, a scene is often a central moment from which the narrative can proceed in any direction. In such cases, the scene is actually anti-linear. The coincidence of TF and TS is then no more than appearance.

A very clear example of this paradox is *L'étranger* by Camus. This novel, in which chronological sequence is maintained, consists almost entirely of scenes. These scenes cannot possibly coincide completely with the time of the fabula. After all, the latter covers quite a few days. In fact, they are pseudo-scenes, scenes which are presented in a strongly accelerated manner, with a myriad of invisible ellipses. This lack of synchrony is even explicitly indicated, as Meursault, the protagonist, regularly consults his watch to ascertain that it is, again, much later. The same thing happens in the Dutch novel *The Evenings*, contemporary with Camus' novel. The scenes, usually slow-paced, are used in these novels to indicate the rapidity of time together with the immeasurable emptiness in spending it: giving the suggestion of too little time reflects an excess of time. The scene is the most appropriate form to do so.

Slow-Down

Slow-down is a tempo that stands in direct contrast to the summary. In practice this tempo occurs very seldom. Difficult if not impossible as it is already to achieve synchrony in a scene, because the presentation is soon experienced as too slow, imagine slowing down even more. Still, the theoretical possibility of this tempo cannot be ignored. Although it is, in general, set aside for use in small sections of the narrative only, it can nevertheless have an extremely evocative effect. At moments of great suspense, slow-down may work like a magnifying glass. This is the case, for instance, in *L'après-midi de Monsieur Andesmas,* where at the end a few seconds of the fabula span pages. The occasion is the long-awaited arrival of Monsieur Andesmas' daughter. The girl's voice, her footsteps, can all be heard, and still it takes a terribly long time before she actually appears. This last event we are not even allowed to see. As if to indicate that her late arrival is definitely too late for her father, as proof that he has lost her, the arrival itself is not presented at all. Consequently, it occurs outside the story and, strictly speaking, outside the fabula. The fabula of the novel spans the time just after her departure to the time just before her return.

Sometimes, a brief slowing down occurs within a scene, in such cases often reinforced, by, for instance, a subjective retroversion. Imagine the arrival of a visitor or a letter. In the short time between the ringing of the bell and the opening of the door, the actor is bombarded by all sorts of thoughts, his nerves are taut – a whole life passes through his mind and it takes pages before he actually opens the door.

Rare as it may be, cases of slow-down rank among the classical passages of world literature. One of such classics is the first kiss that Marcel, the protagonist of *A la recherche,* bestows on Albertine, the object of his obsessive love, repulsion, jealousy, and possessiveness alternatively.

The passage is remarkable for a great numbers of reasons, one of which is its insistence on the difficulties of seeing, to which I will return later. The kiss becomes the crucial example of the impossibility of seeing: 'suddenly my eyes ceased to see, then my nose, crushed by the collision, no longer perceived any odour, and, without thereby gaining any clearer idea of the taste of the rose of my desire, I learned, from these obnoxious signs, that at last I was in the act of kissing Albertine's cheek.' This impossibility, which seems here to be absolute, is the final result of a whole development, stretched out in time, of an entire 'study' of the sensorial imperfection of the body, and in particular, of the lips as a tool for gaining knowledge, a true epistemological instrument. The difficulties that intervene are of various different orders: the perception is displaced, the object is transformed, the skin as a surface breaks up into 'coarse grain':

> At first, as my mouth began gradually to approach the cheeks which my eyes had recommended it to kiss, my eyes, in changing position, saw a different pair of cheeks; the neck, observed at closer range and as though through a magnifying glass, showed in its coarser grain a robustness which modified the character of the face.   II 378

The slow-down is necessary because instead of the act of kissing itself, the relevant element in the fabula, it is the nuances of perception that accompany it that the narrator is describing.

The story overrules the fabula here. And those nuances are too complex to present them in scenic simultaneity. An entire drama of vision inserts itself between fabula and story. For the magnifying glass does not improve close-up vision; it modifies it. The object seen is a different one, and this displacement continues until the perception is reduced to nothing. The lens, however, allowed too much to be seen. But this operation nonetheless functioned by splitting the vision into multiple elements. All these elements are so detailed that presenting them takes more time than a simple kiss. What ultimately happens here, as often in Proust, is that the fabula disappears under the weight of the story, so that a miniature new fabula appears to insert itself, pushing the banality of events away and replacing it by the exciting discovery of perceiving what is hardly perceptible.

Pause

Pauses occur much more frequently. This term includes all narrative sections in which no movement of the fabula-time is implied. A great deal of attention is paid to one element, and in the meantime the fabula remains stationary. When it is again continued later on, no time has passed. In that case, we are dealing with a pause. Pause has a strongly retarding effect; yet, the reader easily forgets that the fabula has been stopped, whereas in a slow-down our attention is directed towards the fact that the passage of time has slowed down.

In various periods of literary history, different opinions have been held about pauses. In Homer, pauses are avoided. Often descriptions of objects are replaced by retroversions, which also have a slowing-down effect, but still replace the broken line of time by another temporal sequence.

This is the case during the explanation of Ulysses' scar, by which his old nurse recognizes him on his return. The shield of Achilles is described in retroversion, while it is being made, thus becoming a case of description motivated on the level of the fabula. Similarly, Agamemnon's armour is described while he is putting it on, so that we can here no longer refer to an interruption, but to a scene.

During the period of naturalism, the pause was less of a problem; the explicit goal of these novels was to sketch a picture of reality. In order to do that a good many object descriptions were necessary, while the flow of the fabula-time was of secondary importance. Lengthy descriptive sections and, to a lesser extent, generalized, argumentative expositions are certainly not exceptions in the novels of this period. The pause was an accepted tempo. And when such descriptions led to excessively long interruptions of the fabula, their presence was justified by tying them to the vision of an onlooker.

Post-naturalist novelists adopted this last solution. Whenever a long description had to be inserted, they made sure that the seam was hidden. In Zola's novels, this takes the following form. An actor looks at an object, and what s/he sees is described. The passing of a certain amount of time is thus implied, so that such descriptions do not constitute a real pause, but a scene. That flow of time is indicated by means of a verb of perception – usually *to see* – supported, in many cases, by adverbs of time: *firstly, subsequently*, and *then finally* all suggest the passing of time, even if everything else indicates that there can hardly be any passing time. The pause is thus concealed.

In modernist narrative the pause is frankly adopted. Many novels by Virginia Woolf, to mention one of the best-known cases, alternate the presentation of slow, unimportant events with lengthy descriptive passage. The difference between the presentation of events and the description of objects is often hard to make out, so that the entire story moves on like a long descriptive flow. The following passage from *The Waves* bears this subtle movement out:

And then tiring of pursuit and flight, lovelily they [the birds] came descending, delicately declining, dropped down and sat silent on the tree, on the wall, with their bright eyes glancing, and their heads turned this way, that way; aware, awake; intensely conscious of one thing, one object in particular.
Perhaps it was a snail shell, rising in the grass like a grey cathedral, a swelling building burnt with dark rings and shadowed green by

the grass. Or perhaps they saw the splendour of the flowers making a light of flowing purple over the beds, through which dark tunnels of purple shade were driven between the stalks.   53

The presentation of a minuscule event – the descent, then rest of the birds – progresses into a description of the birds sitting on their respective perches. As in the Proust passage of the kiss, the fabula is snowed under by an account of an act of perception which takes over. The rhythm is slow, but whether the stillness that results is a pause in the fabula or, on the contrary, completely covers the fabula-time of the act of perception cannot be made out. The exploration of the nuances of perception is characteristic of modernist narrative.

With postmodernism, the question of narrative rhythm along these lines loses its meaning altogether. In her novel *Blood and Guts in High School*, Kathy Acker seems to mock any attempt to establish temporal equivalences between fabula-time and story-time. This does not mean that the story has no narrative rhythm. On the contrary, it seems hasty and fragmented, frantic and verging on the incoherent. In other words, it is by disrupting the correlation between fabula and story in this respect that the novel achieves its postmodern 'feel.' Here are a few passages to get a sense of this. The first passage, about a character, Janey, who works in a hippy East Village bakery, shows how Janey has to 'forget' her self in order to be able to work. In the workplace she is addressed as a function, not as a person. She tersely verbalizes this lack of self that comes with being a labourer: 'I am nobody because I work' (37). Later she explains this condition of being nobody when working:

> I had to do all the counter work. My father stopped sending me money. I had to work seven days a week. I had no more feelings. I was no longer a real person. If I stopped work just for a second, I would hate. Burst through the wall and hate. Hatred that comes out like that can be a bomb.
>
> I hated most that I didn't have any more dreams or visions. It's not that the vision-world, the world of passion and wildness, no longer existed. It always is. But awake I was disconnected from dreams. I was psychotic.   40

As one critic wrote: 'When Janey tells about the abortions in her life, she immediately makes clear that they should not be seen as dramatic moments in a life story. She tells about her abortions because they have for her symbolic value.' This critic cites the following two passages:

I'm not trying to tell you about the rotgut weird parts of my life. Abortions are the symbol, the outer image, of sexual relations in this world. Describing my abortions is the only way I can tell you about pain and fear ... my unstoppable drive for sexual love made me know. 34

I didn't know how much these abortions hurt me physically and mentally. I was desperate to fuck more and more so I could finally get love. Soon my total being was on fire, not just my sex, and I was doing everything to make the non-sexual equivalent of love happen. 35

The critic comments: 'She explicitly tries to prevent the reader from turning the narration of her abortions into a narrative event, that is into part of a plot' (Van Alphen 1997b).

In spite of the difficulty in grasping different narrative tempi and making statements about rhythm, then, this concept is important because in all its lack of precision it is helpful in characterizing different modes of narrative *historically*. The question of the delimitation and definition of descriptive and argumentative sections as opposed to narrative sections has been discussed in the previous chapter. Here it is only relevant to note that such sections disrupt the flow of time and function, therefore, as pauses.

5: Frequency

A third aspect often distorts the two aspects of time treated above, order and rhythm. French theorist Gérard Genette labels this aspect *frequency*. By this he means the numerical relationship between the events in the fabula and those in the story.

The phenomenon of repetition, which is the one under discussion here, has always had a paradoxical side. As I suggested for the example of Borges' quotation of *Don Quixote*, even two literally identical texts are not really identical. Similarly, two events are never exactly the same. The first event of a series differs from the one that follows it, if only because it is the first and the other is not. Strictly speaking, the same goes for verbal repetition in a text: only one can be the first. Yet a series such as

a I went to bed early. I turned in betimes. I was in bed before dark.

will be seen as a repetition of one and the same event: the actor went to bed early. Obviously, it is the onlooker, and the reader, who remember the similarities between the events of a series and ignore the differences. When I here refer to a repetition, I mean different events or alternative presentations of events, which show similarities. The most recurrent frequency is the singular presentation of a singular event.

b She came at length and opened the door to her sister's importunities.

Kate Chopin, 'The Story of an Hour,' *Portraits*

However, a story entirely constructed of such singular presentations would create a highly peculiar and ragged effect. Usually, a combination of this and other possible frequencies is employed.

A second frequency occurs when an event happens more often and is presented as often as it occurs. Thus, there is a repetition on both levels so that, again, we should really term this a singular presentation. This is not the case if the event occurs often and is presented often, but not as often as it 'really' occurs. If something happens every day in the course of three months, and it is presented five times, numerical disproportion results. Whether such a frequency creates a strongly repetitive effect or not depends on the nature of the event and the amount of attention paid to it. 'The more banal the event, the less striking the repetition' could serve as a rough guideline.

I refer to a repetition when an event occurs only once and is presented a number of times. Some experimental novels employ this possibility lavishly. Robbe-Grillet's *Le voyeur is* again a case in point. In general, it is used with much more discretion. Moreover, the repetition may be disguised to a certain extent by stylistic variations, as in example a. Sometimes variations in 'perspective' are also used to justify the need for a repetition: the event may be the same, but each actor views it in his own or her own way. This device was used regularly in the eighteenth-century epistolary novel. Another famous example is Faulkner's *The Sound and the Fury.* Every internal retroversion or anticipation that does not fill in an ellipsis belongs to this frequency. These constitute repetitions of something that has already been mentioned before.

The reverse of a repetition is an iterative presentation: a whole series of identical events is presented at once. We have already seen examples of this. Flaubert and Proust make systematic use of iteration. Iterative presentation used to be regarded as subordinate to singular presentation. It was employed to sketch a background, against which the singular events were highlighted. Flaubert was the first writer in Western literature to my knowledge to give iteration a dominant position in his work. Proust went even further: his novel consists for the most part of iterative scenes. These are often so extensive that their iterative nature becomes questionable. One visit, allegedly an example of a long series, is described in eighty pages: the conversations, the gestures, the guests, everything is presented in detail. It is no longer credible that such a visit is an example of weekly visits, performed year in year out. This then is a case of pseudo-iteration; a form through which Proust marked his modernist anti-realism.

There are three forms of iteration. If they are generalizing and are concerned with general facts that also exist outside the fabula, then they come very close to situation-descriptions. The opening of Dickens' *Oliver Twist* is a good example: the scene in the poorhouse is an instance of what it was like, in general, in the poorhouses of that time, apart from the fabula of this poor little boy. One may also highlight events which are related to a specific fabula but which exceed its time span. These we could call external iterations.

c And yet she had loved him, sometimes.   'The Story of an Hour'

This love has sometimes, though not often, been felt, but is mentioned only once. The period intended lies outside the borders of the fabula, and the iteration could therefore be termed external. It is not generalizing, however, as it concerns this one woman, the woman who is the actor in the fabula. In addition, we also find 'normal' iteration. In order to favour a quick, efficient notation I have drawn up a formula, according to which these kinds of frequency may be defined.

1F/1S: singular: one event, one presentation
nF/ns: plurisingular: various events, various presentations
nF/ms: varisingular: various events, various presentations, unequal in number
1F/ns: repetitive: one event, various presentations
nF/1S: iterative: various events, one presentation

Again, iteration functions differently in postmodernist narrative. Acker's *Blood and Guts* contains the following passage:

Of course, daddy and Sally and the boys in his band are given their rooms first. My room is the room no one else in the world wants.

My bedroom is the huge white hexagon in the front left corner of the hotel. It has no clear outside or inside or any architectural regularity. Long white pipes form part of its ceiling. Two of its sides, which two is always changing, are open.

My bedroom's function is also unclear. Its only furniture is two barber's chairs and a toilet. It's a gathering place for men.

Hotel men dressed in white and black come in and want to hurt me. They cut away parts of me. I call for the hotel head. He explains that my bedroom used to be the men's toilet. I understand. My cunt used to be a men's toilet.

I walk out in a leopard coat.   36

The passage appears to begin with a singular event, coated with description. But how often do the 'hotel men dressed in white and black' come in? Does the conflation between 'my bedroom' and 'my cunt' retrospectively turn this event into an iterative one, ironically turning the 'explanation' of the hotel head into an indictment of gender relations? This iterative effect is thereby loaded with meaning. The final sentence is totally unclear in terms of frequency.

6: Characters

Narrative – fiction as well as journalism, informal narratives of everyday life, or films – thrives on the affective appeal of characters. Whether we like them or not, we are compelled to read on because we respond to those paper people. In this section, I use the term *character* for the anthropomorphic figures provided with specifying features the narrator tells us about. Their distinctive characteristics together create the effect of a character. In the course of this section, the difference between the more specific term *character* and the general, abstract term *actor* at issue in the next chapter will gradually become clearer. To begin with, more often than not a character resembles a human being and an actor need not necessarily do so. What that resemblance means in narratological terms, and what its limitations are, will be discussed later. For the moment, let us assume that a character is the effect that occurs when a figure is presented with distinctive, mostly human characteristics. In this view, an actor in the fabula is a structural position, while a character is a complex semantic unit. As readers, we 'see' characters, feel with them and like or dislike them. These characters are only reducible to actors in a process of abstraction.

On the level of the story, characters differ from each other. In that sense they are individual. On the basis of the characteristics they have been allotted, they each function in a different way with respect to the reader. The latter gets to know them more or less than other characters, finds them more or less appealing, identifies more or less easily with them. The aim of this section is not to determine (define) the characters (who are they?), but to characterize them (what are they and how do we find out?).

Why Characters Resist Us

Characters resemble people. Literature is written by, for, and about people. That remains a truism, so banal that we often tend to forget it, and so problematic that we as often repress it with the same ease. On the other hand, the people with whom literature is concerned are not real people. They are fabricated creatures made up from fantasy, imitation, memory: paper people, without flesh and blood. That no satisfying, coherent theory of character is available is due to this anthropomorphic aspect. The character is not a human being, but it resembles one. It has no real psyche, personality, ideology, or competence to act, but it does possess characteristics that make readers assume it does, and makes psychological and ideological descriptions possible. Character is intuitively the most crucial category of narrative, and also most subject to projection and fallacies.

It is fair to say that characters do not exist. Yet, narratives produce 'character-effects.' The character-effect occurs when the resemblance between human beings and fabricated figures is so great that we forget the fundamental difference: we even go so far as to identify with the character, to cry, to laugh, and to search for or with it, or even against it, when the character is a villain. This is a major attraction of narrative. But it also leads us to asking questions that are not only frankly impertinent and irrelevant ('How many children had Lady Macbeth?') but that reduce the narrative to flat realism. This is a risk, for example, when we identify so much with characters in *Beloved* that we absolutely insist on the natural status of Beloved or, for the very same reason – the need for clarity – her supernatural status. Attempts to understand characters' behaviour often inspire psychological criticism where such criticism is clearly not adequate to account for the literary or cinematic qualities of the text.

Attempting to explain events in biblical narratives that seemed incongruous to the modern reader, for example, biblical critics tended to qualify actors who fall into a trap as 'dumb' or 'stupid' characters, or transgressive actors such as Eve in the creation story as wicked characters. This kind of response has produced the myth of primitivism in scholarship on ancient and folk literature, as well as on geographically and culturally removed literatures. This is a major ideological pitfall. It is also a literary-historical pitfall, for it obscures the characteristics of the mode of story-telling so different from our modern sensibility.

It is not out of a misplaced formalism, but rather with a view to overcoming this flattening tendency, that I suggest restricting our investigation to only those facts that are presented to us in the actual words of the text. Rather than producing formalist descriptions, such restraint produces rewarding surprises, unheard-of possibilities, and innovative social attitudes to emulate. Characters give most literary pleasure when they are allowed to resist their readers, rather than overruled and forced to conform to their expectations. Such wiping away of the dust of interpretive traditions makes even millennia-old texts appear with shining novelty. But within the material of the story – the entire mass of information presented to us by the narrating agent – more confusion occurs. When we come across a detailed portrait of a character that has already been mentioned, we are justified in saying that that information – that portrait – 'belongs to' the character, it 'creates' the character, maps it out, builds it up. A certain measure of coherence results. But relying on the analogy between character and human being, readers tend to attach so much importance to coherence that this material is easily reduced to a psychological 'portrait' that has more bearing on the reader's own desire to 'recognize' the character than on the interchange between story and fabula.

It is crucial to take enough distance from this anthropomorphism, for instance, to understand that Proust's Albertine is a 'paper person' in the true sense. She is an object of the protagonist's obsession, does what he thinks she does, and when he no longer needs her to make his point about the relation between jealousy, love, and knowledge, she dies in an unlikely accident. Once we accept that she has no psychological depth of her own, we not only grasp the specifically Proustian construction of character – which is crucial for an appreciation of the work – but also the aesthetic and epistemological thrust of the narrative. In contrast, a realistic reading of this character as a 'real girl' will only frustrate us, make her irritating and antipathetic, and the CN a selfish monster (this has actually been alleged against Proust in all seriousness). What the character as analogue to humans loses in appeal, it gains in literary excitement. Proust's masterpiece is much more fascinating when allowed to play with its paper people than when reduced to realist, moralist norms.

Moreover, a story contains other information that, though connected less directly with a certain character, contributes as much to the image of that character that is offered to the reader. What a figure does is as important as what he or she thinks, feels, remembers, or looks like.

Another drawback of a certain critical tradition is the division of characters into the kinds of categories literary criticism is so fond of. Forster's classical distinction between round and flat characters, which has been employed for more than seventy years, was based on psychological criteria. Round characters are like 'complex' persons, who undergo a change in the course of the story, and remain capable of surprising the reader. Flat characters are stable; stereotypical characters that exhibit/contain nothing surprising. Even if such classifications were to be moulded into manageable distinctions, they would still only be applicable to a limited corpus: that of the psychological narrative.

Entire genres, such as fairy tales, detective fiction, and popular fiction, but also ancient literature such as biblical or Qur'anic stories, as well as a modernist novel like Proust's and postmodern novels that mock precisely such categories, thus remain excluded from observation or aesthetic appreciation because all their characters are 'flat.' Indeed, Proust's Albertine is explicitly presented as flat – a flatness that, precisely, constitutes the complexity of this figure, if not her 'density.' To get a sense of the relevance of character analysis on the basis of an endorsement of its impossibility, let us take a look at how this character emerges. Albertine is first noticed by Marcel, and 'chosen' to be his love object, on the basis of an image of her at a distance, on the beach. This is no easy selection. The first description of her hardly singles her out:

> But I could not arrive at any certainty, for the face of these girls did not fill a constant space, did not present a constant form upon the beach, contracted, dilated, transformed as it was by my own expectancy, by the anxiousness of my desire, or by a sense of self-sufficient

well-being, the different clothes they wore, the rapidity of their walk
or their stillness.   II 867

The description of Albertine is not simply an account of the perception of her by the narrator. Others evoke her first – as 'the famous
"Albertine"' (I 552), then as 'You've no idea how insolent she is, that
child' (I 643). Both prefigurations, if I may call them that, occur while
the narrator is still pining for Gilberte, his first love. The real 'sighting'
of Albertine – there is not yet a meeting – occurs in an extended de-
scriptive-reflective passage that takes no less than ten pages, in 'Place-
names: The Place' of *Within a Budding Grove*.

It begins with 'In the midst of all these people ...' (I 847), and ends
when Marcel enters the hotel ('I went indoors,' I 856), with the end of
his stroll, hence, in terms of the event in the fabula, quite arbitrarily.
This piece is an astonishing allegory of the difficulty of describing due
to the impossibility of knowing other people. The problems of *distinction* and its eventual arbitrariness are at the heart of the event and they
highlight the fundamental artificiality of character. Let me just select
– arbitrarily, artificially! – a few moments from this extended passage.
And the length of the passage is motivated by a struggle to keep abreast
of an accelerated temporality that rules the novel's combined tempo-
ralities of fabula, discourse, and reading.

The phrase '*In the midst* of all these people ... the girls *whom I had
noticed* ...' introduces a description of the girls' collective movement
through space as they walk towards the narrator. In the fabula the latter
is diegetically walking towards, in the text 'speaking' about, and in the
story, 'reading' the *spectacle* of the girls. When he sees them from closer
proximity, the rationale for the collective description is rendered in a
combined terminology of classification and aesthetics: 'Although each
was *of a type* absolutely different from the others, they all had *beauty*; ...
I had yet not individualized any of them.' The struggle for distinction is
rendered in a nightmare that resembles a parody of descriptive detailing, and explained through the effect of time: 'I saw a pallid oval, black
eyes, green eyes, *emerge*, I did not know if these were the same that had
already charmed me *a moment ago*, I could not relate them to any one
girl whom I had set apart from the rest and identified' (847).

The narrator experiences the incapacity to distinguish as a lack
('want'), but also as a source of beauty. Thus he is placed outside of
himself and his subjectivity as perceiving agent: 'And this *want*, in my

vision, of the demarcations which I *should presently* establish between them *permeated* the group with a sort of *shimmering* harmony, the *continuous transmutation* of a fluid, collective and *mobile* beauty' (747–8). The source of beauty is the negation of distinction, yet time lifts a prescriptive finger ('should presently'). Clashing with this routine temporality is the temporality that inheres in the group: 'continuous transmutation,' the mobility that is the site of beauty. Clearly, a stable character endowed with permanent beauty is not going to result from this descriptive dystopia.

The rhetorical make-up of this initial stage of the production of the character-effect is reconfirmed throughout the passage (e.g., 'to the delight of the other girls, especially of a pair of green eyes in a doll-like face...' 849). But even when distinction is achieved, the result is emphatically not closer to an individualizing and stabilizing character description. 'By this time their charming features had ceased to be indistinct and jumbled' (850) confirms the narrator in an uncharacteristically short, summing-up sentence, but

> I had dealt them *like cards* into so many heaps to compose ...: the tall one who had just jumped over the old banker; the little one silhouetted against the horizon of sea with her plump and rosy cheeks and green eyes; the one with the straight nose and dark complexion who *stood out among the rest* ...

Curiously, the first act of distinction is hidden in a sub-clause ('who stood out'), whereas the actual description of the chosen one is couched in an emphatically parallel series ('the one with the straight nose'). The next step is based on the usual (deceptive) appearances and negativity: 'a girl with brilliant, laughing eyes and plump, matte cheeks, a black polo-cap crammed on her head, who was pushing a bicycle ...' is cast as belonging to the popular classes, as being of light virtue, and rather vulgar. One of the motivations for the negative judgments that accompany the descriptions – in terms of both social class and ethical judgments – is the continuous adjustment that problematizes appearance. Another, I propose, is to isolate for consideration the ethics of representing the other as such, which ultimately leads to an ontological assessment. Ideological reduction appears, in effect, to result from character description.

But distinction on the level of the fabula – the represented object – is not enough to facilitate a successful emergence of the character. Even after this crucial moment of election, the narrator continues his musings on the impossibility of individualizing:

> Though they were now separately identifiable, still the *interplay of their eyes*, animated with self-assurance ... an invisible but harmonious bond, like a *single* warm shadow ... making of them a whole as homogeneous in its parts as it was different from the crowd through which their procession gradually wound.   851

And for hundreds of pages, the narrator continues to struggle with the impossibility of knowing his elected other.

In *The Prisoner*, Albertine, who has lost her former, fixed quality of beach photo, consists only of a series of snapshots:

> ... a person, scattered in space and time, is no longer a woman but a series of events on which we can throw *no light*, a series of insoluble problems   99–100; emphasis added

The shift from the typically modernist preoccupation with epistemological uncertainty ('no light') to the ontological doubt that results when one radically thinks through what epistemological doubt entails ('is no longer a woman') announces postmodernism, and the philosophically rich phrase 'scattered in time and space' (disseminated) with its Derridian overtones articulates that shift. That 'woman' as 'other' falls prey to a true lunacy of the snapshot is, of course, no coincidence. This dissolution in visual, flat seriality is only aggravated as Marcel tries to counter it and 'fix' Albertine by means of 'light' thrown on her, and on paper. Thus she ends up *becoming* (ontology) the sheet on which the images (epistemology) of jealousy (psychology) are going to be fixed:

> For I possessed in my memory only a series of Albertines, separate from one another, incomplete, a collection of profiles or snapshots, and so my jealousy was restricted to a discontinuous expression, at once fugitive and fixed ...   145–6

With the word 'memory' keeping the issue also on the level of epistemology, ontological 'fugitivity' is presented here as a perversion of memory. The final words here, in French 'à la fois fugitive et fixée,' define quite precisely the nature of the series of snapshots, and explain the specific use of this poetic in the novel. The importance of eroticism is crucial: the object of this fugitive fixing is the love object of whom the focalizing narrator is unable to fix the sexual orientation. Obviously, Albertine's 'flatness' can in no way be considered a lack of 'density.' On the contrary, it is of essential importance for this 'dense' novel that she be flat. I propose to generalize this. Both fugitive – as a being – and fixed – in the words of the novel that capture it – the character is an effect that makes us believe in the human nature of a creature that is constantly resisting that humanity, in favour of other important insights it has to offer. This is the game of make-believe in fiction – a game that is, according to the specific insights it produces, truer than truth.

I am concerned here with establishing a framework for the characterization of specific narrative characters, as a way in which to explain at least partly the character-effect. This framework must be as simple as possible. A summary of the kinds of information the readers have at their disposal in order to construct an image of a character, and a summary of the information they actually use while doing so, should make this possible. But in this discussion even more than in the rest of the concepts offered in this book, it is important to realize that much remains resistant to analysis. And, rather than considering that resistance a failure of narratological analysis, I emphasize that it is the evidence of the success of such an analysis.

The so-called extratextual situation creates yet another ambiguity. This concerns the influence of reality on the story, in so far as reality plays a part in it. Even if we do not wish to study the relations between text and context as a separate object of analysis, we cannot ignore the fact that direct or indirect knowledge of the context of certain characters contributes significantly to their meaning. The character President Eisenhower in Coover's *The Public Burning* is not the factual president of the United States, Eisenhower as we know him from historical evidence. But the impression we receive of that character depends to a great extent on the confrontation between our own image of Eisenhower and the image that the story offers, which in its turn is determined by another context. The influence of data from reality is all the more difficult to determine since the personal situation, knowledge, background, historical moment, and so on of the reader are involved here.

Finally, the description of a character is always strongly coloured by the ideology of critics, who are often unaware of their own ideological hang-ups. Consequently, what is presented as a description is an implicit value judgment. And here the realistic tendency promoted by the anthropomorphism of characters can play nasty tricks. Characters are attacked or defended as if they were people that the critics like or dislike. To make matters worse, author and character are viewed as one and the same. Existentialist criticism tended to do this. Emotions flared at the publication of Nabokov's *Lolita*. Humbert's mentality was all wrong; the man was an immoral hypocrite, and quotations from the text could prove this. If, however, we examine all the utterances of the character-bound narrator, then, to say the least, a much more problematic picture emerges. And even if this narrator is an immoral hypocrite, this does not then mean that the entire novel is immoral, or was ever meant to be. A good deal more needs to be considered to back up the claim of immorality, always limited to the context in which the particular morality is generally accepted.

These problems should be neither denied nor ignored, as a formalist approach would do. Rather, they should be clearly formulated and brought to bear on other issues. Ideological discussions and value judgments should not be censured, but should be conducted with insight into the many issues involved. Only then can they be discussed, and this can only benefit the analysis. The discussion below may help to make this procedure a little bit easier.

Predictability

While the preceding section expanded character, this one reduces it. Both moves are necessary and productive. On the basis of bits of information the character becomes more or less predictable. These data determine him or her, mostly so inconspicuously that the reader processes the information without giving it a thought. To begin with, there is information that is 'always-already' involved, that relates to the extra-textual situation, in so far as the reader is acquainted with it. As a matter of fact, the only moments that one realizes that some information is not 'in' the text are precisely, when one fails to make a connection by lack of information. I shall treat that section of 'reality' or 'the outside world' to which the information about the person refers as a *frame of reference*. Few readers will fail to sense the brief moment of laughter when reading, in Karen Harper's mystery novel *Black Orchid* (1996), '"What's the name of that gray-haired boy who's president right now?" Hattie asked.' We really don't need the next sentence, '"Bill Clinton, Grandma," Jordan told her' (68). Readers share the frame of reference in which it is not only elementary knowledge who ran the United States at that time, but also that Clinton's gray hair is like a pointer that identifies him. The answer, rather than identifying Clinton, serves to characterize Hattie's relationship to her grandmother, a relationship of affectionate resignation. This frame is never entirely the same for each reader, or for reader and writer. By frame of reference I here mean information that may with some confidence be called communal. For most American readers, Coover's Eisenhower fits into a frame of reference of that kind. But so does the connection between 'snow' and 'cold weather' if not 'northern countries.'

Historical characters are often brought to life in novels. Napoleon we even meet quite regularly. Legendary characters, like King Arthur or Santa Claus, also fit into a frame of reference. Historical characters are not more strongly determined than legendary ones. On the contrary, legendary characters are expected to exhibit a certain stereotypical behaviour and set attributes; if the story were to depart too far from these set characteristics, they would no longer be recognizable. If presented in opposition to the referential characteristics, however, such 'deviant' characters can be a powerful trigger of surprise, suspense, or humour. Santa Claus loves children; his whole status as a legendary character is based on that. A Santa Claus who sets out to murder people is blatantly a fiction, or as the case may be, a fake. This possibility is used in Francis Ford Coppola's film *The Godfather*, based on Mario Puzo's 1969 novel. The film begins with a peaceful Santa Claus scene in a shopping area, shattered by a murder.

This scene set the tone for numerous imitations, so as to form a network of intertextual relations if not an altogether new discourse. It is taken up in the television series 'Picket Fences,' which borrows this fiction, as an acknowledgment of the way *The Godfather* made it a popular tradition. This effect was brought about yet again, in a case of heterogeneous discourses à la Bakhtin. The 1997 action film *Turbulence* by Robert Butler makes this discursive mix the continuous line of the story. In this film at least three discourses are mixed: Christmas, with its ideology of peace and gift giving; sophisticated, modern air transportation, including the fear of flying; and the terror stories of serial killers. Throughout this extremely terrifying film, Christmas decorations remind the viewer of this interdiscursive clash. The differences among these are not glossed over but, on the contrary, foregrounded in character presentation. When Carl, an African-American flight attendant wearing a Santa Claus hat (Gordy Owens) is confronted by the killer, the clash enhances the artificiality of both. 'Christmas' becomes a shifter where meanings change gear.

Where historical characters are concerned, the possibilities are somewhat greater. Because we are more confident about the identity of such a character, an unfamiliar side can be shown and will be accepted more easily: a tyrant during a fit of weakness; a saint in doubt or in temptation; a party-going revolutionary. But here too the possibilities are limited because of the frame of reference. A mature Napoleon presented as a poor wretch would create a very odd effect: he would no longer be Napoleon. In yet another way, mythic and allegorical characters fit a pattern of expectation, established in the basis of our frame of reference. The goddess of justice cannot make unfair decisions without destroying her identity as a character. Only for those who know that this character is conventionally blind will a wide-eyed goddess of justice be a problem. All these characters, which we could label referential characters because of their obvious slots in a frame of reference, act according to the pattern that we are familiar with from other sources. Or not. In both cases, the image we receive of them is determined to a large extent by the confrontation between, on the one hand, our previous knowledge and the expectations it produces, and on the other, the realization of the character in the narrative. Opting for a referential character implies, in this respect, opting for such confrontation. The ensuing determination, and the extent to which it is realized, is therefore an interesting object for study.

There is another reason for such studies. The expectations aroused by the mere mention of a historical or mythical character are also traps for the reader. We tend to notice only what we already know, unless the deviation from the expectation is strongly enhanced. An amusing case is Sophocles' King Oedipus. Owing to the success of Freud's psychoanalysis, we all 'know' Oedipus. He's the guy with the Oedipus complex, of course. He killed his father and desired his mother. Well, that is precisely not the case. Oedipus the character does not have an Oedipus complex, for two opposed reasons. First, because he did nothing of the sort; he did not know the old man he killed was his father, and so his act of killing did not make him a parricide. Neither did he know that the queen was his mother. Today we would say: these people were only his biological parents; his actual parents were the kind shepherd and his wife who raised him. But if this argument fails to convince, the opposite one will: he has no Oedipus complex because he acted upon his desires, whereas an Oedipus complex emerges, precisely, out of the repression of that desire. And if neither of these reasons is convincing, that is because the question – does Sophocles' Oedipus have an Oedipus complex? – is one of those 'How many children had Lady Macbeth' questions.

Characters don't have an unconscious, only people do. Psychoanalytic criticism does not, or should not, consist of diagnosing characters but of understanding how texts affectively address the reader on a level that comes close to unconscious preoccupations. In general, returning to the ancient texts about the mythical characters that have fed our culture's clichés and prejudices is exciting and valuable. Let me give one example.

The myth of Narcissus is traditionally attached to narcissism, a psychoanalytic concept that has taken on ordinary meaning, more often than not used in a moralizing way. A narcissistic person over-indulges in self-love and self-interest. Narcissus, as the myth has it, died because he did not recognize himself; nor did he perceive the mirror for what it was: a boundary between reality and fiction. The erotic effect of the image worked on him, but not the formative one. In Ovid's *Metamorphoses,* when his mother, the river Liriopa, consulted the seer Tiresias and asked whether her son would live to old age, the answer was: 'If he does not know himself' ('Si se non nouerit,' 346). Self-knowledge, which supposedly entails wisdom if spiritual, kills when 'carnal,' erotic; or so it seems.

Yet, later on, the opposite seems to be the case. The *denial* of carnal knowledge is presented by Ovid as Narcissus' fatal failure: 'he falls in love with an image without body' ('spem sine corpore amat,' 417). Imputing bodily existence to what is only a visual image – or, as the case may be, water – he condemns himself ('corpus putat esse quod unda est,' 417). This story of 'death and the image' is about the denial of the true, natural body.

Prefiguring his imminent demise, Ovid's Narcissus enacts the soon-to-occur rigor mortis:

> He remains immobile, his face impassive, like a statue sculpted in marble of Paros. (Adstupet ipse sibi uultuque inmotus eodem haeret, ut e Pario formatum marmore signum.)   418–19

'Ut signum': he becomes like a sign – an iconic sign of a sign – as an enactment of radical constructivism: a character is a construction, not a person. As opposed to common lore, Narcissus is not wrong in admiring himself: 'He admires everything that makes him admirable' ('cunctaque mirator quibus est mirabilis ipse,' 424). His tragedy is not brought about by excessive self-love so much as by naïve realism: 'what you are seeking does not exist' ('quod petit est nusquam,' 433). He does, in the end, recognize that he loves himself, and, destroyed by the sense of tragic hopelessness that he has inflicted so often upon others, he begins his slow descent into death.

Rather than blaming him – or the narcissism named after the mythical figure – for moral shortcoming or formative failure, I propose to take Ovid's Narcissus as an allegory of the reader who conflates character and person. Referential characters are more strongly determined than entirely fictional characters. But, in fact, every character is more or less predictable, from the very first time it is presented onwards. Every mention of the identity of the character contains information that limits other possibilities. Reference to a character by means of a personal pronoun alone limits its gender. And, in general, this then sets off a whole series of limitations. A *he* cannot find himself unintentionally pregnant. A *she* cannot, in general, become a Catholic priest. In so far as they are traditionally determined, these limitations are subject to change.

One of the earliest inspirations of feminist literary studies was the insight that, in much traditional literature, women only function as protagonists in certain types of fabulas, in which the goal pursued is a characteristic of the character itself (happiness, wisdom) and not a concrete object that would necessitate a long journey or a physically taxing ordeal.

When a character is indicated with 'I' these gender restrictions do not (yet) apply, but in that case other restrictions are possible. The character, the I, is not presented from a spatial distance, which, in turn, involves all sorts of other limitations. When the character is allotted its own name, this determines not only its sex/gender (as a rule) but also its social status, geographical origin, sometimes even more. Names can also be motivated, can have a bearing upon some of the character's characteristics. To this category belong not only names such as Tom Thumb and Snow White. Agatha Christie's Poirot has a pear-shaped head. Miss Marple is not only a woman, but is also unmarried, and that state implies a number of stereotypical qualities conventionally connected with elderly unmarried ladies: inquisitiveness, a great deal of spare time, reliability, innocence, naivety, qualities necessary for the development of the fabulas to which the character leads. In fact, because of the inseparable link between the title Miss and the name Marple – reason also to consider the 'Miss' a proper name – this character is also highly referential.

A portrait, the description of the exterior character, further limits the possibilities. If a character is old, it does different things than if it were young. If it is attractive, it lives differently from the way it would live if it were unattractive, or so the reader tends to assume. Profession, too, greatly determines the frame in which the events take place or from which they receive their meaning. A thatcher falls from a roof (*L'assommoir*, Zola); sooner or later a miner will be trapped in a shaft that has collapsed (*Germinal*, Zola; *Sans famille*, Malot) if he doesn't die of some kind of lung disease; a soldier dies at the front or is sent to faraway countries (*A Farewell to Arms*, Hemingway). None of these determining factors is in fact determining at all. The fact that profession, sex, external factors, or quirks of personality are mentioned creates an expectation. The story may fulfil it, but may just as easily frustrate it. Either way, character features activate the reader.

Genre plays a part in a character's predictability. A detective must, in principle, find the murderer. This genre-bound expectation is sometimes broken; for instance, in *The Locked Room* by Maj Sjöwall and Per Wahlöö, where the murdering character is arrested for another crime and the mysteries are never entirely solved. The alterations to which a genre is subject are influenced by the interplay between the evocation, satisfaction, and frustration of expectations. The stronger the determination, the greater the shift away from tension generated by questions concerning the outcome and towards the tension generated by the question whether the character will realize its own determination and/or break away from it. A character's predictability is closely related to the reader's frame of reference in which it seems to 'fit.' But the effect of this predictability also depends on the reader's attitude with respect to literature and the book he or she is reading. Is she strongly inclined to 'fill in' or will she let herself be led by the story? Does she read quickly or does she interrupt the reading often to stop and think about it?

What I am suggesting here as information about a character's predictability can only provide clues to its potential determination. Thus we can analyse the way in which possible determination emerges in the story. In many ways, we afterwards conclude that a certain detail about a character was related to an event, or to a whole series of events. Establishing connections, coherence, in this way is not the same as signalling predictability beforehand. Predictability makes it easy to find coherence, it contributes to the formation of a unified image of one character out of an abundance of information. But it is not the only way in which that image is formed. We can distinguish various relations between bits of information, on the basis of which an image of a character is also formed.

Predictability is not necessarily in tension with suspense. It can be deployed to produce suspense. Early on in the film *Turbulence*, the serial killer Ryan Weaver (Ray Liotta) is called the Teddy Bear Killer. His m.o. (modus operandi of serial killers) is to give a teddy bear to the women right before killing them. When he enters the home of his girlfriend and gives her a teddy bear, the expectation that he will kill her is raised, then quickly dismissed as the police enter the house to capture him. Later, when the unpiloted Boeing 747 is approaching the area of Los Angeles, the killer, who has already wreaked deadly havoc in the plane, gives the heroine Teri Halloran (Lauren Holly) a teddy bear. We know, then, that the moment of ultimate danger and confrontation is approaching. It is only Teri's status as heroine – and her competence in dealing with the monstrous killer – that can save her. Indeed, this repetition is an effective rhetorical tool to produce suspense, rather than diminishing it.

Construction of Content

When a character appears for the first time, we do not yet know very much about it. The qualities that are implied in that first presentation are not all grasped by the reader. In the course of the narrative the relevant characteristics are repeated so often – in a different form, however – that they emerge more and more clearly. Repetition is thus an important principle of the construction of the image of a character. Only when our attention has been focused on it a few times do we begin to regard, for instance, Frits van Egters' tendency (in Reve's *The Evenings*) to notice baldness in others as typical of this character. And only then do we realize that this characteristic recurs constantly throughout the rest of the narrative.

In addition to repetition, the piling up of data also fulfils a function in the construction of an image. The accumulation of characteristics causes odd facts to coalesce, complement each other, and then form a whole: the image of a character. In *The Evenings* we notice not only Frits' preoccupation with baldness, but his obsession with other signs of decay as well, autumn, illness, old age, death, time. And these facts together convey a clear picture of the character, in the areas where un-connected data might have been striking but would not have been par-ticularly meaningful.

In the third place, relations with others also help to build the image of a character. The character's relation to itself in an earlier phase also belongs to this category. These relations tend to be processed into simi-larities and contrasts. A semantic model to describe these categories is only a reflection of cultural cognitive habits.

Finally, characters change. The changes or transformations which a character undergoes sometimes alter the entire configuration of char-acter as it looked during the analysis of mutual relations. Once a char-acter's most important characteristics have been selected, it is easier to trace transformations and to describe them clearly.

Repetition, accumulation, relations to other characters, and transfor-mations are four different principles which work together to construct the image of a character. Their effect can only be described, however, when the outline of the character has been roughly filled in. This is a constant element in narratological analysis: a dialectic back-and-forth between speculation and verification through open-minded analysis.

Filling In, Fleshing Out

How do we decide which we consider provisionally to be a character's relevant characteristics and which are of secondary importance? One method is the selection of relevant semantic axes. Semantic axes are pairs of contrary meanings. This is a typical structuralist principle with which I have become more uncomfortable lately. I have decided to keep it here, first because there is so little available for character analysis, and second, perhaps more importantly, because it does reflect the way most people, hence, most readers, tend to 'do' semantic categorization. Therefore, it seemed better to present both the model and the critique of it, so that it can be used both to map and to undermine.

Characteristics like 'large' and 'small' could be a relevant semantic axis; or rich-poor, or man-woman, kind-unkind, reactionary-progres-sive. The selection of the relevant semantic axes involves focusing, out of all the characteristics mentioned – usually an unmanageably large number – only on those axes that determine the image of the largest possible number of characters, positively or negatively. Of the axes which involve only a few or even one character, only those are anal-ysed which are 'strong' (striking or exceptional) or which are related

to an important event. Such a selection involves the ideological position of the analyst and also points at ideological stances represented
in the story, and can therefore be a powerful tool for critique. Once a
selection has been made of the relevant semantic axes, it can function
as a means of mapping out the similarities and oppositions between
the characters. With the help of this information we can determine the
qualifications with which a character is endowed (but by whom? by
the story or by the reader? remains an ongoing question, to be continued with 'why?').

Some qualifications belong to a social or a family role. In that case,
determination comes into play. A character is, for instance, a farmer
and a father. Both roles strongly determine what qualifications he receives. In a case like this, no one will be surprised if the character – in
a traditional story – is strong, hard-working, and strict. The opposite
of strong is (let's say for the moment) weak; of hard-working, lazy; of
strict, flexible. The other pole of each of these axes is filled by a character with an equally clear role. It will hardly surprise anyone if the
farmer is contrasted with his weak, effeminate, artistic son. In accordance with prejudice, the young man will be lazy. The qualification
'flexible' is hardly applicable to the son; he does not occupy the kind
of position of power that allows him the choice between strictness and
leniency. This pole will be filled – how could it be otherwise? – by
his mother. Should we now attempt to collect the various qualifications we have isolated for all these characters, we would end up with
a diagram of the following kind, which for the sake of clarity, has been
sketchily outlined.

character qualification / role	strength	diligence	flexibility
farmer/father	+	+	–
student/son	–	–	ϕ
mother	ϕ	ϕ	+

Here + = positive pole
      – = negative pole
      ϕ = unmarked

This results in a picture of a set of characters, strongly determined by social and family roles. The father is not only qualified as strong; he is also the most strongly qualified character. Two of the three qualifications mark him as positive; all three apply to him. The mother plays a less prominent part in accordance with her social position. She is marked by one quality alone, though a positive one. The young man is marked twice, both times negatively. The mutual relations between the characters are immediately visible. In this way, more complexly structured sets of characters may also be mapped out.

But binary opposition itself, as a structure of thought, is problematic. Establishing semantic axes of this kind subjects its object – say, a particular semantic field – to three successive logical moves that each aggravate the damage: reduction, of an infinitely rich but also chaotic field, to two centres; the articulation of those centres into polar opposites; and the hierarchization of these two into a positive and a negative term.

But here, logic catches up with this structure of thought. For the logic of opposition has it that negativity is by definition vague, if not void. It cannot be defined, hence, not articulated, and as a result it remains unmanageable; indeed, wild.

Historiographer Hayden White (1978) has exposed this logic in his analysis of the early modern fantasy of the 'wild man,' the inhabitants of wild nature outside of the control of the city. More specifically, he called the logic of negativity underlying this fantasy, using a term from logic, 'ostentatious self-definition by negation.' White writes:

> They [the concepts] are treated neither as provisional designators, that is, hypotheses for directing further inquiry into specific areas of human experience, nor as fictions with limited heuristic utility for generating possible ways of conceiving the human world. They are, rather, complexes of symbols, the referents of which shift and change in response to the changing patterns of human behavior which they are meant to sustain.   154

White's negative formulation on how concepts based on binary opposition are *not* treated provides a good piece of advice regarding the scepticism necessary to work with this model without endorsing its drawbacks.

Once we analyse which characters appear marked by a certain semantic axis, we can set up, by using such a diagram as this, a hierarchy of strongly and weakly marked characters. If a number of characters are marked by the same axes with the same values (positive or negative), they can be regarded as synonymous characters: characters with the same content. Inconspicuous duplications of characters can thus become visible. But this is an oversimplistic two-way division of axes. It can be useful to determine whether differences of degree and modality are evident within each qualification. Degree can transform a polar scale into a sliding scale: very strong, reasonably strong, not strong enough, somewhat weak, a weakling. Modality can result in nuance: certainly, probably, perhaps, probably not. Especially if synonymous characters have been discovered, these can mean a valuable refinement of the descriptive model.

So far, this model is blatantly ideological. To move beyond believing in the 'truth' of such an analysis, and examine the contents of the character further, we can look at the connections existing between the various characteristics. Are, for instance, certain sexes constantly combined with a certain ideological position? In many seventeenth- and eighteenth-century novels a clear connection can be discerned between the male sex and a military ideology. There is, however, not systematically a connection in the same corpus between the female sex and a pacifist attitude, although sometimes there is (e.g. Corneille's play *Horace*). If not, in female characters the axis militarism-pacifism is not marked. The question arises, in relation to this, whether the fact that a certain character or group of characters (for instance, all the persons of one role) is not marked by a certain axis has any significance. It need not, in my view, be meaningful, but neither need it be meaningless. If in a seventeenth-century novel the women do not take a clear stand either for or against war, this can certainly be regarded as significant: it indicates something about their (lack of) social position. The very binary opposition that is such an ideological trap also helps us to notice ideological positions.

A character exhibits not only similarities to and differences from other characters. Often, there is a connection or a discrepancy between the character, its situation, and its environment. Finally, the description which has been obtained of a character can be contrasted with an analysis of the functions it performs in a series of events. What kinds of actions does a character perform, and what role does it play in the fabula? This confrontation can yield information about the construction of the story with respect to the fabula. Because of a certain event, alterations may take place in the build-up of a character, and internal relations between the various characters change. Conversely, alterations in the make-up of a character may influence events and determine the outcome of the fabula.

Information

How do we come by our information about a character? Characteristics are either mentioned explicitly by the character itself, or we deduce them from what the character does. Actually, we refer to a qualification when the information is given directly by a character. There are various ways this happens. If a character talks about itself and to itself, it is practising self-analysis. We cannot be sure that it is judging itself correctly, and literature shows many such cases: unreliable, deceitful, immature, incompetent, mentally disturbed self-analysts. The genres which are particularly well suited to this manner of qualification are obviously the autobiographical ones: diary, confession, autobiographical novel. In 'The Tell-Tale Heart,' Edgar Allan Poe allows his character to explain why he is not insane, although he has murdered someone, and these confessions clearly demonstrate, because of their negation, the existence of his insanity.

A character can talk about itself to others. If it receives an answer, the qualification becomes plural, deriving from various sources. If one character says something about another character, this may or may not lead to a confrontation. The character under discussion may or may not be present. If it is, it can react, confirming or denying what has been said. If it is not, it may or may not already know what people think of it. A third possibility for explicit qualification lies with a third party outside the fabula: the narrator makes statements about the character. This agent, too, may be a reliable or an unreliable judge. The party, for instance, which presents Dombey in Dickens' *Dombey and Son* as an entirely decent man is unreliable. This presentation involves irony.

When a character is presented by means of her actions, we deduce from these certain implicit qualifications. Such an implicit, indirect qualification may be labelled a qualification by function. The reader's frame of reference becomes a crucial element in picking up such qualifications. A deserter is, say, qualified as either a pacifist or a coward. A revolutionary who participates in a wild party qualifies either as an epicurean or a hypocrite. Moreover, one character can do something to another that qualifies the latter, or that seduces him into qualifying himself. A detective who unmasks a murderer qualifies that character as a murderer. In that case, the qualification is explicit. But before the final arrest takes place the detective can lure his or her victim into a trap, so that the latter qualifies himself as a murderer. She can also, without words, push a gun to his chest, produce a piece of evidence and directly qualify him as a murderer.

If we now involve the various frequency possibilities as well, further differentiation becomes possible. Every qualification is always durative, so that the frequency possibilities are restricted to two. The implicit qualification through action can be split up into potential actions (plans) and realized ones.

The first category of information sources leads to explicit qualification and the second to implicit qualification. Explicit qualifications shed more light than implicit ones, but that light need not be reliable. Implicit, indirect qualifications can be interpreted differently by different readers, as in the case of the deserter. But implicit qualifications may also provide a means of uncovering lies and revealing secrets.

On the basis of this investigation into sources of information, a division can be set up, classifying the character according to the degree of emphasis with which it is qualified. The more ways in which the qualification is communicated, the more frequently a character is qualified, the more emphasis it receives. In conjunction with the number of semantic axes by which it is marked, a classification of characters may be achieved which is somewhat more plausible and more subtle than the old one based on round and flat characters.

The Hero

From the very beginning of the study of literature, it has been customary to refer to the hero of a story. Who is the hero? Lots of problematic features have accrued to the term, so much so that it is better left alone. The reader's ability to identify the hero has been put forward as a criterion. But this differs, in many cases, from reader to reader. Another criterion is the amount of moral approbation that the hero receives from the reader. Again, this varies with each reader. Or does it? As with binary opposition, I am here tempted to explore the implications of such acts of reading rather than turning away from a term that in all its deceptiveness has enough allure to maintain itself. If we believe what a great number of rather smart people have written, the history of literature offers examples of a development of the hero that seem to fulfil this moral requirement.

Nineteenth-century heroes were characters who could survive in a hard and ruthless society, or who attempted to do so but failed. The existential hero is anti-bourgeois and politically committed. Questions concerning the identity of the hero are perhaps not relevant, but are raised so often that they warrant an attempt to formulate criteria by which a decision may be taken. Attempts have been made to define the term more clearly by naming a number of criteria according to which either the hero could be rejected or the reader's intuitive choice could be explained.

But something much more banal may be going on, such as the appeal of a name in the title. If the title of the hero or his or her explicit denomination does not clinch a decision, we can see whether any one character distinguishes itself from the other characters in the following ways:

qualification: comprehensive information about appearance, psychology, motivation, past
distribution: the hero occurs often in the story, his or her presence is felt at important moments in the fabula
independence: the hero can occur alone or hold monologues
function: certain actions are those of the hero alone: s/he makes agreements, vanquishes opponents, unmasks traitors, etc.
relations: s/he maintains relations with the largest number of characters

But 'hero' implies more positive semantics than is warranted. At the very least there is a distinction to be made between the active, successful hero, the hero-victim, and the passive anti-hero (Tommy Wilhelm in Bellow's *Seize the Day*). The hero-victim will be confronted with opponents, but will not vanquish them. The anti-hero will hardly distinguish him- or herself by function, because she is passive. He will, however, meet all of the other four criteria.

The problem of the hero has ideological relevance, if only because of the connotations of the concept itself. It is obvious that heroines display different features from male heroes, black from white heroes, in the large majority of the narratives. The suspicion that the choice of a hero and of the features attributed to him or her betrays an ideological position is a reason not to ignore the problem but rather to study it.

7: Space

Together with character, few concepts deriving from the theory of narrative texts are as self-evident and have yet remained so vague as the concept of space. Only a few theoretical publications have been devoted to it. Here, 'space' is treated as a separate category only to enable specialized analysis. The concept of space is sandwiched between that of focalization, of which the representation of space constitutes in a way a specialized case, and that of place, a category of fabula elements. It is also, obviously, an important aspect of a section I added for the revised second edition, on visuality and narrative, although space cannot be conflated with vision.

Space becomes an issue in Proust's search for Albertine as the unknowable character. Later, when he is already firmly ensconced in his paranoid relationship with Albertine – paranoid, of course, because the descriptive exploration has demonstrated the impossibility of knowledge, hence, of assurance – the narrator describes in minute detail, for example, how, at the beginning of the summer season, his searching eye seeks out the young girls who had so enraptured him before. Now he does not need to distinguish the girl with whom he had so significantly but poignantly said to have decided to 'have his novel.' Yet distinction is still the object of the search. Now, space comes to the fore as an issue of similar magnitude. In the following fragment, the gaze, distant at the beginning of the sentence, moves closer towards the end:

> But I could not arrive at any certainty, for the face of these girls did not fill a constant space, did not present a constant form upon the beach, contracted, dilated, transformed as it was by my own expectancy, by the anxiousness of my desire, or by a sense of self-sufficient well-being, the different clothes they wore, the rapidity of their walk or their stillness.   II 867

The issue of focalization this passage broaches will return shortly. The focalizing subject transforms the incorrect grammatical form of a singular noun (face) accompanied by a plural predicate (these girls) into a zoom effect. And it is a spatial trick. The combination is maintained right to the end of the sentence. It is partially neutralized by the increasingly rapid succession of nouns (clothes – in the plural – rapidity, stillness). The search here is primarily *photographic*. I contend that photography is selected as the mode of this search because it is ambiguously situated between producing and recording a slice of space, a space that fills a vision. Hence, it poses the problem of, precisely, distinction.

Specifically, distinction is not only a spatial issue. It is also a temporal one. If only the model would pose for him, he would be able to fix the lens at the right distance, that is, at the distance necessary to hold the image still. Then, he would be able to take a 'photograph.'

Through photography, Proust challenges the humanistic assumptions inherent in realist literature. Indeed, photography challenges any simple idea of description as distinct from narration. With its glossy, shiny, flat surface, it is neither 'profound' – it has no *depth* – nor stable; it resists any attempt to subordinate description to the service of the humanistic ideal of 'dense' characters, and 'real' space. More strikingly perhaps, in a revisionist appreciation of description, Proust challenges the notion that a connection between appearance and person is possible at all, both in terms of visual bonding and of the flatness and fragmentation that vision also entails.

There are also spatial descriptions generated by the travelling gaze of an external focalizor, who fails to receive recognizable embodiment but in fact anticipates or otherwise represents particular characters' visions. The result is not the analogue of a photograph but of a film; specifically, of that device of the traveling shot that so precisely incorporates the moving image in space. The description of Yonville in *Madame Bovary*, which follows the devastating ending of the first part already quoted – 'Quand on partit de Tostes, au mois de mars, Mme Bovary était enceinte' – is a case in point. It deserves close analysis in view of constituting the travelling gaze that generates it, or rather, the gaze of the travel guide. That gaze binds character to space.

The procedural description is a typical case of naturalizing mimesis as 'make-believe.' While the character manipulates an object, the latter emerges for the viewer. The beginning of Zola's *L'assommoir* displays an entirely theatricalized fight between two women competing for the man who will bring the downfall of the winner. This is the occasion of the descriptive thrust that conjures up the women, the space of the public laundry pit, the extension of the space through the onlooking crowd, and the bone of contention that structures the fabula; the story can unfold after that. This is an excellent example of how spatial arrangement connects discourse to fabula, an arrangement that can be as artificial as it can be naturalizing. But the world that emerges appears, or is made to appear, so fleetingly as to accommodate Roland Barthes' formulation of seduction as 'the staging of an appearance-disappearance.' In other words, between the naturalization of the fabula world and its theatrical, artificial *mise-en-scène* in the story, there is a fine line that is constantly transgressed by fiction, leaving it up to the reader to go along in one direction or another.

To reiterate: the story consists of the operations of arrangement and qualification; the ways the fabula is presented. Due to this process, places are linked to certain points of perception. These places seen in relation to their perception constitute the story's space. That point of perception may be a character, which is situated in a space, observes it, and reacts to it. An anonymous point of perception can also dominate the presentation of certain places. The general question concerning the various points of perception, which lies at the root of every presentation, will be discussed later.

Space Perceived

In the story, where space is connected to the characters who 'live' it, the primary aspect of space is the way characters bring their senses to bear on space. Three senses are especially involved in the perceptual representation of space: sight, hearing, and touch. All three participate in the presentation of a space in the story. Shapes, colours, and sizes are perceived visually, always from a particular perspective. Sounds contribute to the presentation of space. If a character hears a low buzz, it is still at a certain distance from the speakers. If it can understand word for word what is being said, then it is situated much nearer, in the same room, for instance, or behind a thin screen. A church clock sounding in the distance increases the space; suddenly perceived whispering points to the proximity of the whisperer. Thirdly, there is touch. Tactile perceptions usually have little spatial significance. Touch indicates proximity. If a character feels walls on all sides, then it is confined in a very small space. Tactile perception is often used in a story to indicate the material, the substance of objects. Smell can contribute to the characterization of space but less obviously to its experience qua space. Taste is rarely relevant in this context.

With the help of these three senses, two kinds of relations pertain between characters and space. First, the space in which the character is situated, or is precisely not situated, is regarded as the *frame*. Second, the way in which that space is filled can also be indicated. A character can be situated in a space it experiences as secure, while earlier on, outside that space, it felt unsafe.

  a For hours, he wandered through the dark forest. All of a sudden, he saw a light. He hurried towards the house and knocked on the door. With a sigh of relief, he shut the door behind him a moment later.

Both inner and outer space function, in this instance, as a frame. Their opposition gives both spaces their meaning.

These meanings are not fixed. An inner space is often also experienced as unsafe, but with a somewhat different meaning. The inner space can, for instance, be experienced as confinement, while the outer space represents liberation and, consequently, security.

b With a sigh of relief he presently closed the door behind himself. Free at last!

In both examples, the frame has a highly symbolic function. Of course, this is far from always being the case. But culturally, it often is, and the boundary that delimits the frame can be heavily invested with meaning. Narratives can endorse that meaning, reject or change it, or play on different ways in which characters are situated in relation to it. And narrative quite frequently feeds off the horror of the invasion of space that leads to destruction. Buchi Emecheta's *The Rape of Shavi* tells of the future rape-victim, the prospective queen of Shavi, sweeping the entrance of the rapist's cabin as a sign of respect. This sign is mistaken for a sign of humble status, and taking the girl for a maid, the man feels free to rape her, showing how inextricably intertwined are racism, classism, and sexual violence. If Emecheta's fable ends unhappily, it is because misunderstanding – that of the man towards the woman and that of the albino (the novel's name for the whites the Shavians saw for the first time) towards the black culture – is the basis of behaviour. The young woman sweeps the doorstep – the boundary between the man's space and the outside world – as a homage, but:

> Ronje fell on her and, in less then ten minutes, took from the future queen of Shavi what the whole of Shavi stood for. To him, the Shavians were savages and Ayoko was just a serving girl. Though she fought, cried and begged, her pleading was gibberish to him, her resistance enhanced the vengeance he was taking on Shona.   94

The space of Shavi, protected from the outside world by the forest which is in turn a frame, is raped by the whites just as the princess is raped. The characters evolving within this frame and who inhabit this space are both strange, clearly allegorical, and very much 'like' real

people. Noticing both is essential for an interpretation that does justice
to the literary and political qualities of this novel, which, importantly,
cannot be separated. As happens often, rape of women is allegorically
related to invasion and destruction of space. The more allegorical this
fable, the more political becomes its moral.

Remember the descriptive passage from *Nightwood*. It began with, or
better, was framed by, the man looking into the room where a woman
was asleep – an eminently voyeuristic situation based on spatial divisions between private and public space:

> On the second landing of the hotel … a door was standing open,
> exposing a red carpeted floor, and at the further end two narrow
> windows overlooked the square.

The framing is primarily spatial. It is here that the man 'discovers' the
woman he will marry. This frame overdetermines the connections between text (descriptive), story (where seeing, here, is the sole form of
focalization), and fabula (the meeting of the two actors). In the world
narrative conjures up – a world of make-believe – things can happen
because that world is spatial. It gives space to events, so that events can,
as the phrase goes, *take place*.

The objects that can be found in space determine the filling in of that
space. Objects have spatial status. They determine the spatial effect
of the room by their shape, measurements, and colours. A cluttered
room seems smaller, a sparsely furnished room bigger than in fact it
is. Strangely, an empty room seems smaller again. This sensory effect
does not have fixed meanings attached to it. This is culturally specific.
Westerners consider emptiness a challenge: it must be filled, but how?
Japanese, I have been told, see an empty room as storage of endless
possibilities. This difference in interpretation leads to divergent traditions in interior decoration. The way in which objects are arranged in
a space, the configuration of objects, also influences the perception of
that space. In some stories, an object or objects are sometimes presented
in detail. In other stories, space may be presented in a vague and implicit manner.

Content and Function

The semantic content of spatial aspects can be constructed in the same
way as the semantic content of a character. Here, too, we find a prelimi-

nary combination of determination, repetition, accumulation, transformation, and the relations between various spaces.

Determination is again achieved on the basis of the reader's frame
of reference. When a certain event is situated in Dublin, this will mean
something different to the reader who is well acquainted with the city
than to the reader who only knows that Dublin is a large city. The oppressive atmosphere of a dwelling in one of the poorer districts of Dublin is presented in a fairly detailed way in Joyce's *A Portrait of the Artist
as a Young Man*. Those who are already familiar with that atmosphere
will immediately be able to visualize much more, and for them the no-
tations 'in the kitchen' and 'in the parlour' will evoke much more precise images. On the other hand, the unknowing reader has the freedom
to imagine, to construct the kitchen and parlour and test that construction against information provided as we read on.

Determination functions here too on the basis of the general application of characteristics. One big city has a number of characteristics in
common with every big city. This also applies to the country, a village,
a street, a house, and every general category. The more precise the
presentation of a space, the greater the number of specific qualities
added to the general ones, which then become steadily less dominating. But general characteristics never cease to function. Only by means
of general characteristics is it possible to create an image at all.

Spaces function in a story in different ways. On the one hand, they
are only a frame, a place of action. In this capacity a more or less detailed presentation will lead to a more or less concrete picture of that
space. The space can also remain entirely in the background. In many
cases, however, space is thematized: it becomes an object of presentation itself, for its own sake. Space thus becomes an acting place rather
than the place of action. It influences the fabula, and the fabula becomes
subordinate to the presentation of space. The fact that 'this is happening here' is just as important as 'the way it is here,' which allows these
events to happen. In both cases, where both frame-space and thematized space are concerned, space can function steadily or dynamically.
A steady space is a fixed frame, thematized or not, within which the
events take place. A dynamically functioning space is a factor which
allows for the movement of characters. Characters walk, and therefore
need a path. They travel, and so need a large space, countries, seas, air.
The hero of a fairy tale has to traverse a dark forest to prove his courage. So there is a forest.

That space is not present as a fixed frame, but as a passage to be taken, and can vary greatly. From a fast train, the traveller does not see the trees separately, but as one long, blurred line. Proust has masterful passages which explore in detail how speed changes the vision of, and thereby the way of being in, space. Or the sound of a bird suddenly changes the space radically. Space is indicated exactly for this reason, as a space in which the traveller is moving. To put it differently, a traveller in narrative is in a sense always an allegory of the travel that narrative is.

Strategically, the movement of characters can constitute a transition from one space to another. Often, one space will be the other's opposite. A person is travelling, for instance, from a negative to a positive space – or vice versa. The space need not be the goal of that move. The latter may have quite a different aim, with space representing an important or an unimportant interim between departure and arrival, difficult or easy to traverse.

The character that is moving towards a goal need not always arrive in another space. In many travel stories, the movement is a goal in itself. It is expected to result in a change, liberation, introspection, wisdom, or knowledge. It tends to be gender-specific as well: in traditional genres, men travel, whereas women stay at home. As a result, the development of epic literature is bound up with men, that of lyric literature with women. This is not to say that narrative is a men's mode. There is no direct determining line from epic to the novel, and the case can be made that the novel emerged as a women's genre. In this respect, recent revivals of epic emerging out of postcolonial recuperations of space offer a great challenge to any deterministic presuppositions about the development of genres. Epic tends to become bound up less with a glorious mythical past of conquest than with a resistance to such conquests and a renewed attempt of the former colonized to 'take place': to provide the occupied space with a fabula that affirms their own belonging to it. Space then, becomes a site of memory (see 'Focalization').

If such an experiential aim is lacking, even implicitly, the movement, totally aimless, can function simply as a presentation of space. The move can be a circular one: the character returns to its point of departure. In this way, space is presented as a labyrinth, as unsafety, as confinement. The question of how space is experienced by the character in relation to whom it is presented is more important than generalizing answers.

Relations to Other Aspects

Relations between the various aspects on the story level arise because of the way in which they are combined and presented. The same holds for relations between aspects and the various elements of the fabula. The relations between space and event become clear if we think of well-known, stereotypical combinations: declarations of love by moonlight on a balcony, high-flown reveries on a mountain-top, a rendezvous in an inn, ghostly appearances among ruins, brawls in cafés. In medieval literature, love-scenes frequently take place in a special space, appropriate to the occasion, the so-called *locus amoenus*, consisting of a meadow, a tree, and a running stream. Such a fixed combination is called a *topos*. In the literature of later periods, too, certain combinations occur which are sometimes characteristic of a writer, sometimes of a movement, and sometimes even of a novel. The expectation that a clearly marked space will function as the frame of a suitable event can also be frustrated.

The most obvious place to expect examples of the relations between space and character in modern literature would seem to be the naturalistic novel, since it claims to depict the influence of the environment on people. A person's housing is especially connected to his character, his way of life, and his possibilities. In this sense, *A Portrait of the Artist as a Young Man* could also be regarded as naturalistic. Stephen Dedalus is obviously a product of impoverished circumstances. His way of life, his poor diet, his incessant scratching because of lice, his family's constant moves to ever-shabbier neighbourhoods are in complete accordance with the space in which he lives. The spatial position in which characters are situated at a certain moment often influences their mood. A space, situated high up, sometimes causes spirits to be high, so that the character is exalted (Stendhal). A highly situated space, where the character happens not to be, but which it is looking up to, or with which it is confronted in some other way, can depress the character by its very inaccessibility (Kafka, *The Castle*).

In the first image you see a young girl from behind. She is walking on a deserted beach. She is looking down and is paddling a bit with her foot in the wet sand. Her back alone shows depression. She is totally self-enclosed, out of reach, beyond help. A male voice-over begins to explain what is the matter with her. As the beach girl fades

out, we see the authoritative but gentle face of the man who knows:
an American therapist. He explains how abused children don't dare
to speak. Fear of disbelief. Body language is their only means of expression. Then, in the third image, the subject herself, now a woman,
quietly and intelligently explains her case: 'I was about fifteen and
I wanted so much to die.' Then you see her run on the beach. And
then, in a different voice, she reads from a letter: 'Yes, it is true that I
have been raped. So what?' Signed: The Lady.

This is the beginning of an award-winning documentary film, *Denial*,
about a young woman called Brigitte, thirty years old. It is a documentary that shows the phenomenon of multiple personality syndrome:
different personalities split off out of self-defence. The Lady is one
such 'alter': a tough yet well-brought-up lady, who is close to Brigitte's
mother and tries to create some order in the chaos of Brigitte's life.

The intelligent, impressive, beautiful, and brave Brigitte appears before us in her many, diverse appearances, and each alter has a space.
There is the compulsive house-cleaner, who is bossed about by The
Lady and must clean her apartment every single day; with a wet towel,
please, no cheating. We only see her in the confining, overly neat bourgeois apartment. There is The Lady herself, who was conjured up when
Brigitte was twelve, 'to keep things a bit together.' The Lady hates
chaos, and Brigitte's life was in constant danger of becoming chaotic.
The Lady sits on the stone wall in the cloister of Utrecht Cathedral.
There is The Little One, who moves back and forth on a swing, her
hands hidden in her sleeves 'because I don't like hands; hands are dan-
gerous,' and who plays in the yard. The Silent Beach Girl walks the
empty beach between sand and water, because she doesn't like people.
The Tough One, boyish in leather jacket, who is like a coach, encour-
ages the others to sustain the incredible effort to keep going. The Tough
One appears in noisy bars, pool halls, and train stations; it's the only
one who might travel. A whole team of specialists, all indispensable for
that leaden burden: suffering sexual violence. The stable relationship
between space and 'alter' is all this girl can boast as stability. Ignoring
that relationship would be a denial of how this film could be made into
a narrative that we can process.

The relationship between time and space is of importance for the
narrative rhythm. When a space is presented extensively, an interruption of the time sequence is unavoidable, unless the perception of the
space takes place gradually (in time) and can therefore be regarded as an

event. When a character enters a church to sight-see and the interior of the church is presented 'during' its tour, there is no interruption. Spatial indications are always durative (an extreme case of iteration). After all, a permanent object is always involved. In this sense, too, the chronology is always disrupted by spatial indications. Moreover, information concerning space is often repeated, to stress the stability of the frame, as opposed to the transitory nature of the events that occur within it.

Information

As I have said before, space is always implicitly necessary for every activity performed by a character. If a character is cycling, we know that it is outside and is riding on a path or a road. We assume that it sleeps in a bed. In fact, if the information is added that it is sleeping soundly, then we assume that the bed is warm and comfortable.

There are various ways of explicitly presenting information about space. Sometimes a very short indication, without details, is sufficient:

c At home, John puts down the shopping-bag, with a sigh.

d As soon as he had shut the door, John placed the shopping-bag underneath the coat-rack.

In c the indication of space is minimal; we only know that John is again inside, in his own home. Earlier presentations of that house will determine whether we are able to visualize in a more or less detailed way what the space is like in which he is situated. In d we know more, even if this indication is also quite brief. We know that, within the context of Western European floor plans, he is in the hall and that he has not, for instance, walked straight through to the kitchen. So he came in through the front door.

When separate segments of narrative are devoted to the presentation of information about space alone, we have descriptions. The space is then not simply indicated in passing, but is an explicit object of presentation.

I crossed the staircase landing, and entered the room she indicated. From that room, too, the daylight was completely excluded, and it had an airless smell that was oppressive. A fire had been lately kindled in the damp old-fashioned grate, and it was more disposed to go out than to burn up, and the reluctant smoke which hung in the room seemed colder than the clearer air – like our own marsh mist. Certain wintry branches of candles on the high chimney-piece faintly lighted the chamber; or, it would be more expressive to say, faintly troubled its darkness. It was spacious, and I dare say had once been handsome, but every discernible thing in it was covered with dust and mould, and dropping to pieces. The most prominent object was a long table with a tablecloth spread on it, as if a feast had been in preparation when the house and the clocks all stopped together. An epergne or centre-piece of some kind was in the middle of this cloth; it was so heavily overhung with cobwebs that its form was quite undistinguishable; and, as I looked along the yellow expanse out of which I remember its seeming to grow like a black fungus, I saw speckledlegged spiders with blotchy bodies running home to it, and running out from it, as if some circumstance of the greatest public importance had just transpired in the spider community.

Charles Dickens, Great Expectations

This description is linked to the perception of the character: its elaborateness is motivated by the fact that that character is entering this space for the first time. Consequently, the boy is curious and takes in every detail. At the same time, he judges, which is announced in the second sentence. These aspects of the description – the point of perception, the motivation, and the relation between perception and opinion – will be discussed later in this chapter. For the moment, the point to note is that, in such a fragment, space is presented explicitly, as an independent element. In some realistic novels, descriptions of space are executed with great precision. It is important that the realistic aspects in such descriptions be clearly visible: the space must resemble the actual world, so that the events situated within it also become plausible.

Finally, a space is sometimes indicated explicitly, not because of an action taking place in it, but because of an action performed with it. An expression like 'we crashed into a tree' (*Something Very Sorry*, 7) belongs to this category of indications. People do walk into walls, literally and figuratively, if a space is too small, confined. Other examples are to scale a fence, to escape from prison, to lock someone in, to hide something, to clear a path through the jungle, to ascend to heaven, to go to hell. The effect of information about space is not only determined by the way in which it is conveyed. The distance from which the space is presented also affects the image which emerges. If a space is presented from far away, an overview of the whole is usually given, without details. Conversely, a space which is presented from nearby will be described in a detailed way, but the overview will be missing.

Both the image of a character and the image of a space which are offered to the reader are finally determined by the way in which the character and space are seen. The question 'Who is seeing?' is therefore an important aspect.

8: Focalization

Background

The axiom of this section is that whenever events are presented, they are always presented from within a certain 'vision.' A point of view is chosen, a certain way of seeing things, a certain angle, whether 'real' historical facts are concerned or fictitious events. This slanted, or why not say the word, subjective nature of story-telling is inevitable, and denying it constitutes in my mind a dubious political act. Sure, it is possible to try and give an 'objective' picture of the facts. But what does that involve? 'Objectivity' is an attempt to present only what is seen or is perceived in some other way. All comment is shunned and implicit interpretation is also avoided. Perception, however, is a psychosomatic process, strongly dependent on the position of the perceiving body; a small child sees things in a totally different way from an adult, if only as far as measurements are concerned. The degree to which one is familiar with what one sees also influences perception. When the inhabitants of Emecheta's allegorical country Shavi saw white people for the first time, they saw albinos: normal black people with a skin defect.

Perception depends on so many factors that striving for objectivity is pointless. To mention only a few factors: one's position with respect to the perceived object, the fall of the light, the distance, previous knowledge, psychological attitude towards the object; all this and more affects the picture one forms and passes on to others. Story-telling is one form of such passing on. In a story, elements of the fabula are therefore necessarily presented in a certain way. We are confronted with a vision of the fabula. What is this vision like and where does it come from? These are the questions that will be discussed in what follows. I shall refer to the relations between the elements presented and the vision through which they are presented with the term *focalization*. Focalization is, then, the relation between the vision and that which is 'seen,' perceived. By using this term I wish to dissociate myself from a number of current terms in this area, for the following reasons.

The theory of narration, as it has been developed in the course of the twentieth century, offers various labels for the concept here referred to. The most current one is *point of view* or *narrative perspective*. Narrative situation, narrative viewpoint, narrative manner are also employed. More or less elaborate typologies of 'narrative points of view' have been developed, of which I shall include the most well-known in my bibliography. All these typologies have proved more or less useful. They are all, however, unclear on one point. They do not make a distinction between, on the one hand, the vision through which the elements are presented and, on the other, the identity of the voice that is verbalizing that vision. To put it more simply: they do not make a distinction between those who see and those who speak. Nevertheless, it is possible, both in fiction and in reality, for one person to express the vision of another. This is a key feature of language and it happens all the time. When no distinction is made between these two different agents, it is difficult to describe adequately the technique of a text in which something is seen – *and* that vision is narrated. The imprecisions of such typologies can sometimes lead to absurd formulations or classifications which are too rough-and-ready. To claim, as has been done, that Strether in Henry James' *The Ambassadors* is 'telling his own story,' whereas the novel is written 'in the third person,' is as nonsensical as to claim that the sentence:

a Elizabeth saw him lie there, pale and lost in thought.

is narrated, from the comma onwards, by the character Elizabeth; that means it is spoken by her. What this sentence does is to present Elizabeth's vision clearly: after all, she does see him lying down.

If we examine the current terms from this point of view, only the term *perspective* seems clear enough. This label covers both the physical and the psychological points of perception. It does not cover the agent that is performing the action of narration, and it should not do so. Nevertheless, my own preference lies with the term *focalization* for two reasons and despite justly raised objections to the introduction of unnecessary new terminology. The first reason concerns tradition. Although the word 'perspective' reflects precisely what is meant here, it has come to indicate in the tradition of narrative theory both the narrator and the vision. This ambiguity has affected the specific sense of the word. I also find its use in art history too different from the literary one to maintain it in a theory that has also applicability for visual images.

There is yet another, more practical, objection to this term. No noun can be derived from 'perspective' that could indicate the subject of the action; nor is the verb 'to perspectivize' customary. In a subject-oriented theory such as this one, in order to describe the focalization in a story we must have terms from which subject and verb can be derived. These two arguments seemed to me to be weighty enough to justify my choice of a new term for a not completely new concept. Focalization offers a number of extra, minor advantages as well. It is a term that looks technical. It is derived from photography and film; its technical nature is thus emphasized, even if the term is best abstracted from its specific visual slant. As any 'vision' presented can have a strongly manipulative effect, and is, consequently, very difficult to extract from the emotions, not only from those attributed to the focalizor and the character but also from those of the reader, a technical term will help us keep our attention on the technical side of such a means of manipulation. 'Technicality' is just another tool, but a strategically useful one. It helps understand, not only follow our emotions.

The Focalizor

In Southern India, at Mahaballipuram, is what is said to be the largest bas-relief in the world, the seventh-century *Arjuna's Penance.* At the upper left, the wise man Arjuna is depicted in a yoga position. At the bottom right stands a cat. Around the cat are a number of mice. The mice are laughing (see illustration). It is a strange image. Unless the spectator interprets the signs. The interpretation runs as follows. Arjuna is in a yoga position and is meditating to win Lord Siva's favour. The cat, impressed by the beauty of absolute calm, imitates Arjuna. Now the mice realize they are safe. They laugh. Without this interpretation, there is no relation between the parts of the relief. Within this interpretation, the parts form a meaningful narrative.

The picture is quite funny. The comical effect is evoked by the narrativity of the picture. The spectator sees the relief as a whole. Its contents include a succession in time. First, Arjuna assumes the yoga position. Then, the cat imitates him. After that, the mice start laughing. These three successive events are logically related in a causal chain. According to every definition I know, that means this is a fabula.

But there is more. Not only are the events chronologically in succes-

(drawing: Fransje van Zoest)

sion and logically in a causal relation. They can only occur through the semiotic activity of the actors. And the comical effect can only be explained when this particular mediation is analysed. We laugh because we can identify with the mice. Seeing what they see, we realize with them that a meditating cat is a contradiction; cats hunt, and only wise men meditate. Following the chain of events in reverse, we also arrive at the next one by perceptual identification. The cat has brought about the event for which he is responsible because he has seen Arjuna do something. This chain of perceptions also runs in time. The wise man sees nothing, since he is totally absorbed in his meditation; the cat has seen Arjuna and now sees nothing more of this world; the mice see the cat and Arjuna. That is why they know they are safe. (Another interpretation is that the cat is simulating; this doesn't weaken my statements but only adds an element of suspense to the fabula.) The mice are laughing because of that very fact, finding the imitation a ridiculous enterprise. The spectator sees more. She sees the mice, the cat, and the wise man. She laughs at the cat, and she laughs sympathetically with the mice, whose pleasure is comparable to that felt by a successful scoundrel.

This example illustrates quite clearly the theory of focalization. Incidentally, it also suggests that, and how, narratological concepts are relevant for the analysis of visual narrative without absorbing the image in language. We can view the picture of the relief as a (visual) sign. The elements of this sign, the standing Arjuna, the standing cat, the laughing mice, only have spatial relations to one another. The elements of the fabula – Arjuna assumes a yoga position, the cat assumes a yoga position, the mice laugh – do not form a coherent significance as such. The relation between the sign (the relief) and its contents (the fabula) can only be established by mediation of an interjacent layer, the 'view' of the events. The cat sees Arjuna. The mice see the cat. The spectator sees the mice who sees the cat who has seen Arjuna. And the spectator sees that the mice are right. Every verb of perception (to see) in this report indicates an activity of focalization. Every verb of action indicates an event.

Focalization is the relationship between the 'vision,' the agent that sees, and that which is seen. This relationship is a component of the story part, of the content of the narrative text: A says that B sees what C is doing. Sometimes that difference is void, e.g., when the reader is presented with a vision as directly as possible. The different agents then cannot be isolated; they coincide. That is a form of 'stream of consciousness.' But the speech act of narrating is still different from the vision, the memories, the sense perceptions, thoughts, that are being told. Nor can that vision be conflated with the events they focus, orient, interpret. Consequently, focalization belongs in the story, the layer between the linguistic text and the fabula. Because the definition of focalization refers to a relationship, each pole of that relationship, the subject and the object of focalization, must be studied separately. The subject of focalization, the focalizor, is the point from which the elements are viewed. That point can lie with a character (i.e., an element of the fabula), or outside it.

If the focalizor coincides with the character, that character will have an advantage over the other characters. The reader watches with the character's eyes and will, in principle, be inclined to accept the vision presented by that character. In Mulisch's 'Massuro,' we see with the eyes of the character who later also draws up a report of the events. The first symptoms of Massuro's strange disease are the phenomena the other perceives. These phenomena communicate Massuro's condition to us; they tell us nothing about the way he feels about it. Such a character-bound focalizor, which we could label, for convenience' sake, CF, brings about bias and limitation. In Henry James' *What Maisie Knew*, the focalization, whenever it is character-bound, lies almost entirely with Maisie, a little girl who does not understand much about the problematic relations going on around her. Consequently, the reader is shown the events through the limited vision of the girl, and only gradually realizes what is actually going on. But the reader is not a little girl. He does more with the information he receives than Maisie does, he interprets it differently. Where Maisie sees only a strange gesture, the reader knows that he is dealing with an erotic one. The difference between the childish vision of the events and the interpretation that the adult reader gives to them determines the novel's special effect. But the narrator is not a child. James is perhaps the most radical experimenter whose project was to demonstrate that, in the terminology of this book, narrator and focalizor are not to be conflated.

A special case of focalization and perhaps the best justification for the distinction I am making is memory. Memory is an act of 'vision' of the past but, as an act, situated in the present of the memory. It is often a narrative act: loose elements come to cohere into a story, so that they can be remembered and eventually told. But as is well known, memories are unreliable – in relation to the fabula – and when put into words, they are rhetorically overworked so that they can connect to an audience, for example, a therapist. Hence, the 'story' the person remembers is not identical to the one she experienced. This discrepancy becomes dramatic and, indeed, incapacitating in the case of trauma. Traumatic events disrupt the capacity to comprehend and experience them at the time of their occurrence. As a result the traumatized person cannot remember them; instead, they recur in bits and pieces, in nightmares, and cannot be 'worked through.' The incapability that paralyses the traumatized person can be situated on both story and text levels. The events can be so incongruous that no fabula can be 'recognized' as 'logical' enough to make sense, at the moment of occurrence. At the later time of remembrance the subject cannot shape a story out of them. The two moments fail to provide a framework for a meaningful act of focalization. On the text level, even if, thanks to efficacious therapy or other forms of help, memories have been formed – a story has come to cohere – the subject 'lacks words.'

Memory is also the joint between time and space. Especially in stories set in former colonies, the memory evokes a past in which people were dislodged from their space by colonizers who occupied it, but also, a past in which they did not yield. Going back – in retroversion – to the time in which the place was a different kind of space is a way of countering the effects of colonizing acts of focalization that can be called mapping. Mastering, looking from above, dividing up and controlling is an approach to space that ignores time as well as the density of its lived-in quality. In opposition to such ways of seeing space, providing a landscape with a history is a way of spatializing memory that undoes the killing of space as lived. In *Texaco*, Chamoiseau's fictional or allegorical recuperation of Martinique, he has his converted urban planner say, when he gives up destroying the city to build the road 'Penetrante Ouest'(!):

> Razing Texaco, as I was asked to do, would amount to amputating the city from one part of its future, and especially from the irreplaceable richness of memory. The Creole city, which has so few monuments, becomes a monument itself by virtue of the care it puts into the sites of its memory. The monument, here as in all of America, does not rise up monumentally: it irradiates.   369

Marginal as the site is, it must be preserved, the former urban planner concludes, because it is the site of memory of the slaves' art of survival on which this space now bases its future. In this passage, 'rising up' in monumentality, just as much as the allegorically named road 'Penetrante Ouest,' embodies the result of a focalization that is destructive of the past, hence, of the future. Irradiation is the alternative way of being of the space that is focalized from within. As Edouard Glissant, a theorist who influenced Chamoiseau's writing, argued: 'the landscape in the work ceases to be merely a decor or a confidant in order to inscribe itself as constitutive of being' (199). This idea of a historically meaningful, heavily political investment of space can help to interpret stories in which a narratological analysis reveals the intricate relationship between characters, time, and space.

Character-bound focalization (CF) can vary, can shift from one character to another, even if the narrator remains constant. In such cases, we may be given a good picture of the origins of a conflict. We are shown how differently the various characters view the same facts. This technique can result in neutrality towards all the characters. Nevertheless, there usually is not a doubt in our minds which character should receive most attention and sympathy. On the grounds of distribution, for instance the fact that a character focalizes the first and/or the last chapter, we label it the hero(ine) of the book.

When focalization lies with one character which participates in the fabula as an actor, we could refer to internal focalization. We can then indicate by means of the term *external focalization* that an anonymous agent, situated outside the fabula, is functioning as focalizor. Such an external, non-character-bound focalizor is abbreviated EF. In the following fragment from the opening of Doris Lessing's *The Summer before the Dark* we see the focalization move from EF to CF.

> b   A woman stood on her back step, arms folded, waiting.
>
> Thinking? She would not have said so. She was trying to catch hold of something, or to lay it bare so that she could look and define; for some time now she had been 'trying on' ideas like so many dresses off a rack. She was letting words and phrases as worn as nursery rhymes slide around her tongue: for towards the crucial experiences custom allots certain attitudes, and they are pretty stereotyped. *Ah yes, first love! ... Growing up is bound to be painful! ... My first child, you know ... But I was in love! ... Marriage is a compromise ... I am not as young as I once was.*

From sentence 2 onwards the contents of what the character experiences are given. A switch thus occurs from an external focalizor (EF) to an internal one (CF). An alternation between external and internal focalizors, between EF and CF, is visible in a good many stories. In *The Evenings*, Frits is the only character that functions as focalizor. Therefore, the two different focalizors are EF and CF (Frits). A number of characters can also alternate as CF focalizor; in that case, it can be useful to indicate the various characters in the analysis by their initials, so that one can retain a clear overview of the division of focalization: in Frits' case, this would mean the notation CF (Frits). An example of a story in which a great many different characters act as focalizor is *Of Old People*. However, the characters do not carry an equal load; some focalize often, others only a little, some do not focalize at all. It is also possible for the entire story to be focalized by EF. The narrative can then appear objective, because the events are not presented from the point of view of the characters. The focalizor's bias is, then, not absent, since there is no such thing as 'objectivity,' but it remains implicit.

The Focalized Object

In *Of Old People* Harold is usually the focalizor when the events in the Indies are being focalized; Lot often focalizes his mother, mama Ottilie, and it is mainly because of this that we receive a fairly likeable image of her despite her unfriendly behaviour. Evidently, it is important to ascertain which character focalizes which object. The combination of a focalizor and a focalized object can be constant to a large degree (Harold–Indies; Lot–mama Ottilie), or it can vary greatly. Analysis of such fixed or loose combinations matters because the image we receive of the object is determined by the focalizor. Conversely, the image a focalizor presents of an object says something about the focalizor itself. Where focalization is concerned, the following questions are relevant.

1 What does the character focalize: what is it aimed at?
2 How does it do this: with what attitude does it view things?
3 Who focalizes it: whose focalized object is it?

What is focalized by a character F? It need not be a character. Objects, landscapes, events, in short all the elements are focalized, either by an EF or by a CF. Because of this fact alone, we are presented with a certain, far from innocent, interpretation of the elements. The degree to which a presentation includes an opinion can, of course, vary: the degree to which the focalizor points out its interpretative activities and makes them explicit also varies. Compare, for instance, the following descriptions of place:

c Behind the round and spiny forms around us in the depth endless coconut plantations stretch far into the hazy blue distance where mountain ranges ascend ghostlike. Closer, at my side, a ridged and ribbed violet grey mountainside stretches upward with a saw-tooth silhouette combing the white cloudy sky. Dark shadows of the clouds lie at random on the slopes as if capricious dark-grey pieces of cloth have been dropped on them. Close by, in a temple niche, Buddha sits meditating in an arched window of shadow. A dressing-jacket of white exudation of bird-droppings

on his shoulders. Sunshine on his hands which lie together per-
fectly at rest.

Jan Wolkers, *The Kiss*

d Then we must first describe heaven, of course. Then the hundreds
   of rows of angels are clad in glorious shiny white garments. Every
   one of them has long, slightly curly fair hair and blue eyes. There
   are no men here. 'How strange that all angels should be women.'
   There are no dirty angels with seductive panties, garterbelts and
   stockings, not to mention bras. I always pictured an angel as a
   woman who presents her breasts as if on saucers, with heavily
   made-up eyes, and a bright red mouth, full of desire, eager to
   please, in short, everything a woman should be. (Formerly, when
   I was still a student, I wanted to transform Eve into a real whore. I
   bought her everything necessary, but she did not want to wear the
   stuff.)

J.M.A. Biesheuvel, 'Faust,' *The Way to the Light*

In both cases, a CF is clearly involved; both focalizors may be localized
in the character 'I.' In c, the spatial position of the CF ('I') is especially
striking. It is obviously situated on a high elevation, considering the
wide prospect it has. The words 'around us,' combined with 'in the
depth,' stress that high position. The proximity of the niche with the
Buddha statue makes clear that CF ('I') is situated in an eastern temple
(the Burubudur in fact), so that 'the round and spiny forms' (must) refer to the temple roof. The presentation of the whole, temple roof and
landscape, seems fairly impersonal. If the CF ('I') had not been identified itself by the use of the first-person personal pronoun in 'at my side'
and 'around us,' this would have seemed, on the face of it, an 'objective'
description, perhaps taken from a pamphlet or geography book.

On closer analysis, this is not the case. Whether the CF ('I') is explicitly named or not, the 'internal' position of the focalizor is, in fact, already established by expressions such as 'close by,' 'closer,' and 'at my
side,' which underline the proximity of the place to the perceiver. 'Behind' and 'far into' indicate a specification of the spatial perspective (in
the pictorial sense). But more happens here. Without appearing to do
so, this presentation interprets. This is clear from the use of metaphors,
which points to the facts that the CF ('I') attempts to reduce the objects
it sees, which impress it a good deal, to human, everyday proportions.
In this way, the CF ('I') is undoubtedly trying to fit the object into its

own realm of experience. Images like 'saw-tooth' and 'combing,' 'capricious dark-grey pieces of cloth,' and clichés like 'mountain ranges' bear this out. The 'dressing-jacket of white exudation of bird-droppings' is the clearest example. Actually, the image is also interesting because of the association mechanism it exhibits. With the word 'dressing-jacket,' the Buddha's statue becomes human, and as soon as it is human, the white layer on its head could easily be dandruff, a possibility suggested by the word 'exudation.' The realistic nature of the presentation – CF ('I') does 'really' see the landscape – is restored immediately afterwards by the information about the real nature of the white layer: bird-droppings. Thus, what we see here is the presentation of a landscape which is realistic, reflecting what is actually perceived, and at the same time interpreting the view in a specific way, so that it can be assimilated by the character.

Example d exhibits to a certain extent the same characteristics. Here, too, an impressive space is humanized. However, the CF ('I') observes the object less and interprets it more. It concerns a fantasy object with which the CF ('I') is sketchily familiar from religious literature and painting, but which it can adapt as much as it wishes, to its own taste. This is what it does, and its taste is clear, and clearly specific, bound to gender.

Here, too, an association mechanism is visible. From the traditional image of angels, implied in the second or third sentence, the CF ('I') moves to the assumption that angels are women. In this, the vision already deviates from the traditional vision, in which angels are asexual or male. Against the image thus created of asexual male angels, the CF ('I') sets up, in contrast, its own female image, which by now has moved very far away from the image that we have of angels.

And even before the reader realizes that in doing so a link is made with another tradition, that of the opposition angel-whore, in which 'angel' is used in a figurative sense, the word 'whore' itself appears in the text. In this, the interpretive mode of the description manifests itself clearly. The solemn 'we' of the beginning contrasts sharply with the personal turn which the description takes. The humour is here based on the contrast between the solemn-impersonal and the personal-everyday. (Humour does make one uncomfortable if one is not happy with what is being laughed at, but it is still humour.) The interpretive focalization is emphasized in several ways. The sentence in quotation marks is presented as a reaction to the sentence preceding it. Here, the interpreting focalizor makes an explicit entrance. Later this is stressed

again: 'not to mention' is a colloquial expression, and points at a personal subject, expressing an opinion. 'I always pictured an angel as ...'
accentuates even more strongly that a personal opinion is involved.

The way in which an object is presented gives information about that
object itself and about the focalizor. These two descriptions give even
more information about the CF ('I') than about the objects; more about
the way they experience nature (c) or women (d), respectively, than
about the Burubudur temple and heaven. In this respect, it doesn't matter whether the object 'really exists' in actuality, or is part of a fictitious
fabula, or whether it is a fantasy created by the character and so a dou-
bly fictitious object. The comparison with the object referred to served
in the above analysis only to motivate the interpretation by the CF ('I')
in both fragments. The internal structure of the descriptions provides
in itself sufficient clues about the degree to which one CF ('I') showed a
similarity to and differed from the other.

These two examples indicate yet another distinction. In c the object of
the focalization was perceptible. The CF ('I') 'really' sees something that
is outside itself. This is not always the case. An object can also be visible only inside the 'head,' 'mind,' or 'feelings' of the CF – all terms that
project human features and reactions onto a paper person, of course.
And only those who have access to that charater's 'inside' can perceive
anything. This perceiver cannot be another character, at least not according to the classical rules of the narrative genre, but it might possibly be an EF. Such a 'non-perceptible' object occurs in cases where, for
instance, the contents of a character's dream are presented. Concerning
the heaven in d, we can only find out whether that object is perceptible
or not perceptible when we know how the fragment fits into its context.
If the 'I,' together with another person – a devil, for instance – is on an
excursion to heaven, we will have to accept the first part of the description, until the sentence in quotation marks, as 'perceptible.'

Thus, our criterion is that within the fabula there must be another character present that can also perceive the object; if they are the
dreams, fantasies, thoughts, or feelings of a character, then these objects
can be part of the category 'non-perceptible' objects. This distinction
can be indicated by adding to the notation of the focalizor a 'p' or a
'np.' For b we end up with CF (woman)–np; for c, CF ('I')–p, and for d,
CF ('I')–np. This distinction too is of importance for an insight into the
power structure between the characters. When in a conflict situation
one character is allotted both CF–p and CF–np, and the other exclusively
CF–p, then the first character has the advantage as a party in the conflict.

It can give the reader insight into its feelings and thoughts, while the other character cannot communicate anything.

Moreover, the other character will not have the insight which the reader receives, so that it cannot react to the feelings of the other (which it does not know), cannot adapt itself to them or oppose them. Such an inequality in position between characters is obvious in the so-called 'first-person novels,' but in other kinds this inequality is not always as clear to the reader. Yet the latter is manipulated by it in forming an opinion about the various characters. Consequently, the focalization has a strongly manipulative effect. Colette's novel *The Cat* is a strong case: the reader is manipulated, practically by this device alone, into taking the man's side against his wife.

In this respect, the point is to keep sight of the difference between spoken and unspoken words of the characters. Spoken words are audible to others and are thus perceptible when the focalization lies with someone else. Unspoken words – thoughts, internal monologues – no matter how extensive, are not perceptible to other characters. Here, too, lies a possibility for manipulation which is often used. Readers are given elaborate information about the thoughts of a character, which the other characters do not hear. If these thoughts are placed in between the sections of dialogue, readers do not often realize how much less the other character knows than they do. An analysis of the perceptibility of the focalized objects supplies insight into these objects' relationships.

Narrative is also an important element of the rhetoric of scholarship. The following case involves a term that is both an ordinary word – not metaphorical at all – and a concept deployed for cultural analysis. Since in this case the texts stem from an ancient culture – hence, different from our own – the authors were careful not to project anachronistically contemporary norms onto the past. The issue is the question whether in the ancient Middle East something like 'just war' was thinkable, and whether rape could be an acceptable practice therein.

The author, biblical scholar Susan Niditch, struggles with the difficulty that ethical norms differ according to time and place, and the language in which we write about other cultures is also time- and place-bound. In that context she raises the question whether 'just war' – in the biblical framework, 'holy war' – is possible and, if so, whether in such a war the practice we call rape can have a place. Thus she writes about the biblical book of Numbers:

Of course, enslaving the enemy (20:11) and forcing its women into marriage are the terms of an oppressive regime and difficult to imagine under the heading of that which is just.   Niditch 1993

What concerns me in the sentence is that, in the attempt to avoid anachronism, something is nevertheless carried over, a description (equally anachronistic, by the way) of rape. The author wished to avoid that term because of its anachronism, and the concessive clause in which the description 'oppressive regime' occurred was meant to help that avoidance. 'Forcing its women into marriage' is Niditch's attempt to avoid the anachronism. She doesn't want to call the action rape, she argues, because, in the culture under discussion, it was not perceived as such. Even if the war cannot be called just, the taking of women is culturally acceptable, and therefore cannot be called rape. This is undeniably a sound argument. Except for one aspect.

Niditch replaces 'rape' with 'forcing into marriage'; elsewhere, the action is called wife-stealing. As a cultural phenomenon it is in some cultures acceptable and ordinary, and is known in anthropological and historical studies. I see Niditch's point that 'rape' is an obscuring term that fails to address the cultural status of the event. Also, it seems pointless to accuse the biblical culture, three thousand years after the fact, of a violation of human rights and thus feel better about our own behaviour. Yet, the alternative is unacceptable to me. Rather, in the awareness and acknowledgment that the term is 'ours' – and leads to a lot of disagreement in the culture I live in – I would like to take a closer look at the contested term, 'rape.'

That word is more often used as a noun than as a verb – which is my first worry. Like 'secret' in my earlier example, it is one of those nouns which imply a story.' Rape – the action for which we use that term: sexually appropriating another subject without (mostly) her or (also sometimes) his consent – has different meanings in different times and cultures. Its meaning depends on the status of, in particular, women in relation to men, and the status of the individual subject in relation to the community and its juridical organization. It is thinkable that the action concerned is interpreted as rape by one part of the culture at stake, and not at all by another part. Cultures that differ from 'ours' tend to look more homogeneous and more coherent at a distance than they probably are. That deceptive vision is, precisely, the basis of ethnocentrism.

Focalization plays its part. Therefore, I assume that within each community, large or small, ancient or recent, far or close, differences

increase as one's vision approaches. Rape implies an event, if not an
entire story with a number of episodes.

Forging a noun out of a verb – nominalization – makes the concept
analysable, discussable. That is a gain. There is also a loss. What gets
lost from sight is the active character of the referent, the narrative of action including the subjectivities of the agents involved. When the subject of action disappears, so does the responsibility for the action – with
responsibility having a culture-specific meaning according to the status
of the individual in it. Instead, the entire narrative remains an implication, skipped as it were, in the abbreviation that is the noun. The subject who uses the word is, say, the story's narrator. The subject whose
vision is implied in the word is its focalizor. Then there are the actors.
The process in which all these figures interact, the fabula, is dynamic:
it brings about change. All this is lost when a noun is used instead of a
verb that would necessitate the naming of these subjects.

These aspects can be brought back into view by an analysis of the
noun that takes it as a narrative. The narratological perspective of the
term 'rape' requires that we appoint a narrator. The subject of action,
the rapist, needs to be mentioned. Then, there is the subject into whose
body the action is done, in whom it brings about change. Reflection on
the nature and the extent of that change warrants an amount of attention not triggered by the noun. Then, this is the meaningful question:
who is the focalizor? Is it the rapist, who would be likely to refer to his
action differently, or the raped one, the victim who experiences the action? Or is it the narrator, and if so, does this agent identify with either
one of these two positions?

The noun doesn't tell, and I don't want to answer the question in any
general way. The point is in raising it. The realization of this narrative
duplicity seems more productive than the unreflected choice of one of
the possible answers. That, though, is what Niditch does by adopting a
description she considers more fitting for the ancient culture. This is a
gesture of cultural relativism. That relativism is, in fact, condescending.
For if we take other cultures as seriously as our own, then the phenomenon in question deserves at least recognition as an event with 'a difference within,' an internal divisiveness which the quick narratological
analysis clearly indicates.

The item replaced and displaced, obscured, is a story with several
agents, a variability of interpretation, and a difference of experience.
What is sex, or theft, or lawful appropriation for the one may still be

a violation of subjective integrity for another – whether culturally accepted or not; but who, then, is the culture? Such an analysis and recognition of the narratives and the subjective meanings they entail do, at least, disturb the academic as well as the social dilemma between ethnocentrism and relativism. And, while at least acknowledging, not repressing the inevitable anachronism of cultural analysis, they also enable a comparative, trans-historical perspective on present-day occurrences of rape in, and as, war – including in the same region.

Levels of Focalization

Compare the following sentences:

  e Mary participates in the rally.

  f I saw that Mary participated in the rally.

  g Michele saw that Mary participated in the rally.

In all three sentences it is stated that Mary participated in the rally. That is a clearly perceptible fact. We assume that there is an agent which is doing the perceiving, and whose perceptions are being presented to the reader. In f this is an 'I,' in g it is Michele. In e no party is indicated. Consequently, we assume that there is an external focalizor situated outside the fabula. This could be an EF or a CF ('I'), which remains implicit in this sentence but manifests itself elsewhere. We can thus analyse:

  e EF–p

  f CF('I')–p

  g CF (Michele)–p

The dash indicates the relation between the subject and the object of focalization. However, the difference between these sentences has not yet been expressed completely. Sentences f and g are complex sentences. The focalization, too, is complex. The analysis, as it is given here, only applies to the subordinate clause. In f it is stated that 'I' saw, and in g that Michele saw. Who focalized that section? Either an EF or a CF. We

can only conclude that from the rest of the story. For f the possibilities
are:

1 EF–[np CF ('I')–p]: an external focalizor focalizes the CF ('I'), which
   sees. 'Seeing' is a non-perceptible action, in contrast to 'looking,'
   so the complex focalized object is np. That object consists itself of a
   focalizor, CF ('I'), which sees something that is perceptible.
2 CF ('I')–[np CF ('I')–p]: a so-called 'first person narrative,' in which the
   external focalizor remembers afterwards that at a certain moment in
   the fabula, it saw Mary participating in a rally.

The first possibility exists in theory, but will not easily occur, unless the
sentence is in direct speech, and the CF ('I') can be identified as one of
the persons speaking (temporarily). In g only the first formula is possible: EF–[np CF (Michele)–p]. This is easy to see once we realize that a
personal focalizor cannot perceive a non-perceptible object, unless it is
part of that object, is the same 'person.'
    Two conclusions can be drawn from this. Firstly, it appears that vari-
ous focalization levels can be distinguished; secondly, where the focalization level is concerned, there is no fundamental difference between
a 'first-person narrative' and a 'third-person narrative.' When EF seems
to 'yield' focalization to a CF, what is really happening is that the vision
of the CF is being given within the all-encompassing vision of the EF. In
fact, the latter always keeps the focalization in which the focalization of
a CF may be embedded as object. This too is explicable in terms of the
general principles of narratology. When we try to reflect someone else's
point of view, we can only do so in so far as we know and understand
that point of view. That is why there is no difference in focalization between a so-called 'first-person narrative' and a 'third-person narrative.'
In a so-called 'first-person narrative' too an external focalizor, usually
the 'I' grown older, gives its vision of a fabula in which it participated
earlier as an actor, from the outside. At some moments it can present
the vision of its younger alter ego, so that a CF is focalizing on the second level.
    If we wish to include the question of levels in the analysis, we can use
an elaborate system of notation, as I have done here. That is useful if
we wish to know what the relationship between the various focalizors
is like: who allows whom to watch whom? If, however, we are only
concerned with the relationship between the subject and the object of
the focalization – for instance, in f between CF ('I') and Mary, or in g

between CF (Michele) and Mary – then it is easier to remind ourselves of the fact that we are dealing with an embedded focalization, because at any moment the narrative may return to the first level. In that case, it is simple to indicate the level with a number following the F. For f this would be CF2 ('I')–p and for g CF2 (Michele)–p.

Briefly, it appears that the three sentences each differ one from another, in various ways. There is always one sentence that differs from the other two. Thus e differs from f and g in focalization level. Consequently focalization in e is singular and in f and g it is complex. And e and f differ from g as far as 'person' is concerned. In both cases it can be an EF or a CF ('I'). Finally, e and g differ from f because in f an EF cannot simply be assumed without doubt. This is only possible if the sentence is in direct speech.

We assume, therefore, a first level of focalization (F1) at which the focalizor is external. This external focalizor delegates focalization to an internal focalizor, the focalizor on the second level (F2). In principle there are more levels possible. In these sample sentences it is clear where the focalization is transferred from the first to the second level. The verb form 'saw' indicates that. Such markers of shifts in level we call *attributive signs*. These are signs which indicate the shift from one level to another. These signs can remain implicit. Sometimes we can only deduce them from other, less clear information. In example c, the description of the view on and from the Burubudur, we needed the preceding passage to find the sign with which the shift was indicated explicitly. In d a whole sentence – 'Then we must first describe heaven of course' – is used to indicate that the internal CF is now going to give its own vision of heaven. Verbs like 'see' and 'hear,' in short all verbs that communicate perception, can function as explicit attributive signs.

There is yet another possibility. The external EF can also watch along with a person, without leaving focalization entirely to a CF. This happens when an object (which a character can perceive) is focalized, but nothing clearly indicates whether it is actually perceived. This procedure is comparable to free indirect speech, in which the narrating party approximates as closely as possible the character's own words without letting it speak directly. An example of such a 'free indirect' focalization, or rather, ambiguous focalization, is the beginning of the story 'Lady with Lapdog' by Chekhov:

h 1 The appearance on the front of a new arrival – a lady with a lapdog – became the topic of general conversation. 2 Dmitri Dmitrich Gurov, who had been a fortnight in Yalta and got used to its ways, was also interested in new arrivals. 3 One day, sitting on the terrace of Vernet's restaurant, he saw a young woman walking along the promenade; she was fair, not very tall, and wore a toque; behind her trotted a white pomeranian.

4 Later he came across her in the park and in the square several times a day. 5 She was always alone, always wearing the same toque, followed by the white pomeranian, no one knew who she was, and she became known simply as the lady with the lapdog.

This fragment as a whole is focalized by an external EF. In the third sentence a shift of level takes place, indicated by the verb 'to see.' In sentence 4, level 1 has been restored. But in sentence 5 it is ambiguous. This sentence follows the one in which it was stated that Dmitri meets the lady regularly.

The description of the lady which follows would, according to our expectation, have to be focalized by that character: CF2 (Dmitri)–p, but there is no indication signalling that change of level. In the second part of the sentence focalization clearly rests again with EF1. The first part of sentence 5 is focalized both by EF1 and by CF2. Such a double focalization, in which EF 'looks over the shoulder' of CF, we may indicate with the double notation EF1/CF2. Such a part of the story might be called a hinge, a fragment with a double, or at any rate ambiguous focalization in between two levels. It is also possible to distinguish between double focalization, which can be represented as EF1+CF2, and ambiguous focalization, in which it is hard to decide who focalizes: EF1/CF2. In h this difference cannot be established. In view of the development of the rest of the story, EF1+CF2 seems most likely.

Suspense

Suspense is a frequent fact of experience, yet difficult to analyse. In so far as suspense is a psychological process, nothing need be said about it here. If, however, we define suspense as the effect of the procedures by which the reader or the character is made to ask questions which are only answered later, it is possible to get some grasp of the various kinds of suspense in terms of focalization.

These questions may be asked and answered within a short space of time, or only at the end of the story. It is also possible that some questions are solved fairly quickly, while others are shelved. If suspense is to develop, then the questions will, somehow, be recalled repeatedly and the answers postponed. In the paragraphs dealing with order, I noticed that suspense can be generated by the announcement of something that will occur later, or by temporary silence concerning information which is needed. In both cases, the image presented to the reader is manipulated. That image is given by the focalizor. In principle, it coincides with the image that the focalizor has itself; for this reason the latter has been compared to a camera.

But the focalizor's image can be limited. This is the case when the characters 'know' more than the focalizor. That 'knowing more' must, of course, appear later. It is also possible for the focalizor to falsify an image by, for instance, leaving out certain elements, hiding them from the reader. In such a case, the characters also 'know more' than the reader. The focalizor can also be in the possession of information which the characters do not know; for instance, about the origins of events. Then the reader, along with the focalizor, knows more than the character. The reader can thus receive an image that is just as complete or incomplete, more complete or less complete than the image the characters have of themselves. The focalizor determines that. If we now attempt to analyse suspense according to the 'knowledge' of reader and character on the basis of information provided through the focalizor, four possibilities emerge.

When a question is raised (who did it? what happened? how will it end?), it is possible that neither the reader nor the character can answer it. This is the opening situation of almost every detective novel. It is also possible that the reader does know the answer, but the character does not. The tension, in this case, is different. The question is not what the answer will be but whether the character will discover it for itself in time. This is the suspense that lies at the root of a threat. A character makes a mistake. Will it realize this in time? There is someone standing behind it with an axe. Will it turn round in time? Conversely, it can also be the case that the reader does not know the answer and the characters do, as in *Of Old People*. The answer can then be gradually revealed, in various phases and by means of various focalizors (Harold, the old people themselves, and the others, each one according to its own knowledge), or in the form of a puzzle, if the information is revealed, but is not marked as data, as in a detective novel. When, finally, reader and character are both informed of the answer, there is no suspense.

Hence, when a question is evoked, the possibilities that the answer is known are thus:

reader – character – (riddle, detective story, search)
reader + character – (threat)
reader – character + (secret, for instance *Of Old People)*
reader + character + (no suspense)

In each of these forms of suspense one might analyse in turn, if necessary, which character knows the answer, and through which channel of focalization (EF1 or CF2) the reader learns the answer.

9: Visual Stories

As I suggested with the examples of films and other visual images, there is no reason to limit narratological analysis to linguistic texts only. The narrativity of films is obvious, even though the manner in which best to analyse them is not. Film narratology is a rich and diverse field, to which other studies are devoted. In art history, however, narratology is not very popular. This is understandable, as art historical interpretation has often relied on the narratives that the image allegedly 'illustrates,' thus subordinating visual to literary narrative.

Although focalization is not by definition vision-based, it seems the obvious place to begin easing in some elements of a 'visual narratology.' What has been said about any narrative holds for images as well: the concept of focalization refers to the story represented and the concept of narrator to its (material) representation. Focalization acts as the steering perspective on the events (or fabula). Although its basis in the notion of perspective seems to make its transposition to the realm of the visual simple, such a transposition is not unproblematic.

I would like to suggest the idea of visual stories by citing, not the innummerable readings of classical painting as 'word-for-word' translations of well-known biblical and historical narratives – roughly, the tradition known as iconography – but a case of the reverse relationship. In a wonderful book of short stories called *Silence Please!* eleven authors have published widely divergent narratives. These texts only have in common their inspiration in the visual work of the Spanish artist Juan Muñoz. This collection is the more significant as Muñoz's work is known as anti-narrative. His installations of architectural structures within which sculpted figures are grouped in such a way that they do not communicate with one another invariably entices critics to call his work 'silent.'

The stories in the volume do not describe his work – as the reverse of illustration. Nor do they talk about it, or adopt the themes of it. Instead, they create stories that somehow emanate the same visual qualities as Muñoz's works: isolation, finesse, what the editors call 'staged contingencies' (7); episodes in which 'the sculpture is implicated' (8).

In addition to the obvious need for a film narratology, I see three specific areas in which a visual narratology can be usefully embraced. First, the analysis of visual images as narrative in and of themselves can do justice to an aspect of images and their effect that neither iconography nor other art historical practices can quite articulate. Second, the comparison of literary narratives and films based on them can be developed as a form of cultural criticism that does not privilege the literary 'source.' Third, perhaps most unexpectedly, attention to visuality is tremendously enriching for the analysis of literary narratives.

Visual Narratology in a Nutshell

Briefly, in order to make the concept operational for visual art, it is best to provisionally forget the mythical or historical fabula and instead start with the work itself, keeping in mind the following:

1 / In narrative discourse, focalization is the direct content of the linguistic signs. In visual art, it would then be the direct content of visual signs like lines, dots, light and dark, and composition. In both cases, as in literary stories, focalization is already an interpretation, a subjectivized content. What we see is before our mind's eye has already been interpreted. This makes room for a reading of the complex structure of focalization.

2 / In linguistic narrative there is an external focalizor distinguished in function, not identity, from the narrator. This external focalizor can embed an internal, diegetic narrator. For the analysis of narrative, this relation of embedding is crucial. In visual art, the same distinction between external and internal focalizor holds, even if this distinction is not always easy to point out.

3 / In narrative, the fabula is mediated, or even produced, by the focalizors. Similarly, using the concept in analysing visual art implies that the event represented has the status of the focalized object produced by focalizors. In the case of an internal focalizor, the 'reality'-status of the different objects represented is variable and contingent upon their relation to the focalizer.

4 / Thus, the same object or event can be differently interpreted according to different focalizors. The way in which these different

interpretations are suggested to the reader is medium-bound, but the principle of meaning-production is the same for verbal and visual art. In *Madame Bovary*, the heroine's eyes are variably dark, black, blue, and grey, according to the internal focalizor with whom we watch her. The words conveying these incompatible descriptions do not themselves betray the difference between focalizors. Flaubert could simply have been indifferent or careless. But in order to make sense of the work as it is, only the hypothesis of different focalizors, substantiable in a textual analysis, can account for these differences.

5 / As we have seen in narrative discourse, the identification of the external narrator with an internal one can produce a discursive conflation called Free Indirect Discourse. This conflation can also occur on the level of focalization, something like Free Indirect Thought or Perception. The identification between the external focalizor in visual images and an internal focalizor represented in the image can similarly give rise to such a conflation, which would then strengthen the appeal to identification.

Novel and Film

The question of a truly visual story and its relation to what art historians call iconography is most clearly relevant for comparative analysis of novels and films based on them. Again, this is not a matter of 'illustration' or of 'faithfulness.' 'Translation' of a novel into film is not a one-to-one transposition of story elements into images, but a visual working-through of the novel's most important aspects and their meanings. For instance, if a novel addresses political issues in a specifically powerful way, the film, through totally different means, without following the visual indications offered in the novel, may still address the same issues with comparable power. Examining if this is done successfully requires, on the part of the critic, a narratological analysis as well as an engagement with film as visual medium. The following example offers a reflection on the relations between narratology and iconography. Through it I hope to suggest ways to articulate criticism in this domain without endorsing the hierarchical subordination of visuality to language that has pestered the study of art.

Why did I, and many critics, consider Steven Spielberg's film *The Color Purple* an ideological and artistic failure, in spite of its obvious attractions to a large audience? I contend that this was so because the movie failed to represent the iconographic basis of the combative ideological position that Walker's novel proposed as well as the narrative sources used to articulate that position. Ignoring iconography, it ignored the novel's embeddedness in, and response to, a cultural tradition that is deeply narrative.

Alice Walker's bestselling novel *The Color Purple* refers directly to the double tradition of abolitionist and of self-assertive literature, to Harriet Beecher Stowe's *Uncle Tom's Cabin* and the tradition of slave-narratives. For example, when *Color* addresses the problem of education it evokes both slave-narratives and *Tom:*

> 'Why can't Tashi come to school?' she asked me. When I told her the Olinka don't believe in educating girls she said, quick as a flash, 'They're like white people at home who don't want colored people to learn.'   162

The theme of learning is represented in *Tom* as in slave-narratives; it is acutely discussed by Frederick Douglas in his autobiography, and the very existence of slave-narrative as the exemplary genre of persuasive texts points to the function of writing and reading for emancipation.

But while *Color* refers directly to *Tom* and indirectly to slave-narratives, it does not merely 'repeat'; it puts *Tom*'s religiosity in its place by juxtaposing it to elements of black religious culture. And in so far as the characters in *Color* repeat the characters of *Tom*, they are critically feminist rewritings of them. Celie is a female Tom ('I ain't never struck a living thing,' 43). Her attempt to spare her little sister Nettie from rape by their father by offering herself to him is her version of Tom's Christlike self-sacrifice. Nettie is the female George who lifts herself up from humiliation, and like him she travels to Africa. The almost life-long separations between Celie and Nettie and between Celie and her children repeat the plot around George, Eliza, and Eliza's mother and sister, reunited as in the comedy-based romance. And Celie's husband has much of Legree, Tom's cruel master, including the flicker of hope for conversion towards the end. Sophia with her strength and sense of humour as weapon incarnates the insubordinate Cassie, the proud slave who manages to save herself with Tom's help. All this is not a matter of visuality but rather of intertextuality.

But the allusions to *Tom* and to all it stood for are more subtle and complex than just the cast of characters indicates. The language, events, and conversations all respond to the choices made by Stowe and show the limits of Stowe's choices and more radical possibilities. The novel is effective because it balances and intertwines critically the discourse of modern popular culture, the context of the double oppression of black women, and the antecedent of the particularly effective 'sentimental' social novel. How can that critical engagement be visualized in a film? This was Spielberg's challenge.

We can now see that Spielberg's film simplifies and alters all these connections. Because of this, as a visual representation of Walker's novel it is arguably both racist and sexist, as the representation of the character of Sophia alone demonstrates. The film provides visual instances of those generic conventions of the social novel which relate the genre to sentimentality. Thus on the level of external focalization, it visualizes 'sentimentality' in bright colours, counter-light, soft focus, picturesque setting. Those characteristics of the social novel which Walker uses polemically to represent critically the relationship between sexism and slavery are stripped of their critical content, are merely repeated, endorsed without any subtlety, sense of humour, or critical perspective; most important, they are repeated without resonance with the other texts.

Rejecting the idea of a visual narratology, one could be led to argue that the visual medium of film – and the popular character of Spielberg's film – made it impossible to work in Walker's critical allusions. I don't believe this is true. Ignoring what made the novel critical resulted in the film being uncritical. The film now comes to support negative ideological positions. Two examples will illustrate how Walker's attempt to connect racism and sexism is turned, in the film's visualization, into the very racism and sexism her novel critiqued through focalization.

If taken as a twentieth-century documentary view, Walker's representation of Africa is rather naïve; what made it effective was not its realistic adequacy but its relationship with the combative pre-text. Stripped of this relationship, it is open to imperialist recuperation. With Spielberg, Africa comes to stand under an enormous orange sun; thus visually represented it is insistently focalized as unreal. Reduced to a postcard, Africa cannot fulfil the function of object of melancholic longing as well as utopian desire that it has in Walker's novel through its intricate relationship with *Uncle Tom's Cabin*. The slave-narratives and the critical response to contemporary taste which replaced realism in Walker's novel disappear from sight. We are left with kitsch, which, under Spielberg's benevolent and competent direction, easily picks up a connotation of black folklore as seen through white prejudice.

The representation of black sexism without the reference to slavery allows the distanciation which results in the too eagerly adopted view that blacks are more sexist than whites. The father-daughter rape that informed the novel from the start is hardly present in the film, and neither is the alternative the novel proposed: the erotic friendship between Celie and Shug, the wife and the mistress. That these themes have been sacrificed in order to reach a larger audience may be justifiable. But these gender-relations form the background for other elements which become over-emphasized in the film. Thus the figure of Sophia, who recalls Cassie, Tom's more combative and female alter ego, has changed dramatically between the novel and the film.

Without the intertextual relationship to Tom on the one hand, and the contemporary context of the questioning of gender-relations on the other, Sophia's insubordination is an easy target for cheap comic visual effects. Spielberg introduces her as a gigantic woman, an overwhelming mother-figure who is dragging her husband-to-be along like a child through the fields, when the latter is supposed to introduce his fiancée to his father. The scene is focalized from afar and from above and accelerated, all devices for comical effect. Thereby, allusion to Charlie Chaplin and silent comedy film supersedes the allusion to Cassie and thus to *Uncle Tom's Cabin* as a whole. Spielberg's Sophia is irretrievably ridiculous from the start, and so are, then, her insubordination, her husband, and her revolt. Visual effect is used to neutralize the critical potential of the novel. Seen in this way, the film can be criticized on its own terms as visual artifact while its flaws can be illuminated through comparison with its narrative pretext. Yet, this comparison respects the specificity of each medium.

The point of comparing novel and film, then, is not to make aesthetic assessments of 'faithfulness' to the source text. Rather, taking novel and film as equally embedded in the culture in which they function, the comparison can help to articulate what they each, through their own narratological make-up, have to say to their audiences. Their relationship is an intertextual as well as an interdiscursive one.

Vision in Language

Finally, let me briefly indicate the importance of attention to visuality, especially in focalization, as a motor of narrative. Whereas the nineteenth-century novel can be characterized by an increasingly elaborate appeal to visual display – Flaubert is a striking example, Zola no less – modernist literature is particularly visual. The passage quoted from

Woolf's *The Waves* is a good case. The description of Robin when Felix first sees her, in *Nightwood*, insists on the visuality by means of the comparison with paintings by the Douanier Rousseau. As I have suggested, modernism's interest in questions of knowledgeability or epistemology lends itself to an exploration of vision.

The following passage from Proust's *A la recherche* blends this concern with vision with a foregrounding of focalization as a subjectivizing technique. It seems appropriate, then, to end this chapter with this case. The passage demonstrates that the question 'Who sees?' is dramatically made meaningful by the complementary questions, 'Who is being seen?,' 'Who is not seeing?,' and 'What kind of act of seeing is at stake?' It is also a good case for the way narratological analysis can make periodization much more meaningful.

Entering the room without announcing his presence, the narrator tells us, 'I was there, or rather I was not yet there since she was not aware of my presence, and ... she was absorbed in thoughts which she never allowed to be seen by me' (II 141). The protagonist CN is paying an unexpected visit to his grandmother, who, unbeknownst to him, is near her death. This is a critical examination of visual focalization. It is also a good example of what Kaja Silverman called 'heteropathic identification' – identification based on going outside of the self, as opposed to idiopathic or 'cannibalistic' identification, which absorbs and 'naturalizes' the other. Heteropathic identification is associated with a risk of alienation, but enables the subject to identify beyond the normative models prescribed by the cultural screen, and is thereby socially productive. This identification never stops appealing to the narrator-protagonist, even while it exposes him to obvious risks.

The narrator-protagonist is examining his own status as witness, the specific kind of focalization he is involved in:

> Of myself – thanks to that privilege which does not last but which gives one, during the brief moment of return, the faculty of being suddenly the spectator of one's own absence – there was present only the witness, the observer, in travelling coat and hat, the stranger who does not belong to the house, the photographer who has called to take a photograph of places which one will never see again. The process that automatically occurred in my eyes when I caught sight of my grandmother was indeed a photograph.   II 141

The voyeur is constantly in danger, since alienation robs him of his self when he is not interacting with the other. Proust's use of photography to articulate this theory of vision makes this passage an appropriate allegory for the relation between modernism, vision, and narrative focalization. The contemplation of the spectacle afforded by the other is a photographic act. For a brief instant, the looking I/eye wavers between the disembodied retinal gaze of linear perspective and the colonizing mastery it affords, and the heteropathic identification that takes him out of himself with body and soul to 'become' other. The *spectre* – both spectacle and phantom refer to 'lost time.' It is exactly what the subject inevitably is himself.

The passage gradually develops a more hostile, if not violent, language, leading at the end of this worrying amplification to the description of the mental photograph that will always be with the narrator:

> I saw, sitting on the sofa, beneath the lamp, red-faced, heavy and vulgar, sick, vacant, letting her slightly crazed eyes wander over a book, a dejected old woman whom I did not know.   II 143

The 'truth' of photography is this stranger, this unknowable person, cut off from the familial, affective gaze by photography. Thus, Proust's story is a sharp analysis of the very focalization it deploys. However, the theory of this itself takes a visual, photographic form. In the middle of the passage on the mental photograph of the grandmother we find this strange comparison, which both explains the photographic effect and embodies it:

> But if, instead of our eyes, it should happen to be a purely physical object, a photographic plate, that has watched the action, then what we see, in the courtyard of the Institute, for example instead of the dignified emergence of an Academician who is trying to hail a cab, will be his tottering steps, his precautions to avoid falling on his back, the parabola of his fall, as though he were drunk or the ground covered in ice.   II 142

The comparison mercilessly dramatizes what remains of the puppet that is the other, divested of the protection of perceptual and affective routine. The wonder at the photographic look also historicizes this particular act of focalization. At the end of this chapter, what better caution could we hope to find, in one of literature's richest and most visual narratives, to underscore the relevance of a disabused, politically alert analysis of focalization?

The dynamics of focalization is at play in every visual text that contains traces of the representational work, as seen and interpreted by the viewer, since it is precisely in those traces that the text becomes narrativized. In principle all texts contain such traces, but some display them more openly than others.

Finally, an example where many of the issues and concepts of this chapter come together in a convincing case of a visual story. At the occasion of the 2007 film *Atonement* after Ian McEwan's novel, the question was raised in the press why so many of this author's novels ended up in cinematic form. The answer is easy to give as soon as one opens a novel by this hand, such as, for example, *Enduring Love* (1997), a novel about a stalker and the ending of a relationship. The qualifier 'enduring' clearly produces a double meaning, referring to the temporal qualifier of duration and to the progressive form of the verb 'to endure' as 'to suffer,' referring to a focalizing qualification. 'Love' is durable, and it can be suffered. With reference to the romantic tradition of idealized love, the title warns us of the downside of this conception of relationships.

On all levels – text, story, and fabula – the novel begins with an accident: a balloon is adrift and a rescuer falls to his death. The opening paragraph of the novel runs as follows.

The beginning is simple to mark. We were in sunlight under a turkey oak, partly protected from a strong, gusty wind. I was kneeling on the grass with a corskscrew in my hand, and Clarissa was passing me the bottle – a 1987 Daumas Gassac. This was the moment, this was the pinprick on the time map: I was stretching my hand. And as the cool neck and the black foil touched my palm, we heard a man's shout. We turned to look across the field and saw the danger. Next thing, I was running towards it. The transformation was absolute: I don't recall dropping the corkscrew, or getting to my feet, or making a decision, or hearing the caution Clarissa called after me. What idiocy, to be racing into this story and its labyrinths, sprinting away from our happiness among the fresh spring grasses and the oak. There was the shout again, and a child's cry, enfeebled by the wind that roared in the tall trees along the hedgerows. I ran faster. And there, suddenly, from different points around the field, four other men were converging on the scene, running like me.

On all levels, also, the novel is concerned with visuality as the motor of story-telling. While there is only one narrator uttering this sentence, it is easy to imagine the scene, the backdrop, the cast of characters. The CN (Joe) is, it seems, writing the film script already. The first sentence is a temporal indication, stipulating that the story is to begin. This is a meta-narrative commentary on the narrative about to unfold. There follows a starkly visual description, where light and the visual consequences of wind accompany a zoomed-in scene of two people about to begin a picnic. This is a description waiting to be interrupted. As indeed happens, with the next sentence, 'This was the moment, this was the pinprick on the time map,' which, again meta-narratively, appears to position the story in time. Although it does nothing of the sort, not in real time that is; only *qua* temporal interruption of a situation that itself is only the product of descriptive discourse. If only for this reason already, the narrative is a fiction.

Verb forms do their temporal work. 'We were' initiates a descriptive passage, 'I was kneeling' and Clarissa 'was passing' slow down the actions, ordinary as they would normally be. The description zooms in on the date and name of the wine, indicating a memory trace of great detail that suggests another kind of temporal stop, that of a traumatic event. 'I was stretching' and the description of physical sensations continue this work of rhythmic change. The first event is one of perception, a focalization: 'we *heard* a man's shout.' There follows a verb of action – 'running' – and another meta-narrative commentary that further qualifies the story that follows as labyrinth.

With 'The transformation was absolute' the narrator insists on the nature of the event and its decisive importance. Events take over from focalization, before embedding focalization in themselves. The negative formulations, 'I don't recall dropping the corkscrew, or getting to my feet, or making a decision, or hearing the caution,' tell both the actions undertaken and the repression of these in memory, as well as the acceleration of rhythm. The interruption of the peaceful, pastoral scene suggests a cinematic shot/reverse shot: 'We turned to look across the field and saw *the* danger.' The spectator sees the two figures, sees them turn, then sees what they see: the definite article that accompanies the sight suggests that danger is already determined as the one that will set this story in motion. The acoustic environment is eminently suitable for cinematic translation. For example, 'a child's cry, enfeebled by the wind' places focalization at a distance.

The second paragraph continues this cinematic mode of story-telling:

I see us from three hundred feet up, through the eyes of the buzzard we had watched earlier, soaring, circling and dipping in the tumult of currents: five men running silently towards the centre of a hundred-acre field.

The image is all there. The reference to an earlier act of focalization – seeing the buzzard – also serves as a metaphor of danger. Solidarity with the child in the balloon and yet positioning embedded focalization ('I see us ... through the eyes') introduces retroversion and psychological distance. A distance that also splits the CN from the CF and the actor, for Joe is telling this, seeing it but with the eyes of another creature, and he is one of the men running. 'Silently' indicates the effect of distance and its cinematic nature. And so it continues. As the description was waiting to be interrupted, so this novel was waiting to be put into film. The story of this novel is not a film script but it is such a strongly visual and sensory vision of the events that the film director must have been unable to resist.

10: Remarks and Sources

Most of the topics that have been discussed in this chapter are part of the traditional 'theory of the novel.' In various countries, at various periods in the history of literary theory, and according to various principles, concepts have been developed, often independently of each other, which were presented under the deceptive title 'theory of the novel.' This title is deceptive for two reasons. The novel is probably the most heavily researched textual form. The concepts and distinctions that have emerged from this research usually have a more general scope. In so far as genre distinctions were taken into account, the novel was in these studies contrasted sometimes with drama, sometimes with poetry, and sometimes with the novella or short story. By using the term 'theory of the novel' to indicate sometimes (but not always) a much larger area of narratology, critics obscured the precise position of the novel with respect to other genres and types of text. Consequently, it is sometimes difficult to see to which area distinctions apply.

In the second place, the term 'theory of the novel' is deceptive because there can be no system as is presupposed by the term 'theory.' As I said, work was done in very different contexts on various components of the 'theory of the novel.' We have already seen that Müller and his disciples concerned themselves with the temporal relationships in the novel. In Anglo-Saxon countries work was done at another time, primarily on 'point of view' theories. Müller worked with technical, quantitative criteria. The 'point of view' theories were based mainly on psychological criteria. It seems difficult to imagine that these two groups of investigators were working on the same theory. Before reference could be made to a theory, all those different distinctions and concepts had to be brought together in one system.

One attempt to place all the traditional narratological distinctions together within one systematic, theoretical framework is formed by Genette's 'Discours du recit' (1972). This author joins the different time aspects and focalization in one frame, in which he also places the narrative text. The highly different origins of the various aspects made it difficult to allot them all a place in a systematic theory of the story level. I have tried to solve this problem by retaining a clear point of departure. That point of departure was the question how information about the fabula is shaped and presented to the reader. The more technical aspects within this framework (such as various time aspects) could be placed, but so could aspects such as the image of a character and space. Here the questions were specified: what kind of information do we get? how do we get it? how do the various elements and aspects function in relation to each other?

That last question as to how the elements and aspects function is finally determined by focalization. Focalization is a central concept in this chapter. It has an overarching position with respect to the other aspects. The significance of certain aspects cannot be viewed unless it is linked to focalization. Moreover, focalization is, in my view, the most important, most penetrating, and most subtle means of manipulation. Analyses of newspaper reports which aim at revealing the hidden ideology embedded in such reports should involve focalization in their investigation, and not restrict themselves to so-called content analysis, i.e. the semantic analysis of content.

I have made remarks here and there, and especially in this chapter, concerning the relations between fiction and reality. I have not devoted a special section to this issue, because it is not narratological *per se*. Instead of seeing in every narrative a representation of reality – a reading posture that leads to flat realistic judgments – I have insisted that this relationship is important as a tool for critique. I have used the concept of make-believe with reference to Kendall L. Walton's book on fictionality (1990). Walton's study is limited to representational art and thus tends to stay closer to the questions of realism than I do. But within that self-chosen limitation it is the most useful take on this issue that I know of.

The theory of anachrony has been further developed since Lämmert in 1955 first made an extensive study of it. The most systematic exposition of this subject, and of the other time aspects too, has until today been that of Genette just mentioned. Genette considers every variation on a set pattern a (rhetorical) figure, an attitude which is reflected in the title of his book *Figures III*. Within the framework of that theory, it is understandable that he sought to express such figures in terms which would fit into the technical terminology derived from Greek rhetoric. Since such terms, which do indeed have advantages, appear rather cryptic and, consequently, tend to repel, I attempted to avoid them, and at most mentioned them in conjunction with English terms, unless no adequate English term could be found.

Actually, Genette's terms are not really as difficult as they appear, because they have been systematically constructed out of several prepositions and the stems of words. For those who wish to use them in further analysis, it is perhaps useful to know how they are structured. The prepositions are *ana* and *pro*, which mean, respectively, 'towards/ from the back' and 'towards/in the front.' *Para* means 'to the side.' The stem *lips* means 'leaving something out' and *leps*, 'adding something.' Thus, we end up with for instance, *paralips* in the sense of 'something is left out on the side (a missing side-track),' and *paraleps:* 'something is added to the side.' For Genette's complete time theory, I refer the reader to the English translation of his work (1980).

Barbara Herrnstein Smith has long ago cautioned against the presupposition that the fabula pre-exists the story (1980). The paradox of the distinction has been explored in detail by Chase (1986), and further theorized by Culler (1981) in psychoanalysis and the mystery novel. Although I maintain the distinction, I fully agree with these analyses of the problem inherent in it.

An important article by Hamon (1977) (from which I have borrowed a great deal in this chapter) deals with characters. In this article, Hamon treats the most important aspects of the characters, and places them in a semiotic framework. His later book (1983) is based on the same model. His division of the characters into signifier and signified I find a bit problematic.

Booth discusses the unreliable narrator (1961). The best-known study of space is still the philosophically and psychoanalytically tinted *Poetics of Space* by Bachelard (1957). Uspenskij (1973) broaches interesting aspects of this problem. Lodge (1977) discusses a series of location descriptions, which are, in his view, progressively more poetic.

An important philosophical study of space is Lefebvre (1991). De Lauretis (1983) offers a feminist critique of Lotman's (1977) semiotic interpretation of space. Many studies use the distinction between place and space in a sense that I reversed here. The reason for my reversal is that place, in narrative, equals location, the topological specification of where things happen, while space fleshes out the specific look and feel of that place, like the setting of a film or theatre play. But the reverse is just as arguable. For important narratological analyses of space/place, see Hoving (2001). A wonderfully inspiring social-scientific view of space is offered by Michel de Certeau (1984).

Friedman's typology of narrative points of view (1955) is based on various criteria (amount of information, 'perspective,' identity and attitude of the narrator) and is, consequently, less systematic than could be wished. The same goes for Booth's well-known fifth chapter. Both contain, however, a good many interesting insights. The distinction between narration and focalization is introduced by Genette (1972). For a critical discussion, and a theoretical justification of the ideas presented here, Bal (1991). A good survey of narratology, which is also based on a (somewhat different) distinction of three layers and which discusses focalization and character interestingly, is provided by Rimmon-Kenan (1983). Lanser's use of the term 'focalization' is somewhat loose (1981). An important recent study which presents a thorough overview and analysis of many of the subjects of this chapter was published by Fludernik (1996). Chatman, who takes a different approach from mine, offers a narratology of film (1990). He prefers to use a different term for the focalization by the fabula-external agent than for the internal one. He speaks of the narrator's 'slant' to indicate the former form of focalization, of 'filter' for the latter. See also Chatman (1995) and his textbook (1992). Also different, but especially relevant for the historicizing aspect of focalization and narration, is Rimmon-Kenan (1996).

For a clear exposition on memory and trauma in relation to narrative incapacitation, see Van Alphen (1997a), especially chapter 2. This study is in turn inspired by Hartman (1996).

Film narratology has long been attached to the names of David Bordwell (1985; 1989) and Edward Branigan (1992), whose work is not really compatible with this book. Different but compatible is Kaja Silverman (1983), who explains, with the concept of 'suture,' a filmic version of internal focalization. The term 'heteropathic identification' is developed in her later work (1992, but especially 1996). In general her work has many connections with narratology as developed here, because my focus on subjectivity is quite congenial with her psycho-analytic orientation. A very good recent textbook for film narratology by Verstraten (2006) is forthcoming in English. That book takes the narratology presented here as its starting point; hence, it is an excellent companion to this book. Its primary strength is that, while relating all cinematic concepts to the ones discussed here, it develops them for and through cinema, with all the differences this entails.

Alpers and Baxandall offer a good discussion of the problems of a naïve projection of narrativity on visual art (1994). Mitchell (1995) is devoted to the problematic relations between visual art and literature. I have developed this problematic extensively elsewhere (1991).

The example from Homer is taken from the *Iliad* of Homer, translated with an introduction by Richmond Lattimore (23rd edition; Chicago and London: University of Chicago Press, 1974). Mulisch's 'What Happened to Sergeant Massuro?' is from *Hudson Review* 14 (1961). The kissing scene from Proust is a case I discuss at length in my book on visuality in Proust (1997). The page references in the examples from Proust are to *Remembrance of Things Past*, trans. C.K. Scott Moncrieff and Terence Kilmartin (New York: Vintage Books, 1982).

The passages from Acker come from *Blood and Guts in High School* (New York, 1978) in the edition *Blood and Guts in High School, Plus Two* (London: Picador, 1984). The passages and the commentary were borrowed from an article by Ernst van Alphen, 'Fucking Literature: On Excess and Sublimity in Kathy Acker's Narratives' (1997b).

The oldest known source of the myth of Narcissus is Ovid's *Metamorphoses*, book 3, 80–6. Ovid exploits to the full the literary potential of the auditive mirroring in the figure of Echo, as a sonoric embodiment of the visual mirroring that, in literature, cannot be presented in such a concrete manner. See, for a specific focus on Echo, a brilliant analysis by Spivak (1993a). The example from *Texaco* is from Patrick Chamoiseau, *Texaco* (Paris: Gallimard, 1992). The theoretical text this novel relies on is Edouard Glissant's influential *Le discours antillais* (Paris: Editions du Seuil, 1981). The example has been borrowed from Natalie Melas, whose book as a whole is also important for many of the issues raised here (2007).

Denial: Portrait of a Woman with Multiple Personalities is a documentary film from 1993, directed by Tom Verheul, Jura Film Production (in the collection of the Museum of Modern Art, New York). The example of

Niditch is from Susan Niditch, 'War, Women, and Defilement in Numbers 31,' *Semeia* 61 (1993), 59–75.

I have developed the example of *The Color Purple* in more detail (1991).

The collection of Juan Muñoz stories is *Silence Please!: Stories after the Works of Juan Muñoz,* edited with an introduction by Louise Neri (Dublin: Irish Museum of Modern Art/Scalo, 1996). Ian McEwan's novel has been quoted from *Enduring Love,* London: TSP.

3

Fabula: Elements

1: Preliminary Remarks

'Innombrables sont les recits du monde.' So begins a now-famous article by Roland Barthes that sparked off a series of new developments in the theory of fabula.

Despite their many different forms, the fact that narrative texts, recognizable as such, can be found in all cultures, all levels of society, all countries, and all periods of human history led Barthes to conclude that all of these narrative texts are based upon one common model, a model that causes the narrative to be recognizable as narrative. Since then, studies of the structure of this general model have been conducted in several different countries simultaneously, and these studies have produced a number of important insights, even if their generalizing claims are often problematic. These studies were often based, either implicitly or explicitly, upon two assumptions.

One frequent assumption was that there exists a homology, a correspondence between the (linguistic) structure of the sentence and that of the whole text composed of various sentences. A homology was also assumed to exist between the 'deep structure' of the sentence and the 'deep structure' of the narrative text, the fabula. This assumption has as many opponents as proponents, because it is also thought damaging. In particularly, scholars of visual arts and film object that it reduces the richness of visual images to a simple story line, while students of, especially, modernist and postmodernist narrative find it meaningless. First of all, it is easier to accept not as a reduction of narrative or image to a linguistic unit – the sentence – but as the idea that the correspondence between the sentence and the text, or between the sentence and the fabula, rests upon a common logical basis. The purpose of the comparison between the fabula model and the sentence model is to expose the logical principles of construction familiar to us from sentence analysis. The comparison is an illustration only, a metaphor that clarifies some things. Taken in any stronger way the assumption is reductive, no doubt about it, which is another reason to handle it with a dose of relativism, if not a grain of salt.

A second point of departure in the search for the universal model for fabula was also a homology. A structural correspondence was assumed to exist between the fabulas of narratives and 'real' fabulas, that is, between what people do and what actors do in fabulas that have been invented, between what people experience and what actors experience. It makes sense if one realizes that if no homology were to exist at all, no correspondence however abstract, then people would not be able to understand narratives. Two arguments have been introduced against this homology.

Firstly, it has been argued that the difference between literature or art and reality has been ignored. However, it is not a question of concrete identity but rather of structural similarity. Pointing out correspondences does not imply that equality is being suggested. Yet, the objection also aims at the tendency to interpret fictional narratives according to their resemblance to 'real life' and to criticize what distinguishes the two domains. This tendency to a near-irrepressible realist impulse bypasses everything that makes artistic narratives special.

Secondly, another objection to postulating the 'real-life' homology is that, in certain types of narrative texts – for example, fantastic, absurd, or experimental – such a homology seems absent; in fact, these texts are characterized by their denial or distortion of the logic of reality. This objection can be addressed in two ways again. The denial, distortion, or, as is now often said, 'deconstruction' of a realistic story-line is something altogether different from its absence. On the contrary, there is clearly something worth denying. The objection can also be countered with the argument that readers, intentionally or not, search for a logical line in such a text. They spend a great amount of energy in this search, and, if necessary, they introduce such a line themselves. Emotional involvement, aesthetic pleasure, suspense, and humour depend on it. No matter how absurd, tangled, or unreal a text may be, readers will tend to regard what they consider 'normal' as a criterion by which they can give meaning to the text, even if that meaning can only be articulated in opposition to that normality. Textual descriptions of postmodern nov-

Mary Longman, *Co-Dependents*, 1966 (cottonwood, leather, copper, rope, paint, wood). Photography by Sharon. From Gerald McMaster, *Mary Longman: Traces* (Kamloops Art Gallery, 1996).

els, for example, clearly point in this direction. In order to understand a text, some sort of logical connection is needed.

The analysis presented on the basis of this assumption is also deployed in visual criticism, even of rather abstract or non-figurative works that seem to yield little narrativity. Mary Longman's 1996 sculpture *Co-Dependents* reminds the viewer of bones. This skeletal aspect makes it a nice case for the skeletal kind of analysis of fabula that this chapter is presenting. This is a metaphor; it should not be taken to mean that the work is 'only' a skeleton. On the contrary, the bonelike texture provides the wooden 'bones' with a patina that shines with age. The sculpture is suggestive of, in Gerald McMaster's words, 'a sexual edge, giving rise to sensuous relationships' (24).

If the two parts that the slingshot-type connection binds can be seen as anthropomorphic actors, the relationship between them is so full of tension, of desire and hostility, push and pull, that they install a per-petual narrativity based on a delicate balance. This delicate balance can be fleshed out – turned into a story – with all the references the material and formal aspects of the work bring along. The allusion to aborigi-nal culture in the bones, slingshot, and earth-colour base provides a charged backdrop for an 'argument' in favour of close relationship. The patina of age infuses the soft-polished wood with claims to a longev-ity that entitles the actors and the people they stand for to a future. McMaster interprets the relational quality of this work to an ecological ethics that reaches beyond the political issue of aboriginality alone. But whatever the further story one wishes to read in this sculpture, it can only be effective in such a way if the anthropomorphism is allowed to enter the visual field.

Certainly, the fabulas of most narrative texts do display some form of homology, both with a sentence structure and with 'real life.' Conse-quently, most fabulas can be said to be constructed according to the demands of human 'logic of events,' provided that this concept is not too narrowly understood. 'Logic of events' may be defined as a course of events that is experienced by the reader as natural and in accordance with some form of understanding of the world. The nature of this ho-mology as well as the degree of abstraction at which the homology still holds true are questions of interest that can have heuristic value: they may point the reader to issues in texts, rather than to decisions of prin-ciple, abstraction, generalization. In other words, this 'realistic assump-tion' is a term of comparison, a measure by which to understand, or alternatively, to marvel at, the truly constructed nature of the fabula.

This point of departure suggests one consequence: everything that can be said about the structure of fabulas also bears to some degree on extra-literary facts. Various investigators in this area even refer to themselves as anthropologists or sociologists, and work not only on lit-erary narratives but quite often on folk tales, rituals, and common cul-tural practices such as table manners, recipes, and political programs.

Consequently, everything that is said in this chapter – and much of the previous chapters – should also be applicable to other connected series of human actions as well as to elements in film, theatre, news reports, and social and individual events in the world. It helps to keep in mind that the theory of elements, even more generally than that of aspects, makes describable a segment of reality that is broader than that of narrative texts only.

So far, the years between writing this book and making the present revisions have not changed my view that fabulas are comparable – not identitical or even similar – transculturally and transhistorically, even if my interest in such generalization has declined. And yet, more than before, I feel that the *point* of doing all this is not so self-evident. Instead, I would like to foreground, in this chapter in particular, the difference between the presentation of 'tools' and the demonstration of 'what they're for.' This difference is that between an intellectual loyalty to a disabused structuralism and an equally strong conviction that I, too, must make clear what purposes, other than intellectual rigour for its own sake, narratology can serve. Here is an example, then, to set this slightly different stage for the concepts that follow. In an attempt to demonstrate the point of a distinct analysis of fabula, I will simultaneously make an argument about interdisciplinarity; in this case, the interaction – not conflation – between narratology and anthropology.

In a famous article, Clifford Geertz presented a few case-studies meant to provide insight into the fundamental problem of anthropology, that of the relations between ethnographer and autochthonic subject. The issue Geertz chose in order to to discuss this problem is precisely the concept that lies at the heart of that problem as well as at the heart of narratology: the concept of *subject*. As Geertz demonstrates, both the content of the concept of subject – what defines an individual in a given society – and the structural properties of the system of interpersonal reference vary greatly according to different cultures. Hence, the very notion of subjectivity, so central in narratological considerations of, for example, description, but also of agents in the fabula, cannot be given a fixed, universal meaning.

But the different concepts of the subject Geertz describes are more clearly demonstrated in the person-to-person interaction in which he perceived them, in (social) drama if you wish, than in the ethnographic narrative itself. For there, while exposing the different conceptions of the subject, Geertz constantly doubles up the Balinese, Javanese, and Moroccan voice with his own, which he leaves for the purpose of the demonstration blatantly ethnocentric. Thus he explains how the Balinese widower represses his grief and derives his subjecthood from the denial of mourning, and how the Moroccan person is indicated through a network of features of kinship, profession, and location, but he does so in a structure built on the Western concepts of person, the ethnographic third-person narrative.

A subtle narratological analysis of anthropological material can go a bit further, precisely because such an analysis temporarily brackets both ends of the embedding reality, the reality of the events 'out there' and the reality of the ethnocentric reporter; for the duration of a prior analysis, the narratologist presupposes that the narrative is structurally self-sufficient, hence, fictional. I have experienced the usefulness of such an integration of anthropological eagerness for understanding real otherness and a narratological discipline of structural textual analysis in my studies of the Hebrew Bible, particularly the Book of Judges, which poses a number of acute problems of alterity.

I was particularly struck by the fact that three concepts referring to women seemed inadequately rendered, in translations and commentaries, by modern Western concepts: *virgin, concubine, prostitute;* not a haphazard series. The problem with *virgin* was that the immediate contexts of its occurrence systematically overdetermine the concept, adding apparently redundant phrases like 'who have not known a man' (e.g. Judges 11); with *concubine,* that no primary wife is mentioned (e.g. Judges 19); with *prostitute,* that the certainty of paternity – that Jephthah, the alleged son of a prostitute, knows who his father is – seems to contradict the very idea of prostitution (again Judges 11 and 19). These three figures have a predominant role in the fabulas of the Book of Judges. In each of these cases, the fabula seemed determined by precisely these opaque figures.

My first response to these problems was, let's say, 'anthropological.' For just as Geertz became particularly suspicious in the face of a concept that is so central in Western culture, the individual subject, so I became suspicious in the face of the concurrence of these three concepts indicating female status in a culture of the past, translated into modern patriarchal terms. In other words, these translations seemed too smoothly to endorse the notion that patriarchy is a monolithic, transhistorical social form.

But my second response was narratological. A close analysis suggested a different structural context – a different type of fabula – for 'virgin' on the one hand, for 'concubine' and 'prostitute' on the other. 'Virgin' became continuous with two other terms referring to young women, according to age/life phase. 'Concubine' and 'prostitute' became synonyms, of which the projected features of 'secondariness' and 'harlotry' could be suspended, since no element of the fabula whatsoever had any relation to such notions. These decisions were motivated by structural properties of the narratives. For example, the noun rendered as 'virgin' is either hilariously overdetermined in Judges and then spoken by a male voice who seems obsessed by it, or not connected to a fabula about what we consider to be virginity at all and then spoken by a female voice.

Compare, for example, Judges 21:12: 'found ... four hundred young girls, virgins, that had not known man by lying with him,' where the external narrator speaks and the focalization also remains external so that the women do not focalize their own fate, to 11:37: 'leave me alone two months, that I may depart and wander upon [towards] the mountains, and lament [until] my "virginity" [?]' where the 'virgin' herself (Jephthah's daughter) expresses her view of self. The one juxtaposition of 'virgin' and 'concubine,' in 19:24 ('Behold, my daughter the "virgin" and his "concubine"') is revealing, in favour of the earlier separation as well as of a different interpretation of 'virgin.' I considered the word as referring to a life phase – sexually ripe, but not yet married girls – rather than to a state – bodily integrity. The speaker and focalizor ('behold') here is the father of the one woman and host of the other.

The issue is to protect the male guest from gang-rape by offering a more attractive alternative. Now, if being a virgin in the now-common sense were a recommendation to the rapists, then being a concubine in the common sense would not be. The host would have been well advised to leave the women's status unspecified. Unless the terms refer to age: two mature women, sexually useable, hence, rapeable, but still pretty 'fresh.' Incidentally, it is necessary to keep in mind who is doing the focalizing.

The two other concepts also change their meaning according to fabula. Here the usefulness of the provisional suspension of both contemporary and modern reality becomes visible. Suspending moral views of sexual lasciviousness as well as assumptions about ancient Hebrew life often based on projection, and looking at the fabulas for which these terms are used, reveals a structurally recurrent combination, in which the terms referring to female status are linked up with the father's house, inheritance, and displacement (mostly literally, travel). The key is the location of marital life. In all cases where these terms occur in

Judges, the status of the female partner is at stake, and that status is related to her not living or not staying in the house of the 'husband,' but staying or going back to the house of her father.

The terms, then, must not be related to a moralistically loaded concept such as prostitution or a class-bound, condescending concept like concubinage – the apparent display of the father's wealth, in Judges 19, hardly imposes the view that this woman has been sold by her poor relatives to serve as secondary wife. Instead, the original question of translation, through narratological analysis, is turned over to anthropology. The terms must be related to the issue of marriage forms. Judges displays other symptoms of a violent transition from patrilocal (wrongly called matriarchal) marriage to virilocal marriage (e.g. Judges 15), and the hypothesis that this tension underlies the narratives as well as the uses of the problematic terms helps explain the most obscure passages, in particular of the book's final section.

What is the interdisciplinary interaction going on here? Let us assume that I learned from Geertz to suspend the content of the category of the subject. For he suggested we take apparent incongruities as evidence of otherness, not of stupidity. Thus, anthropology 'came first.' As a result, I refrained from wondering what Jephthah's daughter may have thought of her imminent death, as a modern realistic psychologism would entice one to do, and instead took her words as indicators of some sort of ritual behaviour. Through considerations of fabula, the meaning of the term could then be related to phase rather than state. But I could only do this because, in a second move, I had related the detached term to narrative structure. This second move is the one Geertz does not make; instead, he narrates in the double voice I have pointed out.

In the second case – re *concubine* and *prostitute* – the transaction between the two disciplines is different. Narratological analysis of the fabula 'came first.' The structural property found – systematic connection between female status and marriage location, inheritance, and property – again covers an anthropological topic. But that background is a matter of established knowledge, not of method. The methodological issue is in the suspension of reality that narratological structural analysis entails. That suspension, paradoxically, is necessary in order for the less ethnocentric view of reality – of otherness – to emerge. In other words, narratology and anthropology, here, are constantly and polemically intertwined.

This kind of interaction between narratology and anthropology is the more relevant as it addresses implicitly the major challenge posed to narratology: that of, precisely, the social embedding of narrative – in other words, its relationship to reality. As we have seen, privileging structural analysis over a reflection theory of language has in fact helped to reach reality, by a detour that made it more rather than less accessible. What is at stake is the intertwining of three ideologies and their influence on real lives: the ancient male ideology according to which women's value is derived from bodily integrity, the ancient female ideology according to which shifts in life-phases are crucially important moments, and the modern ideology which projects sexual exclusivity as the major issue of an ancient narrative. Narratological analysis helped disentangle these. Thus it helped do justice to otherness. It also, albeit implicitly, makes it easy to see the nature of the otherness in sameness: that is, to what extent these modern translations are informed by an ideology that is male, and thus represses female concerns.

So, if the case for the relevance of fabula analysis has been made, let us begin working out the procedure. The material that constitutes the fabula can be divided into 'fixed' and 'changeable' elements – objects, on the one hand, and processes on the other. *Elements* may be understood as not only the actors who are more or less stable in most fabulas, but also as locations and things. *Processes* are the changes that occur in, with, through, and among the objects; in other words, the events. The word *process* emphasizes the ideas of development, succession, alteration, and interrelation among the elements. Both sorts of elements – objects and processes – are indispensable for the construction of a fabula. They cannot operate without one another.

2: Events

Selection

I have defined events in the introduction as 'the transition from one state to another state, caused or experienced by actors.' The word 'transition' stresses the fact that an event is a process, an alteration. Trying to establish which sentences in a text represent an event is the beginning of a fabula analysis. This appears an arid, technical endeavour but is already an interpretive step.

Many sentences refer to elements that may be considered processes. These same elements can often be objects as well as processes, depending upon the context. Such a selection results in an enormously large number of elements, impossible to work with. Moreover, the elements can only be compared with one another – a step that is necessary if relationships are to be established – if they display at least some correspondences with one another. I shall successively discuss three criteria, each of which further limits the number of events to be investigated, and each of which further develops a different aspect of the definition of events given above.

Change

Compare these two sentences:

a John is ill.

b John falls ill.

The first sentence describes a condition, the second a change. The difference can be seen in the verb. So we can begin by examining the series of events in which sentence b might occur. Imagine that the preceding text segment read as follows:

c John was cleaning his house.

John's illness interrupts his activity and, as such, indicates a change. But in that case, sentence c can precede either sentence a or sentence b equally well.

d John was cleaning his house. John is ill.

Is just as intelligible as

e John was cleaning his house. John fell ill.

In both cases the cleaning activities are interrupted, although in neither case is this explicitly stated. Sentences d and e differ in the same way from, for example, a text segment such as:

f John was cleaning his house. John fell ill and therefore had to stop cleaning.

The explicit relationship established in segment f is only implied in d and e. The relationship between c and a, or between c and b, is decisive for an analysis of the events; it is only in a series that events become meaningful for the further development of the fabula.

According to this view, it is pointless to consider whether or not an isolated fact is an event. The linguistic form in which the information is embodied can be an indication, but it is not always decisive. Furthermore, the general assumption that every event is indicated by a verb of action doesn't work either. It is, of course, possible to restate every event so that a verb of action appears in the sentence as, for example, with the verb 'stop' in sentence f. This provides a convenient means of making explicit any implicit relationships between facts, and can lead to a preliminary selection of events. As a result, however, the number of possible events becomes still too large.

Choice

In the article by Barthes mentioned above, the author distinguished between functional and non-functional events. Functional events open a choice between two possibilities, realize this choice, or reveal the results of such a choice. Once a choice is made, it determines the subsequent course of events in the developments of the fabula. Compare the following text segments:

g Liz leaves her house to go to work.
  She turns left and walks straight ahead.
  She arrives at eight-thirty.

h Liz leaves her house to go to work.
  She walks straight ahead, and crosses the street.
  Unconscious, she is carried into a hospital at eight-thirty.

Again, something is implied in both text segments: in g, that Liz successfully covered a certain distance; in h, that she was run down while crossing the street. If, soon after eight-thirty, something happens at work that influences the further development of the fabula, then the statement 'she turns left' may be considered to constitute an event: because the actor chose a certain route, she arrived in time to make the following event possible.

Should that not be the case, it does not mean that turning left has no significance. It cannot be included in the succession of functional events, but it can point to some particular characteristic of the actor in question. For example, it can indicate a punctual attitude towards work, a preference for a certain route, or leftish political views; this depends upon the network of meaning in the text as a whole. However, for the purpose of this analysis, the selection of functional events, this text segment doesn't matter. In segment h, something happens that most probably has consequences for the rest of the fabula. The actor is run down, something that would not have happened if she had chosen the other route. In turn, the accident presents a number of alternatives. Was Liz hit intentionally or not? If so, by an acquaintance or by a stranger?

Questions such as these could form the subject for a detective story. The sentence 'She walks straight ahead and crosses the street' indicates a functional event. But even if the result of segment h is more spectacular than that of segment g, this does not imply that such an event as that in segment h always satisfies the criterion. If this text segment is unrelated to the rest of the fabula and refers instead only to the world in which the fabula occurs – the accident can, for example, illustrate traffic congestion during the rush hour – then the choice in segment h between turning left and crossing the street is not a functional event. This is why the analogy with the sentence only goes so far; it is also why analogy with 'real life' cannot determine the result of the analysis.

As with the selection in the previous section, an intuitive decision is often necessary here. That an agreement may, however, be reached is demonstrated in the analysis that Chatman conducted using this method in his analysis of a narration from Joyce's *Dubliners*.

Confrontation

A third criterion for selecting events has been suggested by Hendricks. In a programmatic article, Hendricks presents a promising method for extracting the structure of the fabula from the text via formal procedures. One of his most important points can help to formalize and further refine Barthes' method so that the number of functional events is further reduced. Hendricks' point of departure is that the structure of the fabula is determined by confrontation. Two actors or groups of actors are confronted by each other. Every phase of the fabula – every functional event – consists of three components: two actors and one action; stated in the logical terms, two arguments and one predicate; in yet another formulation, two objects and one process. Linguistically, it should be possible to formulate this unity as: two nominal and one verbal component. The structure of the basis sentence would then be:

subject – predicate – (direct) object

in which both the subject and the (direct) object must be actors, agents of action.

According to this third criterion, only those segments of the text that can be presented by such a basis sentence constitute a functional event. Compare the following text segments:

i Liz writes a letter.

j Panting from exhaustion, John sat down. The entire room had been washed. He felt that he had earned a reward, so he poured himself a cup of coffee, dropped in two cubes of sugar, added a bit of evaporated skim milk, and took the most recent book from the *True Romances* down from the shelf. 'Great books for relaxing after work,' he said to himself. 'Not too difficult.' But the housework had been too strenuous, and he simply could not concentrate.

k John kills a fly.

l John kills a woman.

According to the logical criterion, sentence i is lacking one component. There is a subject, a predicate, and a direct object, but this last component (a letter) is not an actor. The necessary confrontation is, then, impossible. But writing a letter is an activity which presupposes an addressee, just as hiding a secret presupposes someone from whom one is hiding. The letter is written to someone. Although the second actor is not specifically named in this sentence, his or her existence is implied. Consequently, sentence i can be rewritten with the help of surrounding text segments: Liz writes (a letter to) John (or, to the tax inspector, her employees, her friend). Because it is possible to rewrite the sentence in this manner, we may consider it relevant to the structure of the fabula.

This same possibility is not implied in segment j. Despite the numerous actions performed by John, and the lifestyle which they suggest to the reader, John remains an isolated agent of action. His actions are not considered to be functional events because they do not bring about any change in the relation between John and another (group of) actor(s). Instead of considering this a lack, it is a (negative) sign of the life of people living in isolation.

Sentences k and l share a common subject and predicate; both sentences can provide just as much information about the character of the subject, but the difference between the two is clear. Here again, the nature of the direct object itself cannot provide a definite answer. Again, the answer as to whether either the fly or the woman may be considered an actor depends upon the context. It is quite possible to imagine a fabula in which John is continually confronted by a fly, as in La Fontaine's fable 'Le Coche et la Mouche,' for example; on the other hand, a murder can serve to illustrate a character trait and have no influence whatsoever on the development of the fabula, as in the short story 'The Man That Turned into a Statue' by Joyce Carol Oates. In this text, a woman who can in no way be considered an actor is murdered.

Relationships

According to the definition used in this study, a fabula is 'a series of logically and chronologically related events.' Once we have decided which facts we wish to consider events, we can then describe the relationships which connect one event to the other: the structure of the series of events. Structuralist methodology tells us how. Starting from Barthes' assumption that all fabulas are based on one model, we can begin to search for a model that is so abstract that it may be considered universal – until, that is, the model in question is either rejected or improved. This model is then 'laid upon' the text investigated; in other words, we examine the way in which and extent to which the concrete events can be placed in the basis model.

The purpose of this method is not to force the text into a general model and then to conclude that the text is indeed narrative. Such a procedure has given structuralist narratology a bad name. It could at best be useful for testing doubtful cases when trying to specify the corpus. Rather, a confrontation between a concrete fabula and a general model allows the description of the structure of the fabula of the text in question to be formulated more precisely, so that the specific structure is placed in relief and made visible. A 'perfect fit' as well as any deviations from the basis model can influence the meaning of the text.

One model that makes ample provision for this possibility is that suggested by Bremond. It must be remarked here that Bremond begins from the second postulate discussed in section 1: according to him, the narrated universal is regulated by the same rules as those which control human thought and action. These rules are determined by logical and conventional restrictions. A logical rule is, for example, that effect succeeds cause; thus, the hero dies after the bullet strikes him. A conventional restriction is, for example, that a worker is not rich.

The two sorts of restrictions have to do with each other; conventional restrictions could be seen as the interpretation, by historically and culturally determined groups, of logical rules in concrete situations. Also included among the conventional restrictions are the traditional rules to which texts of specific genres must conform; for example, a classical tragedy takes place in the mythical upper-class circles of kings and gods. Conventional restrictions are based in ideological and political assumptions. This is more obvious for older texts, or texts from other cultures, than for what is close by, because we might simply not see that what is 'normal' for one reader need not be so for others. For example, the convention that was broken by Madame de Lafayette's heroine in *The Princess of Cleves*, who – unheard of! implausible! – told her husband that she was in love with someone else, would hardly be felt by today's readers. 'What's the fuss about?' could be the response of any reader insensitive to the cultural difference between the seventeenth-century French upper classes and many segments of today's European societies.

As much as it is a mistake to take conventional restrictions for universal rules, so the opposite tendency, to shrug off any norm that one doesn't share, makes reading a very limited experience, and reading texts from other cultures seem tedious. It is, therefore, even or perhaps precisely today, worthwhile to test one's own norms against what can be gleaned from different narrative artifacts, by asking the question of the model's 'fit.'

As is true of every model, Bremond's model is abstract. This implies that he presents terms which can represent a large number of events; the events from every distinct fabula can be 'translated' into these abstract terms. In this way, the relations among the events can be made visible. The next section contains a brief reproduction of this model. This is then followed by a short survey of a few other principles for determining relations.

The Narrative Cycle

A fabula may be considered as a specific grouping of series of events. The fabula as a whole constitutes a process, while every event can also be called a process or, at least, part of a process. Theories are sometimes old, if not tenacious. According to Aristotle as well as Bremond, three phases can be distinguished in every fabula: the possibility (or virtuality), the event (or realization), and the result (or conclusion) of the process. None of these three phases is indispensable. A possibility can just as well be realized as not. And even if the event is realized, a successful conclusion is not always ensured. The following example illustrates these possibilities:

   a Liz wants to earn a diploma.

The following alternatives are possible:

   1   Liz wants to earn a diploma (a possibility)

   2.a She prepares for the exam (realization)
   2.b She does not prepare for the exam (no realization)

In b, the cycle is prematurely completed; in a, the third phase begins:

   3.a She passes the exam (conclusion)
   3.b She fails the exam (negative conclusion which can lead to the recommencement of the cycle)

These phases cannot always be explicitly found in the text, as is demonstrated in example b:

   b John wants to offer his girlfriend a lovely dinner. The beef Stroganoff tastes delicious. (The butcher was closed so John serves a sandwich.) (The beef was excellent but, unfortunately, burnt.)

The preceding has been conceived as an elaboration of Barthes' criterion for selection. Bremond calls this first grouping an elementary series. These series are combined with one another. The combination of elementary series into complex series can assume a variety of forms. The processes can occur one after the other. In this case, the result of the first process is also the beginning (virtuality) of the new process.

   c John is tired (= he can rest)
     He rests (= he feels fine again)

He feels fine (= he can work again) = John feels fine (= he can work)
He works (= he becomes tired)
He is tired (= he can rest), etc.

The processes can also be embedded in another process, as, for example, when one possibility opens another, or when one realization leads to another possibility.

d John is tired (= he can fall asleep)
   John falls asleep = John can forget about his exam
                      He forgets about his exam
                      He fails
   John feels fine again

In this example, the first series, the *primary series*, leads to an improvement in John's condition, and the *embedded series* leads to a deterioration. As is apparent from this example, the so-called primary series is not necessarily more important than the embedded series in order for the fabula to proceed; the embedded series is probably more important in this example. Such situations can characterize the *style* of a fabula. When, for example, important events are continually embedded in everyday, banal events which are the cause of the important events, an effect of determinism is likely to occur. It can, for example, be read as an expression of fatalism, of the impotency of man against the world, or of an existential view of life. On the other hand, a 'minimalist' fabula where the important events remain unstated but 'colour' the seemingly unimportant, everyday events, tends to become pregnant with importance.

In d, a causal relationship can be indicated or implied between the primary series and the embedded series. This is not always the case. The embedded series often provides a specification of the primary series.

e Peter insults John
   John is angry   = John asks for an explanation
                                  Peter explains
   John is no longer angry = John understands

In this example, asking for an explanation is a specific form of being angry. It is also possible to express anger in another way, for example, by hitting someone; in this case, another embedded series with another specification of the primary series would evolve.

There are innumerable possibilities for succession and embedding, so that an infinite number of fabulas can be formed. Bremond's further structuring of these series is based upon his definition of narrative texts which is as follows:

> A narrative consists of a language act by which a succession of events having human interest are integrated into the unity of this same act.
>
> Bremond 1973, 186

With regard to the fabula, this definition distinguishes itself from the definition given earlier in this *Introduction* only by the addition of 'human interest.' Because this difference is actually a theoretical issue, and, in fact, one of reception, I will not discuss the issue further at this point. But it deserves some thought that so many narratives hold the reader's attention by precisely some form of 'human interest.'

One division based on human interest is that between processes of improvement and processes of deterioration. Both sorts are possible, both can be realized or not, and both can conclude successfully or not.

Example e represents a possible deterioration which is avoided by an embedded improvement. In example d, the process of improvement contains an embedded deterioration, while example c represents an improvement and a deterioration immediately following each other.

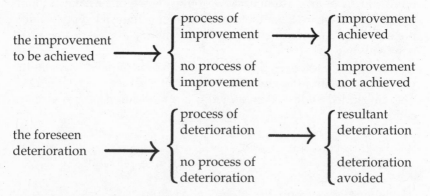

The various processes of improvement or deterioration, grouped in certain combinations, together constitute a *narrative cycle*. Each of the various processes has its own semantic contents. Applying a semantic label to an event makes it easier to compare the structures of different fabulas with one another. For example:

the fulfilment of the task
the intervention of allies
the elimination of the opponent
the negotiation
the attack
the satisfaction

It is quite easy to conceive of other possibilities at the same level of abstraction. When seen as the theoretical abstractions of concrete events, these possibilities can be found in many texts. Satisfaction, for example, can take the form of punishment, revenge, or reward, and these sorts of satisfaction can, in turn, be further specified.

The same applies to processes of deterioration. Bremond cites:

the misstep
the creation of an obligation
the sacrifice
the endured attack
the endured punishment

A misstep can, for example, take the form of a mistake, an error, a social blunder or a moral lapse, or a crime – and naming it in any of these terms is an interpretive step of consequence. And these variations can then assume other concrete forms. The initial situation in a fabula will always be a state of deficiency in which one or more actors want to introduce changes. The development of the fabula reveals that, according to certain patterns, the process of change involves an improvement or deterioration with regard to the initial situation.

Other Principles of Structure

The events selected can be related to one another in a variety of ways. For this reason, it is best not refer to *the* structure of a fabula, but to *a* possible structure. Bremond's model can be used as a basis, but it can also be left out of consideration, not because it would be invalid but because we can foresee that the results would not be very relevant to the fabula in question.

The following suggestions are not further elaborated. They are presented in order to give an idea of the multitude of possibilities, and, in so doing, to make clear that structures are formed by the investigating subject on the basis of selected events combined with other data. These possibilities are intended to give some impression of the ways in which we can introduce structures into a collection of elements. This does not imply that it makes no difference if we work at random. The structures can only be built on the basis of data; the relationship between the data and what is done with it is only convincing if made explicit, and some degree of relevancy will be foreseeable for the student to be interested in undertaking the analysis at all. Although the weather in Virginia Woolf's *To the Lighthouse* is often cold and raw, it does not seem relevant to contrast the events that occur in cold weather with those that occur in good or neutral weather conditions in order to establish a principle of structure.

First, the events can be grouped on the basis of the identity of the actors involved. If the chronological order is maintained or reconstructed, the fabula is segmented into phases. For example: actor A is the subject from event 1 through 6, actor B is the subject from event 7 through 15, etc. (see section 3, below, for the term 'subject' in the fabula). The same can be done on the basis of the object, the actor who experiences the action. The events in which the two most important actors are confronted by one another can be contrasted with events in which only one of these two actors is involved with another, secondary, actor, and so on.

Second, classification is possible on the basis of the nature of the confrontation. Is there verbal (spoken), mental (via thoughts, feelings, observations), or bodily contact? Are these contacts successful, do they fail, or is this impossible to determine? Such data can help to discover meanings in many difficult modern texts. If, for example, the contact between the two most important actors is predominantly mental and unsuccessful, we could conclude, if other data confirmed our conclusion, that the theme is alienation, a pre-eminently twentieth-century theme. The relationship between bodily and mental contact can suggest another theme.

Third, the events can be placed against time lapse. Some events can occur at the same time, others succeed one another. These latter form a linked series, sometimes interrupted by a span of time in which nothing occurs, at least nothing that is narrated. 'She used to be an Art Teacher' implies a long period of time between 'being an art teacher' and the current situation, where the mother is a full-time homemaker.

Fourth, the locations at which events occur can also lead to the formation of a structure. Depending on the fabula in question, different oppositions can be relevant: inside-outside, above-below, city-country, here-there, etc. (Lotman 1977, 330; for a feminist critique, see De Lauretis 1983). These possibilities can be combined with one another. We might foresee, for example, that actor A is always the subject when the events occur inside, and actor B when the scene shifts to the outside; or that the contact always or almost always fails in one case while it succeeds in another; or that A especially desires verbal contact and B mental contact. Thus we can make intuitive choice, necessitated by the simple fact that we cannot investigate everything, explicit by means of our analysis. This carries with it the advantage of allowing us to pursue our own interests to a great extent while keeping to the same intersubjectively understandable model of analysis.

3: Actors

In defining the concept of 'event' I already used the term 'actors.' In the selection of events and the formation of sequences, actors always were important elements. In the following, therefore, actors will be regarded in their relation to the sequences of events that – as follows from our definition – they cause or undergo.

Selection

In order to begin to analyse this, it helps first to select which actors must be taken into consideration and which not. In some fabulas there are actors who have no functional part in the structures of that fabula because they do not cause or undergo functional events. Actors of this type may be left out of consideration. What I said earlier also applies here: the initial disregard of an actor does not mean that this actor is without significance. It only means that this particular actor does not form part of the functional category, and therefore need not be taken into consideration. Well-known examples are the porters and maids who open the front doors in many nineteenth-century novels. Such actors act, by opening the door, and thus they fit the definition of actors, but their action does not belong to the category of functional events. Therefore they fall outside the scope of this analysis. Which, not so incidentally, marks their cultural position more devastatingly than their full participation possibly can.

This is not to say that they may not be meaningful as an indication of a certain social stratification; and in that case they contribute to the representation of bourgeois society given in such a novel. They might also serve as an indication of a specific use of space; they guard the boundary between inside and outside, and demonstrate this boundary's permeability. In order to acquire insight into the relations between events, it is necessary to limit the actors to the category of functional actors. In order to do so, one may rely on an earlier analysis of events. If this analysis has been skipped, an intuitive summary of the event may provide a preliminary starting point that might be tested later, for instance by drawing selective samples. This procedure, however, entails a vicious circle when one makes the summary with a certain subdivision of the actors already in mind. A middle-of-the-road solution might be to ask several people to write a summary, and to use the elements they have in common. In the practice of teaching this is a helpful way to engage students in the collective analysis.

Classes of Actors

An important tool for understanding the fabula is the subdivision of its actors into classes. Taking as a basis the presupposition that human thinking and action are directed towards an aim, structuralists such as Greimas have constructed a model which represents the relations to the aim. This model claims universal validity for its operative principle and is not limited to invented fabulas. As such, it offers a good opportunity for reflection on the relations between fiction, reality, and truth. This is not a specifically narratological concern.

As mentioned earlier, the model starts from a teleological relation between the elements of the story. The actors have an intention; they aspire towards an aim. That aspiration is the achievement of something pleasant, agreeable or favourable, or the evasion of something unpleasant, disagreeable or unfavourable. The verbs to wish and to fear indicate this teleological relation and are, therefore, used as abstractions of the intentional connections between elements.

In this model, the classes of actors are called *actants.* An actant is a class of actors that shares a certain characteristic quality. That shared characteristic is related to the teleology of the fabula as a whole. An actant is therefore a class of actors whose members have an identical relation to the aspect of telos which constitutes the principle of the fabula. That relation we call the function. This is a typically structuralist model: it is conceived in terms of fixed relations between classes of phenomena, which is a standard definition of structure.

Subject and Object

The first and most important relation is between the actor who pursues an aim and that aim itself. That relation may be compared to that between subject and direct object in a sentence. The first two classes of actors to be distinguished, therefore, are subject and object: actor x aspires towards goal y. x is a subject-actant, y an object-actant. For instance, in a typical love story the slots may be filled as follows: John – wants to marry – Mary. John is subject, Mary object, and the element of intention of the fabula takes the form of 'wanting to marry.'

The object is not always a person. The subject may also aspire towards reaching a certain state. In Stendhal's novel *The Red and the Black*, for instance, one might see the following scheme: Julien – wants to acquire – power; or: Julien – aspires towards – becoming a powerful man. Other objects of intention found in fabulas are riches, possessions, wisdom, love, happiness, a place in heaven, a bed to die in, an increase in salary, a just society; you name it. Thus the actant, and also its concrete embodiment the actor, are, in theory, disconnected from the embodiment in a person. This is implied in our structural approach. However, since, as was said earlier, the principle of the fabula resides in its aspect of intention, the practical result is that the subject is usually a person or a personified animal (in animal fables), not an object.

The following examples give an impression of the multiplicity of possibilities which can be 'translated' into this basic structural scheme:

actor/actant-subject	*function*	*actor/actant object*
a John	wants to marry	Mary
b Anna Wulf	wants to become	an independent woman
c the old people	want to prevent	the discovery of their crime
d Kinsey Millhone	wants to know	the identity of the muderer
e the killer	wants to avoid	Millhone's discovery
f Marxists	want to bring about	a classless society
g Tom Thumb	wants to have	a safe return
h Scheherazade	wants to prevent	the king's killing her

The reader has undoubtedly recognized in this series a number of well-known fabulas and/or types of fabulas.

The examples have been chosen from very different types of texts: an epistolary novel (a); a feminist novel (b); a nineteenth-century novel (c); a modern detective novel (d and e); a work of social philosophy (f); a fairy tale (g); a story sequence from folk literature (h). I shall return to these examples. At present we only need to realize that it is indeed likely that in very many if not all fabulas, a similar scheme can be pointed to. Which is not yet to say that it helps much to do so.

Power and Receiver

The intention of the subject is in itself not sufficient to reach the object. There are always powers that either allow it to reach its aim or prevent it from doing so. This relation might be seen as a form of communication, and we can, consequently, distinguish a class of actors – consisting of those who support the subject in the realization of its intention, supply the object, or allow it to be supplied or given – whom we shall call the power. The person to whom the object is 'given' is the receiver. The French terms used by Greimas are *destinateur* and *destinataire*, and 'sender' and 'receiver' are their most literal translation. However, 'sender' suggests an active intervention or an active participation, and this does not always apply; that is why 'power' is perhaps a better term.

Often the power is not a person but an abstraction: e.g., society, fate, time, human self-centredness, or cleverness. The receiver may also be embodied in a person. Thus a typology of fabulas might be related to the concretization of this actant: in fairy tales the 'sender' is mostly a person, such as a king who under certain conditions gives his daughter in marriage to the aspiring subject. In psychological novels, a character trait of the subject itself is often the power which either facilitates or blocks the achievement of the aim. In many so-called 'realistic' nineteenth-century novels the class structure of bourgeois society is decisive – one is determined for life by one's social background. It is also possible that several powers are in play at the same time. A combination of a character trait (ambition) and a social power (the division into rich and poor) may conflict as positive and negative power.

The receiver is often the same person as the subject. S/he desires something or somebody for him- or herself. But, since this is not always the case, it is necessary to specify this class of actors. In principle the subject and the power predominate more, or are more active in a grammatical sense, than the object and the receiver, because they are the agents, or the (grammatical) subject, either of the function of intention/evasion or of giving/receiving.

I have already mentioned the possibility of the coalescence of two actants into one actor or the reverse, the concretization of one actant, the power, in several specific powers. This makes us realize that the basis of our model is the principle of numerical inequality; and that this principle, however problematic it may seem, is at once the model's justification. In principle all actants are represented in each fabula: without actants no relations, without relations no process, without process no fabula. But the number of actors is unlimited. It may happen that in one fabula we find only one actor, a heroine who, for instance, is at war with herself, her passions, her madness, and so on. On the other hand, it is also possible that large numbers of actors, whole crowds, armies, or university groups, form together one actant. An example of the coalescence of four distinct actants into two actors is, again, the typical, conventional love story in which the receiver is the longing lover himself and the power coalesces with the object: she 'gives' herself.

He: subject + receiver
She: object + power

The conventional nature of this plot becomes clear when we try to reverse it, and fill both versions out further.

On the basis of this analysis, one gains insight into the relations between the powers that form the basis of the unreversed, conventional version. Seen grammatically, the active subject is passive in his role of receiver: he must wait and see whether he will receive the desired object. On the other hand, the passive object is also subject, and therefore more autonomous, in the role of power. The apparently passive object actant is, as power, the decisive factor in the background. The forces have been equally divided over the two actors. An inversion of roles would, therefore, not mean an inversion of power, and give no reason for the 'he' to panic. But the plot changes as soon as the actant 'power' is placed elsewhere. The symmetry is gone, and the development of the plot depends on the collusion or lack of it between subject and power.

The examples of the previous sections may now be expanded:

actor/actant-subject	function	actor/actant object
a John	wants to marry	Mary
b Anna Wulf	wants to become	an independent woman
c the old people	want to prevent	the discovery of their crime
d Kinsey	wants to know	the identity of the murderer
e the killer	wants to avoid	Millhone's discovery
f Marxists	want to bring about	a classless society
g Tom Thumb	wants to have	a safe return
h Scheherazade	wants to prevent	the king's killing her

power	function	receiver
a Mary	is prepared	John
b the existing social structure	makes it impossible	for her(self)
c fate/time	make it impossible to hide their disgrace	from themselves and Ottilie
d her psychological insight	allows her to do so	to the benefit of herself, the police, and society
e his obsession and Millhone's insight	make it impossible	for the killer
f history	makes it impossible	for mankind
g his cleverness	brings that about	for himself and his brothers
h her powers of narrative	have that effect	to her own benefit

Helper and Opponent

The categories discussed so far are directly geared to the object, which is object both of desire and of communication. Both relations are necessary for the development of a fabula. But a fabula based on merely these two relations would end very soon: the subject wants something and either gets it or not. Usually the process is not so simple. The aim is difficult to achieve. The subject meets with resistance on the way and receives help. Thus the model distinguishes a third relation which determines the circumstances under which the enterprise is brought to an end.

In analogy with the structure of the sentence, these two actants might be regarded as adverbial adjuncts. They are not related to the object by means of 'a verb,' but relate through such things as prepositions, e.g. *owing to, notwithstanding,* to the function that connects subject with object. These actants are in many respects different from the others. They are not in direct relation to the object, but to the function that connects subject with object. At first sight they do not appear necessary to the action. In practice, however, they are often rather numerous. They determine the various adventures of the subject, who must sometimes overcome great opposition before s/he can reach his or her goal.

It is often difficult to agree on the difference between power and helper. The following points of difference may help to solve this difficulty.

power	*helper*
has power over the whole enterprise	can give only incidental aid
is often abstract	is mostly concrete
often remains in the background	often comes to the fore
usually only one	usually multiple

The same points of difference can be pointed to between a negative power, a power who prevents the subject from reaching the object, and an opponent.

Another issue concerns the reader's sympathy or antipathy, since the relations between actants are not the same as those between actants and reader. The helper is not always the person who acts to bring about the ending desired by the reader. When the subject seems unsympathetic to the reader, the helper will, most likely, be so too; and the sympathy of the reader will go towards the opponent of the subject. If one confuses these two areas of relationship one easily mistakes the division of forces.

This is surely not to imply that sympathy must be eliminated from the reading experience, or from the analysis for that matter. On the contrary; it is, again, in the difference between actantial roles and reader's response that the specific effect of the narrative's fabula receives relief and visibility.

The examples of page 206 may now be expanded. I give only a sample of the many possibilities. In a, for instance, Mary's father might be an opponent if he opposed the marriage; John's good job, Mary's determination, and an interceding aunt could be helpers. In b several of Anna's friends, social prejudice, her employer might be opponents; her best friend tries to give help which is not sufficient to reach her aim. In c the several children, their curiosity, the memories of Harold are opponents; the doctor and those among the children who keep silent, helpers. In d and e helpers of one are the opponents of the other: witnesses, meetings, circumstances that help to bring the solution about, a button left on the scene of the murder, the murderer's alcoholism, a talkative concierge, and more. In f the proletariat is helper and the bourgeoisie opponent. In g the giant's wife and boots are helpers; the nightfall, the birds who eat the crumbs, and the giant's power of smell, which tell him that prey is near, are opponents. In h every story Scheherazade tells is a helper, and the unremitting suspicion and jealousy of her husband opponents.

From these examples it becomes clear that each helper forms a necessary but in itself insufficient condition to reach the aim. Opponents must be overcome one by one, but such an act of overcoming does not guarantee a favourable ending: any moment a new opponent may loom. It is the presence of helpers and opponents which makes a fabula suspenseful and readable.

Further Specification

This model is structural: it describes a structure – the relations between different kinds of phenomena – and not, primarily, the phenomena themselves. As we saw earlier, this model results in a numerical inequality of actors and actants. It is not surprising that one class of actors comprises more than one actor. The reverse, the fact that one actor stands for several classes, can only be understood if one disconnects the concept of 'actor' from that of 'person': this is the reason why the term 'person' is avoided when discussing actants and actors.

I have already indicated some causes of the numerical inequality between actors and actants. The relationship between subject and object is the most important; it is the motor of the fabula. It can be aimed at the appropriation of someone, something, or, on the other hand, a quality in oneself. In the first case the object is a separate actor, in the second it is not. In the first case the relationship is objective, aimed at an outside object; in the second case the subject aims at (an aspect of) the subject itself; the relationship is subjective. In some cases this entails the further splitting or merging of actors and actants. The merging of the power with the object and the receiver with the subject occurs with frequency. One also notes the merging of power with subject when a character trait of the subject is of overriding importance. Perhaps we may take it as a rule that the greater the fabula's orientation towards the actual outside world, the greater the number of actors; to the degree in which the fabula is subjective, oriented towards the subject, the number of actors decreases.

Doubling

Some fabulas have different subjects who are in opposition: a subject and an anti-subject. An anti-subject is not an opponent. An opponent opposes the subject at certain moments of the pursuit of his or her aim. It is this incidental opposition which determines the structural position. An anti-subject pursues his or her own object, and this pursuit is, at a certain moment, at cross purposes with that of the first subject. When an actant has his or her own program, his or her own aims, and acts to achieve this aim, s/he is an autonomous subject. It is also possible that a fabula has a second subject that does not come into opposition with the program of the first subject, but is entirely independent from it, or s/he may, consciously or not, give incidental aid or opposition to the achievement of the first subject's aim. In that case there are moments in the fabula when the different lines touch or cross. (Using a different terminology, we would speak of the difference between the various episodes of one plot, and various sub-plots.) The appearance of a separate subject indicates the existence of a sub-fabula. In Couperus' *Of Old People,* for instance, we might regard some of the children and grandchildren as autonomous subjects. In his struggle to become an artist, Lot needs self-analysis as a helper. This helper proves an opponent when Lot gains insight into the emotional predisposition of his heritage, and when his aims begin to conflict with those of the old people.

It also happens that the power consists of two actants, a positive and a negative one. In naturalistic novels we often note the opposition of a personal will-power to social structure or heredity. It is likely that an extensive analysis of a number of naturalistic novels might give us as a characteristic result the opposition of two powers as a form of fabula intermediate between the subjective and the objective, between the one oriented towards the individual and the one directed towards the outside world.

Competence

Aside from oppositions there are other principles to further specify act-ants. If the process of the fabula can be seen as the execution of a pro-gram, then each execution presupposes the possibility of the subject to proceed to execution. This possibility of the subject to act, the compe-tence, may be of different kinds, which leads to further specification.

Greimas subdivides competence into the determination or will of the subject to proceed to action, the power or possibility, and the knowl-edge or skill necessary to execute the aim. On this basis some critics have distinguished three different kinds of subjects. It makes sense to distinguish the phase of the fabula in which the virtual subject begins to desire the execution of the program; this phase might be seen as the introduction to the fabula. The distinction between power/possibility and knowledge/skill is a second principle of differentiation. The gi-ants, witches, and wolves of the fairy tale are actants of the first cat-egory, Tom Thumb of the second one. It may have struck the reader that in the analysis of example g, the one of Tom Thumb, I have paid little attention to the giant. I have only mentioned his power of smell. It is evident, however, that the giant plays an important role in the fabula, more important than, for instance, his wife or Tom's brothers. Merely classifying him as an opponent would be insufficient as a definition. He has his own program. He wants to find children and eat them. He reaches that goal in part: he finds children and eats them because he has the power to do so, owing to his physical force and size.

Still, he does not fully reach his goal: he eats the wrong children. His program is at cross purposes with that of Tom Thumb, who aims at a safe return home. The giant does not catch Tom Thumb and his broth-ers, because Tom Thumb possesses the second kind of competence, knowledge and skill in the form of cleverness.

It would appear that in this example the specification coincides with the opposition between good and evil powers. In fairy tales this is cer-tainly often the case. It also seems to apply to the classic detective story. Nevertheless, there is an important difference, especially in this respect. Examples d and e show that Kinsey Millhone and the murderer are in opposition. Millhone's competence is one of skill and knowledge. How-ever, so is that of the murderer; and it is in this respect that the detective story differs from the fairy tale. What characterizes the detective story is that the murderer fails in his or her competence: he makes a mistake. The detective novel has attempted to break through the opposition of good and evil, as for instance in the novels of the Swedish team of writers Sjöwall and Wahlöö. It is striking that, especially in those novels, the hitherto fixed division of competence should be broken. The detective often reaches his or her goal by accident or sometimes not at all, as in *The Locked Room*. The 'power' then is not the detective's insight, but fate or serendipity. In other instances the detective reaches the aim through the manipulation of power. If, owing to his or her social position, the culprit is forced into such a tight corner that she is ripe and ready to give him- or herself up to the detective, the latter only needs to dispose of the power to mobilize the police in order to reach his or her aim.

Truth Value

The final factor leading to further specification of actants is that of truth value. By truth value I mean the 'reality' of the actants within the actantial structure. This specification is of importance not only with regard to the subject, but also with regard to the helpers and opponents. Often they are only in appearance what they seem to be; in reality they prove the opposite. A traitor has the appearance of a helper, but reveals him- or herself in the course of the story as an opponent. In the reverse case there are secret helpers: actors who help the subject who believes s/he is dealing with an opponent, or an actor who seems to help the subject while the latter does not realize that this actor is not at all related to his or her own enterprise. According to this specification, certain categories of actors stand out: liars, master figures, false heroes, invisible fairies, but also truth-tellers, false clues, sudden moments of inspiration or misgivings which instigate the subject to take wrong decisions, seducers, etc. The several possibilities are outlined in the following table:

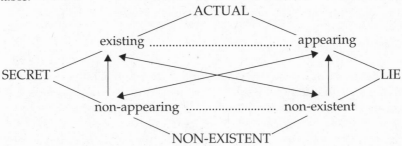

---> implication
.... opposition
<--> contradiction

This table shows the similarities and differences between the possible positions of actors with regard to 'truth.' 'Truth' exists in the coincidence of existence and appearance, of the identity and qualities of an actor on the one hand and the impression she makes, his or her claims, on the other. When an actor is what she appears, she is true. When she does not put up an appearance, or, in other words hides who she is, this identity is secret. When he neither is nor puts up an appearance, he cannot exist as an actor; when he appears to be what he is not, this identity is a lie.

Not only actants but complete actantial schemes may be qualified as 'true' or 'false.' The frequent situation of the subject aspiring towards an illusory goal and finally realizing it might be accounted for in this way.

To this aspect of actantial analysis we might also try to relate a typology. Fabulas which show the predominating influence of a secret in their actantial structure (e.g., certain fairy tales and myths) might be opposed as a separate category to fabulas in which a lie determines structure. *Of Old People* hinges on the structural principle of the secret. So do detective stories. In spy novels the concept of the lie predominates. This division into classes of actors helps us to interpret, to set up typologies to sharpen our definitions of the literary movements, and to contrast fabulas that appear rather similar at first sight but prove different at vital points; on the other hand, it allows us to compare the actantial structures of apparently widely different fabulas. An analysis of this type may show unexpected aspects of meanings.

The supposition that the model outlined above is the only possible one would be absurd. Just as in the case of the analysis of events, there are many other possibilities of approaching the matter which may or may not combine with our model. I briefly list a few below.

Other Divisions into Classes

In whatever way one regards literature or art, whether one values books or films as autonomous works of art, as products of an individual or group, as objects of communication, as a specific form of a sign system, one can never escape the obvious fact that works of art and literature are made by, for, and – usually – about people. Relations between people themselves and between people and the world will therefore almost always be of importance in fabulas. It is possible to describe in every fabula at least one type of relation between actors that is of a psychological or ideological nature, or of both simultaneously. Each of these relations may give a specific content to the relation between subject and power, between subject and anti-subject, but they may also be studied separately from the actantial model. On the basis of the information about the actors contained in the text, one may group them according to those principles which seem important in the frame of reference of the fabula or groups of fabulas under analysis.

First, psychological relations are of overriding importance in psychologically or psychoanalytically oriented criticism and determine the specification of actors into 'psychic instances.' What does it mean to say that one actor relates to another as daughter to mother, as father to son, or son to mother? Attempts have even been made to account for the difference between tragedy and comedy and their effect on the reader: in tragedy the son is guilty about the father, whom he, unconsciously, desires to replace; in comedy the father is guilty about the son and is consequently punished and replaced by the latter. In other cases the relationship between man and wife, or between child and adult, or between strong and weak personalities attracts attention.

Second, ideological relations occur, in addition to psychological relationships, in many if not all fabulas. Whether it is the opposition between feudalism and liberalism, liberalism and socialism, patriarchy and feminism, colonialism and emancipation, or more specific oppositions, actors must always deal with the ideological oppositions of the world in which they move. The opposition between the individual and the collective, or between the individual and the representatives of power, is often of importance both in medieval romances and in nineteenth-century realistic novels. In Kafka's novels this opposition is even the primary thematic centre. Other oppositions of groups result in ideological relationships: black against white, men against women, employers against employees, 'haves' against 'have-nots,' conformists against individualists, the 'normal' against the 'insane.' These oppositions demonstrate that not the categories as such but the categorization, not the differences but the structure of opposition itself is the ideological trap.

Third, all kinds of different oppositions may become important on the basis of data which, at first sight, do not have a psychological or ideological foundation, even if, on further consideration, it becomes apparent that they are often linked to psychological or ideological oppositions. On the basis of physical appearance groups may take shape; fair versus dark or red-haired, an opposition which in works of ideological

fiction seems to coincide with that between good and evil, thus conveying a racist ideology, or its parallel, the opposition of good-but-boring
to exciting-but-evil. On the basis of past experience, heritage, possessions, relationships to third parties, age, and lifestyle, other groups may
take shape which are often also related to psychological or ideological
relationships.

4: Time

Events have been defined as processes. A process is a change, a development, and presupposes therefore a succession in time or a chronology.
The events themselves happen during a certain period of time and they
occur in a certain order. McEwan wrote about 'the pinprick on the time
map.' Some narratives make their point primarily by means of duration. Werner Herzog's 2007 film *Rescue Dawn*, which describes almost
exclusively the captivity, escape, and waiting for rescue of an American
soldier in Vietnam, makes duration its primary fabula; the poverty of
events is the point of this film about waiting.

Duration

The fabula of 'Tom Thumb' occupies a span of some three days. The
first event, the overhearing of the parents' intention to rid themselves
of their expensive children, takes place at night. So does the gathering
of pebbles. The expedition to the wood and the return journey occupy
the day following that night. The next night or, in some versions, a
following night, at some indeterminate time, Tom Thumb again over-
hears his parents, again tries to collect pebbles, but finds himself pre-
vented from leaving the house. The night after that the children get
lost and wander into the giant's den. That night the giant eats his own
children by mistake.

   The next day Tom Thumb and his brothers return home safely in possession of the seven-mile boots, which guarantee a fixed income that
will preclude the repetition of the fabula in the future. The time span
of this fabula forms one continuous whole, possibly with the exception
of the first night, which may be regarded as a prelude to the fabula
proper. In three days the family's life changes substantially, from desperate poverty to happy prosperity. In 'Little Red Riding Hood' the
whole fabula occupies only half a day. The principle narrative of the
Arabian Nights presents a fabula which takes one season; that of *War*

and Peace takes many years. The fabula of the Old Testament lasts many centuries. Kinsey Millhone's investigations are, as a rule, finished in a few days, while Hercule Poirot and Miss Marple usually take longer. Classical tragedy even has rules about time. The time span of its fabula, which should not extend beyond one day and one night, thus functions as an aesthetic criterion or, at least, as a differential criterion with regard to genre.

While 'unity of time' as a generic requirement remains restricted to classical tragedy, the time span of a fabula – which may show such wide differences – is also of significance in the fabulas of narrative texts. A first, general distinction might be that between crisis and development: the first term indicates a short span of time into which events have been compressed, the second a longer period of time which shows a development. In itself neither of these two forms has clear advantages over the other. It has sometimes been said that a development would be more realistic, more in accord with the experience of 'real life.' This seems doubtful, to say the least. In reality too, moments of crisis present themselves, moments during which, in a brief instant of time, the life of persons or an entire nation takes a decisive turn. It depends, moreover, on one's personal views about literature whether one prefers a greater or lesser degree of verisimilitude. It does seem likely, however, that a preference for one of these forms entails a certain vision of the fabula, and, often, of reality. It is likely, therefore, that such a form is meaningful in itself.

Certain types of fabulas are specifically appropriate for either of the two types of duration, or even dependent upon it. (Auto)biographies, Bildungsromans, war novels, frame narratives (*Arabian Nights, Decameron*), and travel histories need a fairly long time span: the most important topic presented is precisely the passing of time. Other narrative texts, however, need a brief period of time, especially when describing a moment of crisis. Classical tragedy and the novels inspired by it are not the only examples. Many modern and contemporary novels and stories have also been written in the crisis form. The novels *La modification* by Michel Butor and *Seize the Day* by Saul Bellow, each a well-known representative of new developments in the post-war novel, have, in this respect, been compared to classical tragedy. Though the fabula of Henry James' *The Ambassadors* covers a period not of twenty-four hours but of several months, one may see it as a crisis nevertheless.

However, the distinction between crisis and development is relative. One form blends into the other. A fabula tends to a greater or lesser degree towards either one of the two forms, or covers the middle ground. Hence, it is often possible to distinguish both forms within one type of text. Sometimes, when this is the case, they can be considered characteristic of a certain sub-form, an author, or a developmental phase of the type. Earlier I suggested a difference between the detective novels of Sue Grafton and Agatha Christie. True, a more systematic analysis of their entire oeuvre would be needed to confirm the impression gained from a relatively small number of their novels. However, the point here is not that in principle a distinction of this kind results in a typology of texts. The preference for a crisis or development does not merely imply a certain vision of reality or a choice of a certain type of texts. Once selected, the two forms have implications for the construction of the fabula.

1.a A development may present, in historical order, as much material as seems fit. It is not by accident that these novels or films are usually rather long.
1.b The selection of a crisis form implies a restriction: only brief periods from the life of the actor are presented. In narrative painting the crisis is a privileged form for the obvious reason that a still image can only accommodate a limited number of events. What art historians call 'the pregnant moment' is the pictorial equivalent of a crisis. Such paintings represent a single moment, but one which can only be understood as following the past and announcing the future.
2.a In a development, the global significance is built up slowly from the strings of events. The insights of the actors, and their mutual relationships, take shape through the quality of events.
2.b In a crisis, the significance is central and informs what we might call the surrounding elements. The crisis is representative, characteristic of the actors and their relationships.
3.a But a development, too, requires selection. It is not an entire lifetime which is presented, but parts from it; parts are skipped, abbreviated, summarized. Films cut from one scene to another. Marleen Gorris' 1995 film *Antonia's Line* marks the development by the physical aging of the characters and the births of children. Other parts are worked out, given an extra-detailed representation. From one novel or film to another we find great differences in this representation of the development.
3.b The crisis, too, hardly ever occurs in its ideal form. Corneille met

with the reproach that his *Cid* was too crowded with events for a twenty-four-hour span; the fight against the Moors, in addition to all the other events, could not possibly have taken place in so brief a time. In narrative – since it is, traditionally, less governed by precept than drama – the basic form is more easily varied and diverged from. In a crisis this does not happen primarily through summary, selection, or highlighting but through asides. Thus we find recollections. In this way the time span of *Of Old People* is extended from one season to sixty years. Or, we encounter references to past and future: at the end of most fairy tales ('Tom Thumb' is no exception), the future of the protagonist(s) is briefly alluded to. There is another kind of diversion that can also serve to extend the time span of the crisis form: a minor actor can become the protagonist in his own fabula; in this way a sub-fabula is created. These possibilities for extending the compass of the crisis and compressing the development are closely linked with the other aspect mentioned: that of chronology.

Chronology: Interruption and Parallelism

Techniques of varying the time sequence by means of elimination, or of condensation of duration, and of the parallel development of several strands of the fabula have a bearing on the chronology of the fabula. Elimination causes gaps in the sequence of chronology. A period of time is skipped, often without being noticed by the reader. What has been eliminated? This is, of course, a nonsensical question, parodied in McEwan's nevertheless earnest 'I don't recall …' The fabula is, after all, nothing but the series of events that are mentioned. No one is likely to wonder what Tom Thumb's profession will be or at what age he started to walk. Still, often omitted events are brought to the fore in other parts of the text. Thus ellipsis – the omission of an element that belongs in a series – gains its power of signification. Robbe-Grillet's *Voyeur* is, perhaps, the most spectacular illustration. In this novel an event which, according to the further information given by the fabula, must certainly have taken place is omitted. It would even seem the most important event of the entire fabula: the sadistic murder of a young girl, probably committed by the protagonist. Throughout the fabula this actor, Mattias, exerts himself in filling this gap in time, establishing an 'innocent' chronology. Until the very end it is not clearly evident that Mattias is the murderer. Consequently, the fabula cannot be fully described.

Though it is not as central as in *Le voyeur*, in other narrative texts ellipsis often has a significant function. The sentence 'when they left Tostes, Madame Bovary was pregnant,' which is so characteristic of Flaubert's style, indicates by the ease with which it passes over the event that the getting, and later having, of children is of very slight importance to Emma Bovary, and the moment at which the child is conceived is of none at all. Indeed, the sexual relationship between Emma and Charles is, through the ellipsis of the event, fully 'represented' as poor. In this case too, at no point in the fabula are we given full certainty about events.

The elaboration of parallel strings of one fabula makes it difficult to recognize one single chronological sequence in that fabula. Several events happen at the same time. It is not always possible to decide whether the coincidence in time is partial or complete. The vagueness of the chronology is, at times, just as significant as its painstaking representation. In Reve's *The Evenings*, events happen exactly chronologically and this chronology is indicated with such accuracy that the suggestion arises of an obsession caused by a surplus of time.

In García Márquez' *One Hundred Years of Solitude* the strict sequence of events is undercut from the inside, and readers who want to keep track of the course of the fabula find themselves powerless in the face of the ever-multiplying story-lines, which make one hundred years into an eternity. In so far as this effect is caused by changes, reversals in chronology, this problem belongs to chapter 2, section 2. What concerns me here is that incomplete information, which is never filled out, leaves gaps in the constructed fabula, and thus blurs our impression of it. Also of importance here is the occurrence of parallelism, and the fact that achronicity, the impossibility of establishing a precise chronology, can be the result of the crisscrossing of several lines.

Logical Sequence

Sequence is a logical concept. It is a matter of logic to suppose that someone who arrives must have departed first; that old age follows youth, reconciliation quarrel, awakening sleep. On the basis of the information offered in the text, it is possible to find the chronology of the fabula even if the order is not sequential.

What is the point of doing so? Chronological sequences are to be distinguished from other logical sequences. It is a frequent misconception that chronological and causal connections are always interrelated. It is true, of course, that one can only kill, hate, or despise one's father after having been engendered, although films like *Back to the Future* suggest otherwise. One may even do so before one is engendered by one's father, but there can also be entirely different reasons for such discrepancies. Another ruling misconception is that what happens first is therefore better. For some people this has been a reason to proclaim the superiority of men over women, on the basis of the account of creation in Genesis 2; for others, on the basis of the same fragment, to denounce the account of creation as sexist. Both parties implicitly base their contention on the assumption that chronological priority entails a qualitative priority.

The poetics of the Bible, however, does not at all encourage such an interpretation. The sequence of events, there, mirrors the process of creation as an ongoing splitting and specifying, much like cells in the human body. Therefore, the first creation of 'man' is rather the creation of an undivided, still elementary proto-human being, subsequently split into female – in fact mentioned first there! – and male. Limiting the analysis to purely chronological connections helps to expose such misconceptions. This is the gain of structuralist analysis.

The time span can be contrasted and compared with chronology. A brief event, e.g. a meeting, succeeds a long-lasting event, e.g. a process of estrangement between two actors. In this order the meeting has or might have another significance and other consequences than it would have had if the order had been inverted. Ordering the events in chronological sequence, one forms an impression of the difference between fabula and story. The interventions in chronology which become manifest can be significant for the vision of the fabula which they imply.

5: Location

Events happen somewhere. The locations where things happen may in principle be deduced. When we read

    a John was pushing his shopping cart when he suddenly saw his
      hated neighbour at the check-out counter

we may assume that the meeting place is the supermarket.

    b Elizabeth crossed the street

indicates a street, whether narrow or wide, long or short.

   c Sighing with pleasure, he sank back into the pillows as she bent
     over him.

This sentence, also, leaves small doubt about the location of action.

When the location has not been indicated, readers will simply supply one. *They* will imagine the scene, and in order to do so, they have
to situate it somewhere, however vague the imaginary place may be.
The Russian critic Lotman has explained this through pointing out
the predominance of the dimension of space in human imagination.
In support of his contention he lists a number of convincing examples
of spatial terms we use to indicate abstract concepts, such as 'infinite'
for an 'immeasurably' large quantity, 'distance' for a deficient relationship between people. Incidentally, even the word 'relation' itself would
seem to support Lotman's contention.

If spatial thinking is indeed a general human tendency, it is not surprising that spatial elements play an important role in fabulas. It is, for
instance, possible to make a note of the place of each fabula, and then to
investigate whether a connection exists between the kind of events, the
identity of the actors, and the location. The subdivision of locations into
groups is a manner of gaining insight into the relations between elements. A contrast between inside and outside is often relevant, where
inside may carry the suggestion of protection, and outside that of danger. These meanings are not indissolubly tied to these oppositions; it
is equally possible that inside suggests close confinement, and outside
freedom, or that we see a combination of these meanings, or a development from one to the other. Thus in French author Colette's novel *Chéri*,
Lea's bedroom is, at first, a safe haven for Chéri, but towards the end
this place becomes a prison from which he escapes with barely concealed relief. The expectation that the home provides safety is a powerful trigger of suspense when the opposite is the case. And sadly, the
issue of the sexual abuse of children has revealed how often the home
is precisely the place of danger.

Another, related, opposition is the one between the centrally located
square, which functions as the meeting place where actors are confronted with one another, and the surrounding world, where each actor has to fend for her- or himself. City and country are contrasted in
many romantic and realistic novels. Emma Bovary's idealization of the
city, projected on Paris, becomes the measure of her involvement, then

disappointment, with a lover in Rouen, the only city to which she has access.

The opposition between city and country can take on different meanings, sometimes as the sink of iniquity as opposed to idyllic innocence, or as a possibility of magically acquiring riches in contrast to the labour of the farmers; or as the seat of power against the powerlessness of the country people. This contrast, too, may reverse itself when it appears that the riches of the city are also limited to a few and the common man in the slums is worse off than the farmer who can, at least, eat his own crops. Or, conversely, the city can be represented as a maddening place ruled by paranoia contrasting with the peaceful, wholesome countryside In the British TV series 'Upstairs Downstairs' the contrast between kitchen and drawing-room represents the radical difference between masters and servants. A public meeting-place such as a pub may function as neutral ground, lending it a social function: a meeting-place for companions in adversity who may gain courage from sympathy and solidarity. On the other hand, it may also be a place to take refuge in alcohol, leading to complete destruction, as in Zola's *Assommoir*.

Spatial oppositions can be much more abstract than the examples mentioned here. When several places, ordered in groups, can be related to psychological, ideological, and moral oppositions, location may function as an important principle of structure. For instance high–low, related to favourable–unfavourable, fortunate–unfortunate, is an opposition which Western literature has inherited from the late biblical vision of heaven and hell, and from Latin and Greek mythology. Far–near, open–closed, finite–infinite, together with familiar–strange, safe–unsafe, and accessible–inaccessible are oppositions often encountered.

Fabulas sometimes centre structurally on a spatial opposition. Thus Robinson Crusoe first flees the oppression of society by going to sea, then he is oppressed by his solitude, and finally he learns to convert his confinement into a form of freedom. Still, the longing for the society which oppressed him, but which also promised safety and protection from the adventure, continues; here we witness the crossing of another pair of opposites.

As I already suggested in chapter 2, a special role is played by the boundary between two opposed locations. Just as in Christian mythology purgatory mediates the opposition between heaven and hell, so the front door may connote a crucial barrier for one intending to penetrate into certain circles. The shop as a transitory place between outside and inside, the sea between society and solitude, the beach between land

and sea, gardens between city and country, all function as mediators. It is possible to be trapped in such places.

Many events are set in vehicles of transportation, such as trains, boats, carriages, airplanes. Consequently these events – murder in Agatha Christie, sex in Flaubert, meetings, quarrels, hold-ups – temporarily suspend the safe predictability and clarity of the social order. This structuring potential of places of transition nourishes the narrative potential of the road 'Penetrante Ouest' in Chamoiseau's *Texaco*. This road inaugurates the fabula but never gets built. Instead of being a connection it was only a 'penetration' of the land. Its destructive nature – for its construction, the entire site of Texaco was to be erased – makes it, and the fabula of appropriation it represented, unacceptable. As a figure for that unacceptability, the woman founder of the community of Texaco, Marie-Sophie, abducts it: she tells the story that will convert the urban planner, makes him give up the construction of the road, and instead, monumentalize the place into a site of memory.

Oppositions are constructions; it is important not to forget that and 'naturalize' them. As deconstructive criticism has amply demonstrated, they are invariably flawed in their attempted logic. And that is very fortunate. If this chapter has relied more than the previous ones on the idea of opposition, this is not because oppositions have a privileged status in reality or art. Structuring often takes the route of opposition as a handy simplification of complex content. The oppositions we expect to function in fabulas can be traps as well as tools. This is the major problem of ideological and political criticism. The very ideological structure – binary opposition – that we use for our critical readings is simultaneously the object of those readings, their main target. The point is not to notice, confirm, or denounce oppositions but to confront the oppositions we notice with those we hold ourselves, and to use the differences between them as a tool to break their tyranny. With such an approach criticism need not prejudge the politics of great literature, or of popular culture, as happens so often. Instead, it helps to realize that criticism is always also, to a certain extent, self-criticism.

6: Remarks and Sources

In this chapter I have outlined objects and processes as the most important elements of the fabula. First events were discussed, then actors. These two categories are considered the most relevant elements. In both cases I first discussed criteria for selection on the basis of which a large quantity of subject matter may be restricted on explicit grounds.

Subsequently the relationship between the remaining elements was taken into consideration. Events were always seen in relation to the actors forming part of it, and the actors in relation to the events they initiate or suffer. With regard to events I paid special attention to different criteria of selection, while in discussing the actors I was primarily engaged in classification. This difference relates to the order in which both subjects were discussed; it is not necessary to discuss again the several criteria for selection when that has been done in the previous subsection, even if with regard to a different subject.

Finally, time and location have only been given summary attention. They have been discussed at greater length in the previous chapter, for these elements are primarily interesting because of the way in which they are ordered and specified in the story.

The different subsections of this chapter show a clear resemblance. In every case I tried to describe the elements in their relationship to each other, and not as isolated units. This approach is structuralist: its assumption is that fixed relations between classes of phenomena form the basis of the narrative system of the fabula. I chose this approach because it offers, among other advantages, that of coherence. The different elements may thus be seen within the framework of one theoretical approach. Since every choice has its disadvantages as well as advantages, objections may be raised against this approach. The one mentioned most often is that it is reductive. This is inevitable: every choice is a limitation. But if that limitation is a starting point, not end point, it can be turned against itself and help us grasp what the ideological distributions of elements are and do. Instead of an ideological foundation, structural analysis then becomes a tool for critique.

A consequence of the approach taken in this book is that a great deal of attention was given to classification. When dealing with determined relationships between classes of phenomena, the ordering principles which form the basis of these classes must be made explicit. Classification, however, is not a self-serving aim for the literary scholar. Its use is instrumental: only when classification helps to provide greater insight into the phenomena constituting the classes is it meaningful in describing the text. Then significance may be derived from the fact that a phenomenon belongs to a certain class. The specific characteristics of one object may be described in the class to which they belong – or to which, against our expectation, they possibly do not belong.

Among other things, it is to emphasize that aspect of the approach that I have, in my examples, selected typological aspects just as often as specific texts. Typologies, however, are often handled implicitly: when saying that a text shows 'such an original vision of society,' one implicitly assumes that a certain outlook on society forms the basis of the class of texts to which that particular one belongs.

On the 'resemblance' or homology between fabulas and reality, the literature is innumerable. Suffice it here to refer to the classical study by Erich Auerbach (1953) which inaugurated a flurry of interest in this subject. A good later study is Prendergast (1986). Mary Longman's sculpture was brought to my attention by Gerald McMaster, who wrote the very suggestive essay in the catalogue *Mary Longman: Traces* (Kamloops, BC: Kamloops Art Gallery, 1996).

The criteria for the selection of events have been derived from Barthes (1977) and Hendricks (1973). A critical application of Barthes' proposals has been made by Chatman (1969). The relations between events have been discussed according to the proposals of Bremond (1973). He distinguishes a third possibility for the combination of elementary series, juxtaposition. I have not included this possibility because to me it seems not of the same order as succession and embedding. 'Juxtaposition' does not result in a complete series of events, but in several visions of one and the same event. This issue was dealt with in chapter 2. The actantial model as it is presented here is derived from Greimas (1966). I have not adopted his later proposal (e.g., 1976) to replace *opponent* and *helper* with the concepts *anti-actant* and *co-actant;* the distinction between anti-subjects – autonomous subjects whose intentions are at cross purposes with those of the first subject – and incidental opponents would be lost. I would prefer to regard the duplication of the principal actant as a possibility, in addition to maintaining the original sixfold model. An alternative to Greimas' model is the less systematic but perhaps more inspiring sevenfold model of Souriau (1956). Most structural models have, to a greater or lesser degree, been inspired by Propp, whose work only became widely known during the 1960s. The early work of Todorov and Van Dijk, some of Doležel's studies (e.g., 1973) and the work of Prince (1983) also belong to this development. Lotman's remarks on location are published in Lotman (1977). I already mentioned De Lauretis' (1983) feminist critique of this view. Fludernik (1996) offers a thorough discussion of the issues of this book, including the topics of this chapter, which motivated students might find interesting.

The example of the Book of Judges was treated extensively in my book *Death and Dissymmetry* (1988). Another example of the use of narratology for anthropology is Elsbee (1982).

Afterword:
Theses on the Use of Narratology
for Cultural Analysis

During the time this book has been used, I have developed an increasing awareness of the cultural embeddedness of narrative. This shift in my interest has been indicated by the addition of somewhat longer examples in the second edition, some of which I have again replaced in the third. I would like to offer, by way of conclusion, some thoughts about the relation of narratology to what has been called 'cultural studies' but what I prefer to call 'cultural analysis.'

Narrative is everywhere, but it isn't always so important.
The present return to narratology is most welcome to a compulsive narratologist like myself. Why this return is occurring, why now, is not so obvious – at least, not if we want to see in it more than regression to the good old days of structuralism. A first reason may simply be the omnipresence of narrative in culture, which logically calls for a method to deal with it. Like semiotics, narratology applies to virtually every cultural object. Not that everything 'is' narrative; but practically everything in culture has a narrative aspect to it, or at the very least, can be perceived, interpreted as narrative. In addition to the obvious predominance of narrative genres in literature, a random handful of places where narrative 'occurs' includes lawsuits, visual images, philosophical discourse, television, argumentation, teaching, history-writing.

In court, two parties each give an account of 'what really happened.' Two opposed accounts of the 'same' event: for people conversant with the practice of law, the notion that narrative is a construction, rather than a reconstruction, must seem pretty obvious, if not 'natural.' Let them talk to historians. In argumentation the story fulfils a function of persuasion, or of variation, distraction, or just poking fun at the right moment, at the opponent's expense. Who's to say that narrative serves

the truth? The omnipresence of narrative makes a case for the importance of narratology only if narrative is crucial in those cultural artifacts
we qualify as wholly or partially narrative. But there lies the problem,
as well as the reason why narratology has traditionally been confined
– more or less – to the category of story-telling, mostly literary, mostly
novelistic.

*The point of narratology is not to demonstrate the narrative
nature of an object.*
For what would the point of such an exercise be? Usually we don't
doubt, don't wonder, about the status of a text, and watching a film we
may or may not be carried away, but it hardly seems important to ask if
what we are seeing is in fact a narrative. Asking whether or not an object 'is' narrative is both obvious and futile, just as the notion that an image 'is' visual hardly calls for visual analysis to make that point. On the
other hand, if so much of culture 'is' narrative, or, if not, at least 'has an
aspect of' narrative, doesn't any invocation of narratology initiate a circular argument that begs the question of specificity? This is why, traditionally, narratology has been used to differentiate 'types' of narrative,
narrative situations, 'modes' of story-telling: authorial versus personal
(Stanzel), heterodiegetic versus homodiegetic (Genette), reliable versus
unreliable narrators (Booth). But what's the point of *that?*

Establishing categories is not continuous with analysis.
Delimitation, classification, typology, it is all very nice as a remedy
to chaos-anxiety, but what insights does it yield? As I have argued at
length in my reply to Genette (1991), the pervasive taxonomical bend
of narratology is epistemologically flawed; it entails skipping a step or
two. Between a general conception of narrative and an actual narrative text – or object – lies more than a classification. The distribution of
actual objects over a restricted number of categories is only meaningful
– if at all – after insight into a text has been gained. Classifying texts as a
method of analysis, therefore, is a circular way of reasoning. There is no
direct logical connection between classifying and understanding texts.
And understanding – if taken in a broad sense that encompasses cognitive as well as affective acts, precisely, not distinguished – is the point.

*Narratology is not an instrument, at least, not for the 'ready-made'
production of knowledge.*
Although it is common usage to talk about concepts as 'tools' for
analysis, understanding is not an operation that can be instrumental-

ly performed. Culture encompasses many different productions and organizations of utterances in language, images, sounds, gestures. These cannot stand on their own. Included in culture is theoretical reflection, narratological and otherwise. This reflection is itself part of the substance of culture; indeed, narrative artifacts are full of it, too. Assuming an instrumentalist position counters this view of culture. It feeds the illusion, typical of enlightenment thought, that the subject can stand outside of what it criticizes, analyses, understands. More down to earth, it tends to present concepts as descriptions of 'things,' mostly elements like words, characters, speaking styles. As a result of the descriptive bias, such concepts, which lack analytical thrust, are unsystematically related.

Instead, narrative is a cultural attitude, hence, narratology a perspective on culture.
What I propose we are best off with in the age of cultural analysis is a conception of narratology that implicates text and reading, subject and object, production and analysis, in the act of understanding. In other words, I advocate a narrative theory that enables the differentiation of the place of narrative in any cultural expression without privileging any medium, mode, or use; that differentiates its relative importance and the *effect* of the narrative (segments) on the remainder of the object as well as on the reader, listener, viewer. A theory, that is, which defines and describes narrativity, not narrative; not a genre or object but a cultural mode of expression.

With such a perspective, cultural artifacts, events, or domains can be analysed closely.
As a book series devoted to cultural analysis has it, 'cultural analysis should not be taken literally – or analytically – as meaning the "taking apart" of culture. Rather, cultural analysts interpret the way in which cultures take things, people, and themselves "apart"' (flyer for the book series 'Cultural Memory in the Present,' Stanford University Press; series editors Mieke Bal and Hent de Vries). Narratology is of great relevance for such a reorientation of, simultaneously, close reading and cultural studies into cultural analysis.

However, such a theory offers, as much as a perspective on culture, a caution against a number of fallacies and risks.
It cautions against the reification of modes as things, so that the belief in the 'truth' of narrative is replaced by a belief in the truth of what things

are narrative. It cautions against a lack of differentiation ('narrative is everywhere') that makes the theory redundant and helpless to promote specific understanding. It cautions against the illusion of objectivity, both in story-telling as witnessing and in analysis as the scientific discovery of the truth. As Gadamer said, and Leith and Myerson reiterate, the point is in the questions, not the answers:

> He [Gadamer] insists that questions are what matter; the 'dominant opinion' threatens questions.   Leith and Myerson 1989, 150

Hence, narratology cautions against a confusion of understanding and axiology, against a sense of value inherent in narrative: either as intrinsically true, hence, good, or as intrinsically false, fictional, manipulative, hence, bad.

The point is to ask meaningful questions.
Rather banal, isn't it? Let's see. In the wake of Gadamer, Leith and Myerson structure the section of their book devoted to interpreting stories around questions. Since this is what I did in this book, a quick comparison may be illuminating. Leith and Myerson's primary question is 'Whose voice is this?' They complicate this question through Bakhtinian dialogism and Derridian deconstruction. They derive from that complication the notion of reading *as* a pursuit – a continuous questioning of – voice: who speaks? They call that strategy 'quotation-reading.'

The second question they raise is 'To what is this a reply?' Reply, they state, can be a move towards, or a polemic against, that to which it is a reply. This, then, allows for more complicating questions. The strategy here is 'reply-reading.' The procedure is excellent: each question entails new questions. The problem is, both key-terms – *voice* and *reply* – are metaphors suggestive of individual and perceptible speech. This implicitly promotes both individualism and language-centrism, both tenacious ideologemes – so much so that even raising the question of their inevitability is hard.

Owing to the many responses the earlier editions of this book have triggered, I have often been compelled to argue why for heaven's sake I needed to make such a fuss about focalization as the third term here; so often that I find it hard to come up with new answers. But perhaps the combined argument against individualism and the concomitant mastery of the speaking 'voice,' and against language-centrism and the concomitant domination of the 'speaking voice,' can carry some weight where logical and ideological arguments could not suffice. To ask, *not* primarily where the words come from and who speaks them, but what, in the game of make-believe, is being proposed for us to believe or see before us, hate, love, admire, argue against, shudder before, or stand in awe of: it's my way of following Gadamer's perpetual questions.

For Those Who Wish to Know More

The following are a few further bibliographical notes, in addition to what was given at the end of each chapter.

Structuralism
The models that derive from structuralism have been critically discussed by Culler (1975) in a clear survey. In a later book (1983), the biases of structuralism are discussed from a still more critical point of view.

Barthes and Greimas
One of the many critical applications of the analytical model of Barthes is Chatman (1969). A simple introduction to Greimas' work does not exist. Courtés' attempt (1976) is not very successful; it does not help in understanding Greimas' theory. It is easier, in fact, to read Greimas' own applications, such as the analysis of a short story by De Maupassant (1976). Though this is not easy to understand, it gives insight into the possibilities of the theory, which is more comprehensive than the actantial model referred to in this text. Greimas and Courtés (1979) present the theory in dictionary form.

Genette
The work of Genette has often been discussed; the best discussion is that of Rimmon (1976). She places the theory in the context of the development of structuralism, and also surveys consistency and practical usefulness. Culler's preface to the English edition (Genette 1980) is a short and clear introduction to all of Genette's work.

Characters
There is little systematic discussion of character apart from the actantial model. The most useful article is that by Hamon (1977). See also his book of 1983. A historical survey of character in the Aristotelian tradition is offered by Walcutt (1966). Like Harvey (1965), he does not go beyond Forster's distinction (1927). Chatman (1972) does criticize the central role of the action in structuralist theories of the character, but he does not offer a viable substitute. Rimmon-Kenan (1983) presents work on character by the Tel Aviv school, among others' Hrushovski's.

Descriptions
Here too, Hamon's contribution is the most systematic one apart from the many analyses of description in which its symbolic importance was especially stressed. A special number of *Yale French Studies* provides interesting suggestions (Kittay 1982). A survey of the problems is to be found in Bal (1982). About the difference between narrative and non-narrative (descriptive and argumentative) parts of the text, see Genette (1969). An extensive new discussion of description appeared in Bal (2004).

Free Indirect Discourse and Personal Language Use
In addition to the work of Banfield mentioned above, see McHale (1978), which discusses the most important suggestions. Doležel (1973) defends the opinion that free indirect discourse is a form of 'text interference.' Ron (1981) discusses it from the point of view of 'deconstruction.' Tamir (1978) discusses several forms of personal narrative from a linguistic point of view.

Focalization
Several publications by Perry (e.g., 1979) consider the problem of 'perspective' in an original manner. Doležel (1980) links it to the problem of authentication, the credibility of various sources of information in a fictional text. In this article, he also broaches the subject of the usefulness of so-called 'possible world semantics' for the theory of literature.

Dialogues
Glowinski (1974) discusses the status of dialogues. In comparison with Pelc (1971), his opinions have been given less theoretical underpinning, but he provides more possibilities for the analysis of the text. The two articles could be combined fruitfully. Bal (1981) discusses dialogue as

an embedded part of texts. For other aspects, see the theory of drama. Platz-Waury (1978) is a simple introduction; Van Kesteren and Schmid (1975) contains a number of important articles. A second collection is in preparation. Segre (1990) is also useful.

The Audience and the Reader

Recently, attention has been paid to the narratee. See the articles by Prince (e.g., 1973). The publications of Iser (e.g., 1978) focus on the reader. Eco (1976, 1979) discusses the reader's activity in building a fictional world while decoding a text. Pratt also discusses a similar problem (1977). Leith and Myerson (1989) is one example of a rhetorical approach to the addressee of narrative.

Narratology and Cultural Studies

Carlisle and Schwartz (1994) offer a representative collection of the use of narratology against a background of larger cultural considerations. See also Bal ed. (1998), where the question of the connection is explicitly foregrounded.

Appendix on Quoted Dutch Novelists

J.M.A. Biesheuvel (b. 1939) comes from a Protestant Christian background. He alternately studied law and worked as a sailor. He is a full-time writer now, performing on TV and giving lectures. In his work, which is partly autobiographical, he plays on his experience as a patient in a psychiatric hospital. Biesheuvel is considered a postmodern writer, of a typically Dutch kind, where intense story-telling, often taking the form of gossip, is thematized. In his plea for the absurdity of human behaviour, of human life, existentialism persists. *De weg naar het licht* (The Way to the Light) appeared in 1977, from Meulenhoff of Amsterdam. The quotation is from the short story 'Faust,' a parodic variation on the Faust motif, full of crazy fantasies caused by psychiatric medication.

Louis Couperus (1863–1923) grew up as one of many children in a family of colonial administrators. His father was severe and demanding, and the child was bound to disappoint him. The family spent several years in the Indies. His many works include psychological novels, symbolic fairy tales, mythological novels, historical novels, often set in a decadent society, short stories, travel accounts, and journalism. His recurrent theme is the predominance of fate in human life. Fate, in Couperus' view, is an almost personified, basically obscure force, impregnated with guilt. The opposition between the north, as cold, somber, male, and bourgeois, and south, as sensual and female, structures many of his novels.

    Of Old People, and Things That Pass (1906) can be considered a typically Dutch variant of Naturalism: hereditary flaws persevere through three generations, guilt is connected with passion and violence is staged in both the Indies and The Hague. The 'old people' are more and more haunted by the murder of the old woman's husband they committed sixty years ago in the Indies, while the secret, after all these years, becomes more and more in danger of revelation.

Harry Mulisch (b. 1927) lived with his German-Austrian father after the divorce of his parents. His mother was Jewish. The war influenced him deeply. Mulisch's philosophy has been elaborated in his entire oeuvre, and explicitly in his *De compositie van de wereld* (The Composition of the World), 1980. For him, art is the only possible way of understanding and knowing the world. Reality only becomes meaningful when it is recreated in art. Language disposes of a magical power that allows the writer to create and to conquer time. Mulisch considers the mystical philosopher Pythagoras to be the first exemplary artist. The collection of short stories *What Happened to Sergeant Massuro?*, published in 1972, contains the story with the same title, which was written in 1955. The story consists of a report, written by Massuro's friend, on behalf of the Ministry of War, in which the friend tries to explain, or rather to understand, the mysterious event that happened to Massuro: his slow petrification during an expedition in the jungle of New Guinea. The personal language-situation is relevant for an understanding of the story, which, in its dense symbolic structure, is reminiscent of *Heart of Darkness*.

Gerard Reve (1923–2006) claimed to have inherited his verbal talent from his father, a Communist journalist, and his romantic feelings from his mother. During the first period of his authorship (1946–56) he wrote realistic symbolic novels, set in a lower-class milieu, often featuring young boys or adolescents. *De avonden* dates from this period (1947). The (anti-)hero of this novel fills up the boredom of his daily life with counting the hours and sharply observing others, his parents and his friends. Reality is presented as a meaningless sequence of details without connections. The novel presents the ten days of the Christmas period in 1946. Nothing happens. Later, the author becomes *the* writer of romantic-ironic feelings, and the works of his later period often take the epistolary form. His ostentatious stance for homosexuality, (iconoclastic) Catholicism, and reactionary political views, including racism, has made him the constant centre of public attention and the source of many controversies. His irony makes his position disturbingly unclear.

He has doubtless contributed importantly to the emancipation of homosexuality in the Netherlands.

Jan Wolkers (1925–2007) was the third son of an orthodox Christian family with a dominant father. Although a relatively successful sculptor, he is most famous as a novelist and writer of short stories. His early work settles accounts with his Calvinist background, as exemplified by his *Terug naar Oegstgeest* (Return to Oegstgeest) of 1965. The uncensored representation of sexuality and sadism, in an atmosphere of guilt and penance, made Wolkers very popular among the young. His later work evolves towards a preoccupation with decay. The best-known novel of this period, *Turks fruit* (Turkish Delight), is internationally known. *De kus* (The Kiss) is the report of a tour through Indonesia, paralleled by a gradual questioning of masculine values and strength. The description of the roof of the Burrubudur temple marks the beginning of physical decay which befalls the I-character's 'superman'-friend. Wolkers is the most popular Dutch writer; significantly, his work has never been seriously studied.

Bibliography

I have given full references in the 'Remarks and Sources' sections for those texts I used only as examples, in order to limit the bibliography to theoretical works directly relevant for the student of narratology, even if some of these are not narratological per se.

Alpers, Svetlana, and Michael Baxandall
– 1994. *Tielpolo and the Pictorial Intelligence.* New Haven: Yale University Press
Auerbach, Erich
– 1953. *Mimesis: Representation of Reality in Western Literature.* Princeton: Princeton University Press
Bachelard, Gaston
– 1957. *La poetique de l'espace.* Paris: Presses universitaires de France
Bakhtin, Mikhail
– 1981. *The Dialogic Imagination.* Edited by Michael Holquist, translated by Caryl Emerson and Michael Holquist. Austin: University of Texas Press
Bal, Mieke
– 1978. 'Mise en abyme et inconicité.' *Literature* 29, 116–28
– 1981. 'Notes on Narrative Embedding.' *Poetics Today* 2:2, 41–59.
– 1982. 'On the Meaning of Descriptions.' *Twentieth-Century Literature* 6:1–2, 100–48
– 1986. 'Tell-Tale Theories.' *Poetics Today* 7:3, 555–64
– 1988. *Death and Dissymmetry: The Politics of Coherence in the Book of Judges.* Chicago: University of Chicago Press
– 1991. *On Story-Telling: Essays in Narratology.* Edited by David Jobling. Sonoma: Polebridge Press
– 1991 (1994). *Reading 'Rembrandt': Beyond the Word-Image Opposition.* New York: Cambridge University Press

- 1994. *On Meaning-Making: Essays in Semiotics*. Sonoma: Polebridge Press
- 1997. *The Mottled Screen: Reading Proust Visually*. Stanford: Stanford University Press
- 2004. 'Over-Writing as Un-Writing: Descriptions, World-Making, and Novelistic Time.' *Narrative Theory: Critical Concepts in Literary and Cultural Studies*, vol. 1, ed. Mieke Bal, 341–88. New York and London: Routledge
Bal, Mieke, ed.
- 1998. *The Practice of Cultural Analysis: Exposing Interdisciplinary Interpretation*. Stanford: Stanford University Press
- 2004. *Narrative Theory: Critical Concepts in Literary and Cultural Studies*. 4 vols. New York and London: Routledge
Banfield, Ann
- 1982. *Unspeakable Sentences*. London: Routledge and Kegan Paul
- 2000. *The Phantom Table: Woolf, Fry, Russell and the Epistemology of Modernism*. Cambridge: Cambridge University Press
Barthes, Roland
- 1977. 'Introduction to the Structural Analysis of Narratives.' *Image-Music-Text*, 79–124. London: Fontana
Benveniste, Emile
- 1971. *Problems in General Linguistics*. Coral Gables: University of Miami Press
Bertens, Hans
- 2001 *Literary Theory*. New York and London: Routledge
Bloom, Harold
- 1973. *The Anxiety of Influence: A Theory of Poetry*. New York: Oxford University Press
Booth, Wayne C.
- 1961. *The Rhetoric of Fiction*. Chicago: University of Chicago Press
Bordwell, David
- 1985. *Narration in the Fiction Film*. Madison: University of Wisconsin Press
- 1989. *Making Meaning: Inference and Rhetoric in the Interpretation of Cinema*. Cambridge, Mass.: Harvard University Press
Bortolussi, Marisa, and Peter Dixon
- 2003. *Psychonarratology: Foundations for the Empirical Study of Liteary Response*. Camridge: Cambridge University Press
Branigan, Edward
- 1992. *Narrative Comprehension and Film*. New York and London: Routledge
Bremond, Claude
- 1973. *Logique du récit*. Paris: Editions du Seuil

Brooks, Peter
– 1984. *Reading for the Plot: Design and Intention in Narrative*. New York: Alfred
  A. Knopf
Bryson, Norman
– 1984. *Tradition and Desire: From David to Delacroix*. New York: Cambridge
  University Press
Carlisle, Janice, and Daniel R. Schwartz, eds.
– 1994. *Narrative and Culture*. Charlottesville and London: University of Virginia Press
Chase, Cynthia
– 1986. *Decomposing Figures: Rhetorical Readings in the Romantic Tradition*. Baltimore: Johns Hopkins University Press
Chatman, Seymour
– 1969. 'New Ways of Analysing Narrative Structures, with an Example from
  Joyce's *Dubliners*.' *Language and Style* 2, 3–36
– 1972. 'On the Formalist-Structuralist Theory of Character.' *Journal of Literary
  Semantics* 1, 57–79
– 1978. *Story and Discourse*. Ithaca: Cornell University Press
– 1990. *Coming to Terms: The Rhetoric of Narrative in Fiction and Film*. Ithaca:
  Cornell University Press
– 1992. *Reading Narrative Fiction*. New York: Macmillan
– 1995. 'How Loose Can Narrators Get? (And How Vulnerable Can Narratees
  Be?)' *Narrative* 3, 303–6
Cohan, Steven, and Linda M. Shires
– 1988 *Telling Stories: A Theoretical Analysis of Narrative Fiction*. New York:
  Routledge
Courtés, Joseph
– 1976. *Introduction à la sémiotique narrative et discursive*. Paris: Hachette
Culler, Jonathan
– 1975. *Structuralist Poetics: Structuralism, Linguistics and the Study of Literature*. London: Routledge and Kegan Paul
– 1981. *The Pursuit of Signs: Semiotics, Literature, Deconstruction*. Ithaca: Cornell
  University Press
– 1983. *On Deconstruction*. Ithaca: Cornell University Press
– 2007. 'Omniscience.' *The Literary in Theory*, 183–204. Stanford: Stanford University Press
Dällenbach, Lucien
– 1977. *Le récit spéculaire: Essai sur la mise en abyme*. Paris: Seuil; translated as
  The Mirror in the Text by Jeremy Whiteley with Emma Hughes. Chicago:
  University of Chicago Press, 1989

De Certeau, Michel
– 1984. *The Practice of Everyday Life*. Trans. Steven Rendall. Berkeley: University of California Press
De Lauretis, Teresa
– 1983. *Alice Doesn't: Feminism, Semiotics, Cinema*. London: Macmillan
– 1987. *Technologies of Gender: Essays on Theory, Film, and Fiction*. Bloomington: Indiana University Press
Dionne, Claude, Silvestra Mariniello, and Walter Moser, eds.
– 1996. *Recyclages: Economies de l'appropriation culturelle*. Montreal: Les Editions Balzac
Doležel, Lubomir
– 1973. *Narrative Modes in Czech Literature*. Toronto: University of Toronto Press
– 1980. 'Truth and Authenticity in Narrative.' *Poetics Today* 1:3, 7–25
Eco, Umberto
– 1976. *A Theory of Semiotics*. Bloomington and Indianapolis: Indiana University Press
– 1979. *The Role of the Reader*. Bloomington and Indianapolis: Indiana University Press
Elsbee, Langdon
– 1982. *The Rituals of Life: Patterns in Narratives*. Port Washington and London: National University Publications
Fludernik, Monika
– 1996. *Towards a 'Natural' Narratology*. New York and London: Routledge
Forster, E.M.
– 1974 (1927). *Aspects of the Novel*. Harmondsworth: Penguin
Friedman, Norman
– 1955. 'Point of View in Fiction: The Development of Critical Concept.' *PMLA* 70, 1160–84
Geertz, Clifford
– 2000. '"From the Native's Point of View." On the Nature of Anthropological Understanding.' *Local Knowledge: Further Essays in Interpretive Anthropology*, 55–72. New York: Basic Books
Genette, Gérard
– 1969. '"Frontières du récit." *Figures II*, 49–69. Paris: Editions du Seuil
– 1972. *Figures III*. Paris: Seuil
– 1980. *Narrative Discourse*. Translated by Jane Lewin, with a preface by Jonathan Culler. Ithaca: Cornell University Press
Glowinski, Michal
– 1974. 'Der Dialog in Roman.' *Poetica* 8:1, 1–16

Greimas, Algirdas Julien
- 1966. *Sémantique structurale*. Paris: Larousse
- 1973. 'Les actants, les acteurs et les figures.' Claude Chabrol et al., eds., *Semiotique narrative et textuelle*, 161–76. Paris: Larousse
- 1976. *Maupassant: La sémiotique du texts: exercices pratiques*. Paris: Editions du Seuil
Greimas, Algirdas Julien, and Joseph Courtés
- 1979. *Sémiotique: Dictionnaire raisonné de la théorie du langage*. Paris: Hachette
Hamon, Philippe
- 1977. 'Pour un status sémiologique du personnage.' Roland Barthes et al., *Poétique du Récit*, 115–80. Paris: Seuil
- 1981. *Introduction à l'analyse du descriptif*. Paris: Hachette
- 1983. *Le personnel du roman*. Geneva: Droz
Hartman, Geoffrey H.
- 1996. *The Longest Shadow: In the Aftermath of the Holocaust*. Bloomington and Indianapolis: Indiana University Press
Harvey, Richard Brown
- 1965. 'Narrative, Literary Theory, and the Self in Contemporary Society.' *Poetics Today* 6:4, 573–90
Hendricks, William O.
- 1973. 'Methodology of Narrative Structural Analysis.' *Semiotica* 7, 163–84
Herman, David
- 2002. *Story Logic: Problems and Possibilities of Narrative*. Lincoln and London: University of Nebraska Press
Herman, David, ed.
- 2003. *Narrative Theory and the Cognitive Sciences*. Stanford: CSLI Publications
Herman, David, Manfred Jahn, and Marie-Laure Ryan, eds.
- 2005. *Encyclopedia of Narrative Theory*. New York and London: Routledge
Hirschkop, Ken, and David Shepherd, eds.
- 1989. *Bakhtin and Cultural Theory*. Manchester and New York: Manchester University Press
Hoving, Isabel
- 2001. *In Praise of New Travelers: Reading Caribbean Migrant Women Writers*. Stanford: Stanford University Press
Hrushovski, Benjamin
- 1976. 'Poetics, Criticism, Science: Remarks on the Fields and Responsibilities of the Study of Literature.' *PTL* 1, iii–xxxv
Iser, Wolfgang
- 1978. *The Act of Reading: A Theory of Aesthetic Response*. Baltimore: Johns Hopkins University Press

Jakobson, Roman
- 1960. 'Closing Statement: Linguistics and Poetics.' Thomas A. Sebeok, ed.,
  Style in Language. Cambridge, Mass.: MIT Press
Jefferson, Ann
- 1983. 'Mise en abyme and the Prophetic in Narrative.' *Style* 17:2, 196–208
Johnson, Barbara
- 1987. *A World of Difference*. Baltimore: Johns Hopkins University Press
Kakandas, Irene
- 1993. 'Are You in the Text?: The "Literary Performative" in Postmodernist
  Fiction.' *Text and Performance Quarterly* 13: 139–53
- 1996. 'Narrative Apostrophe: Reading, Rhetoric, Resistance in Michael
  Butor's *La Modification* and Julio Cortázar's "Graffiti."' *Style* 28: 3,
  329–49
Khanna, Ranjana
- 2008. *Algeria Cuts: Women and Representation, 1830 to the Present*. Stanford:
  Stanford University Press
Kittay, Jeffrey S., ed.
- 1982. *Towards a Theory of Description*. New Haven (special issue of *Yale
  French Studies*)
Lämmert, Eberhard
- 1955. *Bauformen des Erzählens*. Stuttgart: J.B. Metzlersche Verlag
Lanser, Susan Sniaber
- 1981. *The Narrative Act: Point of View in Prose Fiction*. Princeton: Princeton
  University Press
Lefebvre, Henri
- 1991. *The Production of Space*. Translated by Donald Nicholson-Smith. Ox-
  ford and Cambridge, Mass.: Basil Blackwell
Leith, Dick, and George Myerson
- 1989. *The Power of Address: Explorations in Rhetoric*. New York and London:
  Routledge
Link, Hannelore
- 1976. *Rezeptionsforschung: Eine Einführung in Methoden and Probleme*. Stuttgart: Fink
Lodge, David
- 1977. 'Types of Description.' *The Modes of Modern Writing: Metaphor, Metonymy, and the Typology of Modern Literature*, 93–102. London: Edward Arnold
Lord, Catherine
- 1999. *The Intimacy of Influence: Narrative and Theoretical Fictions in the Works
  of George Eliot, Virginia Woolf and Jeanette Winterson*. Amsterdam: Belle van
  Zuylen Institute/ASCA.

Lotman, Jurij M.
- 1977. *The Structure of the Artistic Text*. Ann Arbor: University of Michigan
  Press.
Lubbock, Percy
- 1957. *The Craft of Fiction*. New York: Viking Press
Margolin, Uri
- 1998. Mieke Bal. *Narratology* (review). *Canadian Review of Comparative
  Literature/Revue Canadienne de Littérature comparée*, September–December,
  574–81
McHale, Brian
- 1978. 'Free Indirect Discourse: A Survey of Recent Accounts.' *PTL* 3, 249–87
Melas, Natalie
- 2007. *All the Difference in the World: Postcoloniality and the Ends of Comparison*.
  Stanford: Stanford University Press
Mezei, Kathy, ed.
- 1996. *Ambiguous Discourse: Feminist Narratology and British Women Writers*.
  Chapel Hill: University of North Carolina Press
Mitchell, W.J.T.
- 1995. *Iconology: Image, Text, Ideology*. Chicago: University of Chicago Press
Moser, Walter
- 1981. 'Translating Discourse: Inter-Discursive Mobility in the Early Roman-
  tic Encyclopedia.' *Eighteenth Century: Theory and Interpretation* 22: 1, 3–20
Müller, Günther
- 1968. *Morphologische Poetik: Gesammelte Aufsätze*. Tübingen: Niemeyer
Musser, Charles
- 1984. 'The Travel Genre in 1903–04: Moving Towards Fictional Narrative.'
  Iris 2:1, 47–59
Pavel, Thomas
- 1976. *La syntaxe narrative des tragédies de Corneille*. Paris: Klincksieck; Ottawa:
  Editions de l'université d'Ottawa
Peeren, Esther
- 2008. *Intersubjectivities and Popular Culture: Bakhtin and Beyond*. Stanford:
  Stanford University Press
Pelc, Jerzy
- 1971. 'On the Concept of Narration.' *Semiotica* 2:3, 1–19
Perry, Menakhem
- 1979. 'Literary Dynamics: How the Order of a Text Creates Its Meanings.'
  Poetics Today 1:1, 35–64 and 311–61
Platz-Waury, Elke
- 1978. *Drama und Theater. Eine Einfuhrung*. Tübingen: Max Niemeyer Verlag

Pratt, Mary Louise
- 1977. *Towards a Speech Act Theory of Literary Discourse*. Bloomington and Indianapolis: Indiana University Press
Prendergast, Christopher
- 1986. *The Order of Mimesis: Balzac, Stendhal, Nerval, Flaubert*. Cambridge: Cambridge University Press
Prince, Gerald
- 1973. *A Grammar of Stories*. The Hague: Mouton
- 1983. *Narratology. The Form and Function of Narrative*. The Hague: Mouton
Propp, Vladimir
- 1968. *Morphology of the Folktale*. Austin: University of Texas Press
Rimmon[-Kenan], Shlomith
- 1976. 'A Comprehensive Theory of Narrative: Genette's *Figures III* and the Structuralist Study of Fiction.' *PTL* 1, 33–62
- 1983. *Narrative Fiction: Contemporary Poetics*. London: Methuen
- 1996. *A Glance beyond Doubt*. Columbus: Ohio State University Press
Ron, Moshe
- 1981. 'Free Indirect Discourse, Mimetic Language Games and the Subject of Fiction.' *Poetics Today* 2:2, 17–39
Schmid, Wolf
- 1973. *Der Textaufbau in den Erzählungen Dostoievskijs*. Munich: Wilhem Fink Verlag
Segre, Cesare
- 1990. 'Semiotica y teatro.' *Revista de Filología Hispánica* 6:2, 327–36
Silverman, Kaja
- 1983. *The Subject of Semiotics*. New York: Oxford University Press
- 1992. *Male Subjectivity at the Margin*. New York and London: Routledge
- 1996. *The Threshold of the Visible World*. New York and London: Routledge
Smith, Barbara Herrnstein
- 1980. 'Narrative Versions, Narrative Theories.' *Critical Inquiry* 7, 213–36
Souriau, Etienne
- 1956. *Les 200.000 situations dramatiques*. Paris: Larousse
Spivak, Gayatri Chakravorty
- 1987. *In Other Worlds: Essays in Cultural Politics*. New York: Methuen
- 1993a. 'Echo.' *New Literary History* 24, 17–43
- 1993b. *Outside in the Teaching Machine*. New York and London: Routledge
Stanzel, Franz
- 1971. *Narrative Situations in the Novel*. Bloomington and Indianapolis: Indiana University Press

Suleiman, Susan R., and Inge Crosman, eds.
- 1980. *The Reader in the Text*. Princeton: Princeton University Press
Tamir, Nomi
- 1978. 'Personal Narrative and Its Linguistic Foundation: *PTL* 1:3, 403–30
Todorov, Tzvetan
- 1970. *Introduction à la littérature fantastique*. Paris: Editions du Seuil
- 1984. *Bakhtin: The Dialogic Principle*. Translated by Wlad Godzich. Minneapolis: University of Minnesota Press
Uspenskij, Boris A.
- 1973. *A Poetics of Comparison*. Berkeley: University of California Press
Van Alphen, Ernst
- 1988. 'Literal Metaphors: On Reading Postmodernism.' *Style* 21:2, 208–18
- 1989. 'The Heterotopian Space of the Discussions on Postmodernism.' *Poetics Today* 10:4, 819–38
- 1997a. *Caught by History: Holocaust Effects in Contemporary Art, Literature, and Theory*. Stanford: Stanford University Press
- 1997b. 'Excess and Sublimity in Kathy Acker's Narratives.' *ASCA Brief: Visions and Voices of Otherness*, 190–208. Amsterdam: ASCA
Van Kesteren, Aloysius, and Herta Schmid
- 1975. *Moderne Dramentheorie*. Kronberg/Ts.
Verhoeff, Nanna
- 2006. *The West in Early Cinema: After the Beginning*. Amsterdam: Amsterdam University Press
Verstraten, Peter
- 2006. *Handboek filmnarratologie*. Nijmegen: Van Tilt
Walcutt, Charles C.
- 1966. *Man's Changing Mask: Modes and Methods of Characterization in Fiction*. Minneapolis: University of Minnesota Press
Walton, Kendall L.
- 1990. *Mimesis as Make-Believe: On the Foundations of the Representational Arts*. Cambridge, Mass.: Harvard University Press
White, Hayden
- 1973. *Metahistory: The Historical Imagination in Nineteenth-Century Europe*. Baltimore: Johns Hopkins University Press
- 1978. 'The Forms of Wildness: Archeology of an Idea.' *Tropics of Discourse: Essays in Cultural Criticism*, 150–82. Baltimore: Johns Hopkins University Press

Index of Names and Titles

Index of Concepts

This book is largely about concepts and their usage. For reasons of teaching, many concepts recur throughout this book. Listing all the locations of each concept would make this index useless. To increase its usefulness, page references indicate only those pages where concepts are defined, discussed, or used in a specific theoretical sense that extends their defintion.